REMEMBERING
BRITISH TELEVISION

REMEMBERING BRITISH TELEVISION

Audience, Archive and Industry

Kristyn Gorton and Joanne Garde-Hansen

THE BRITISH FILM INSTITUTE
Bloomsbury Publishing Plc
50 Bedford Square, London, WC1B 3DP, UK
1385 Broadway, New York, NY 10018, USA

BLOOMSBURY is a trademark of Bloomsbury Publishing Plc

First published in Great Britain 2019 by Bloomsbury
on behalf of the
British Film Institute
21 Stephen Street, London W1T 1LN
www.bfi.org.uk

The BFI is the lead organisation for film in the UK and the distributor of Lottery funds for film. Our mission is to ensure that film is central to our cultural life, in particular by supporting and nurturing the next generation of filmmakers and audiences. We serve a public role which covers the cultural, creative and economic aspects of film in the UK.

Cover design by Louise Dugdale
Cover image: Television Store, National Media Museum, Bradford, UK.
Photograph by Iain Logie Baird, March 2016.

A catalogue record for this book is available from the British Library.

A catalogue record for this book is available from the Library of Congress.

ISBN: HB: 978-1-8445-7661-6
PB: 978-1-8445-7660-9
ePDF: 978-1-9112-3905-5
eBook: 978-1-8445-7663-0

Typeset by Integra Software Services Pvt. Ltd.
Printed and bound in Great Britain

To find out more about our authors and books visit www.bloomsbury.com and sign up for our newsletters.

CONTENTS

FIGURES

ACKNOWLEDGEMENTS

t is rare to find someone that you can write with over a long period of time and across a wide range of material. We have been lucky enough to research and write several pieces together having started our careers on the same day at the same institution. We agree, though, that this particular book has been the most challenging, primarily because the terrain underneath us was constantly shifting and changing. Around 2013 we felt strongly that there was something in the air, there was a certain resilience of 'nation' and 'family' to more liberal conversations about tectonic movements within media industries, national contexts and family dynamics. The continued unsettledness during the research phase, while we tried to understand these tensions, meant we had to reconsider our story, re-evaluate our argument and re-affirm our commitment to finishing this book. The fact that we managed to do so reminds us of the strength of friendship, the support of family and the passion we have for television.

Acknowledging all those who have assisted us in the Remembering British Television project, and the research and writing of this book, is a reminder of just how many lines of enquiry the whole project produced. To the British Academy itself, we would like to thank them for validating the programme of research that underpins the work. This programme kicked off with a symposium at the National Media Museum in February 2014 and those who attended opened many avenues to consider. For their invaluable assistance at that event and/or in the interviewing stages we thank Tony Ageh, Marcus Prince, Kenith Trodd, Dick Fiddy, James Patterson, Steve Bryant, Iain Logie Baird, Paul Goodman, Michael Terwey, Chris Perry, Lisa Holdsworth, Helen Wheatley, Helen Wood, Rachel Moseley, Mhairi Brennan, Matt Hills, Chris Hodson, David Pearson, Alan Mackay, Patrick Titley, Peter Ceresole, Mark Helsby, Ed Braman, Ian Macdonald, Lindsay Williams, Charles Fairall, Camilla Wheeler, Georgina Petty, Veena Murray, Anna Crossley, Julie Robinson and Debbie Evans. Colleagues at our universities have been particularly generous with their time, support and advice. Members of the Northern and Midlands Television Research Groups have been sounding boards, with Charlotte Brunsdon and Charlotte Stevens offering insightful comments and reflections. And many thanks, of course, to our partners, Paul and Justin.

Special thanks to Matt Hills for advising on *Doctor Who* fandom and commemoration.

To the editorial staff at the BFI who trusted us to complete the work, many thanks for your patience and kindness.

This book is dedicated to our children (Kate, Jack, Johnny, Matthew, Sam and Josh) who care as much about TV as we do, if not more.

PREFACE

The authors of this book are old enough to remember teaching about television through and with a television set. We carefully compiled VHS recorded tapes and curated for each class a 'playlist' of clips to be replayed on a large cathode ray tube set on wheels. We did not, as we do now, search Box of Broadcasts and YouTube for programmes, select segments, beginnings and endings, and project these through a wide variety of often poorly transcoded digital screens, smartboards, data projectors in a cinema-style setting. Our students did not play the same clips on handheld devices before, during and after class for pre-viewing and re-viewing. In fact, much of our teaching of television in those days, and it was not so long ago, was in small and cosy, dimly-lit rooms. Though we controlled access to past television for our students we were quickly coming to the end of this pedagogic experience, transitioning to DVDs, then memory sticks and now more reliant on the quickly accessible online repository (public, private, fan and hobbyist). While our students would go on to make television, hopefully with a sense of the temporal, spatial and material as much as the aesthetic, historical and political, we were launching degrees in *digital screen media*.

The television set may have disappeared from many universities to be replaced by larger and flatter screens connected to computers; yet, the set remained fixed in the corner of the living room in our homes, quietly and incrementally transforming into a computer and gaming system with each upgrade. There was and perhaps still is a period of doubt about what and where 'is' television in the twenty-first century: its longevity, its limitations, its disappearance and its relationship with its own past (see Auslander 1999; Caughie 2010; Holdsworth 2011). In fact, in the recent book *TV Museum*, Maeve Connolly opens the first paragraph by citing Andreas Huyssen's 1995 book *Twilight Memories* for connecting museums and television on the issue of their contemporary relevance and artefact-uality. She states, 'television has itself acquired the status of a "soon-to-be-obsolete" material object' (Connolly 2014, 3) and later draws on Caughie's 'Mourning Television' article for *Screen* who emphasized that television studies are 'ill-equipped to imagine a different television, one which escapes the "relentless spectacle of the present"' (Caughie 2010, 421). Yet, we cannot seem to ignore this box in the corner of the room and its hidden inter-dependency upon buildings full of tapes and the relationships between organizations and industries. Anna McCarthy reminded us, at the Material Cultures of Television conference in 2016, of all the seemingly 'useless' television boxes (referencing Maxwell and Miller's *Greening the Media* 2012), being dumped, recycled, shipped as e-waste, upcycled and entrepreneurially repurposed (McCarthy 2016). Anu Koivunen also states in reference to Raphael Samuel (1994) who 'saw television as a medium that was constantly looking toward the past', that it is a medium taking opportunities to 'travel down memory lane' by 'revisiting and recycling old film footage' (Koivunen 2016, 5270).

Our own academic study of television has had to be reimagined in the last fifteen years and the demands of our students have had an impact on this. If television was an 'object' in our teaching rooms, materialized as a television set, disconnected from the internet, standing alone and separated from cinematic film (being taught in different kinds of darker rooms), from popular music (practised in studios with sound proofing), from journalism (in news rooms) and gaming (in labs), we did not appreciate this at the time. The clips we curated were part of a whole to be negotiated, the many cables and wires were a health and safety issue, and the light and sound from the box were analogue. Remembering teaching television in this way is to recover its materiality, the labour of putting together collections, footage, clips and personal archives of tapes, the space they took up on the shelves (overwhelming the books), the wearing out of tape heads from endless play, their cueing before class, as well as the cost of transferring VHS to DVD. It was laborious but *we* made the decisions, *we* controlled the selection, the curation and the exhibition (at least in terms of our teaching and research agenda).

Our careers, were we to undertake an auto-ethnographic study of them, have witnessed the transition between the analogue and digital of television at an archaeological level. The German theorist Wolfgang Ernst (2011) offers 'a fresh way of looking into the use and remediation of media history as a material monument instead of a historical narrative' (Parikka 2011, 53). More likely, in the sense of Jussi Parikka (2012), as a *television genealogy* that is part of a wider 'media genealogy: writing counter-histories of such practices, ideas and contexts which are not included in mainstream film and media histories' (Parikka 2011, 54). This book is one attempt to address Caughie's point above on mourning television and to explore the multiple reflections at work personally, professionally, industrially and more importantly in the cultural heritage sector, all of which are dealing with the many afterlives of television.

Caring for past television and what it means to people also acknowledges that we are female scholars and teachers of television. We taught television studies and television history in departments largely dominated by men and by a growing focus upon digital production, technical-vocational media and on a decreasing attention to the gendered politics of narrative, texts and production cultures. While our careers charted television genealogy from the *monument of the set in the room* to the digital clip on any sized screen, we have also been acutely aware of the 'pedagogical problem' on 'the changing role of women in television' that Lynn Spigel (1995) addressed in the late 1990s. A problem that shifted our attention from television history to television memory and television emotion early on in our careers (see Gorton 2009; Garde-Hansen 2011; Garde-Hansen and Gorton 2013). Our students of television, who were just as likely to be female and/or working class, wanted (and still do need) to tell a different story of and in the industry. Their practice and experience of television needs to find role models, no doubt to make their entry into the industry seamless (at least to themselves). More than this, their memories of television may be at odds with the archive and with authorized television histories or new commemorative cultures.

Television memory, then, is concerned with the everyday-ness, the routine, the habits, the rituals and the always-there-visible-invisibility of television in people's lives (see Bourdon 2003 and Collie 2013). Yet, we are also concerned in this book with those organizational actors (museums, archivists, fans and hobbyists, for example) who, like individual academics and increasingly universities and other institutions, work hard (both paid and unpaid) to curate television's memory and/or memories of television. They draw together Bourdon's (2003) 'wallpaper', 'media events', 'flashbulbs' and 'close encounters' into new configurations for remembrance and, as a result, inheritance. As television passes from memory into heritage, tackling the ideal archive as repository, with its gaps and silences, then we find new relationships are forged, new publics are created and new recollections are curated.

Television, in our scholarly and personal experience – two quite different logics – has been in transition, at least technologically, industrially and in consumption terms. Yet, certain continua remain in terms of its study and these pertain to the division between *what* and *how* we want to teach television's history and *what* and *how* our students want to learn from it. The fact that our research has also engaged with other stakeholders: former employees, actors, agents, extras; the audience, fans, collectors and followers; museums, heritage organizations, communities and location scouts, means that like many academics working in media scholarship more broadly, our research and teaching of our popular cultural pasts has had to be both accountable and actionable. Spigel drilled this down some time ago to the 'logic of popular memory' (Spigel 1995, 17) and we have always found this distinction between history and memory productive in creating a space for exploring television's inheritability for different groups, especially those alienated by official accounts or sceptical of expert knowledge. For example, young women in Spigel's argument can find in 'popular memory' a rationale for action:

> As I use the term, popular memory is history for the present … Whereas official history typically masks its own storytelling mechanisms, popular memory acknowledges its subjective and selective status … Popular memory does not set out to find 'objective', 'accurate' pictures of the past. Instead, it aims to discover a past that makes the present more tolerable.
>
> (Spigel 1995, 21)

We agree with Spigel that if 'schools, museums, textbook publishers and other arbiters of social knowledge' provide professional and official histories of television this must be squared and integrated with popular memories of television (Spigel 1995, 21). Joe Moran in *Armchair Nation: An Intimate History of Britain* suggests that television and memory are congruent because the point at which television produces shared and sharable memories is the point at which we also reflect upon the nature of remembering: 'for a programme that millions once watched but which has now faded into the atmosphere like a dream is a neat encapsulation of the elusive quality of memory itself' (2013, 5–6).

All this scholarly reflection was partly the reason why this book was slow to write. The intense *accumulation of memory* – ours as a transnational relationship of an American and British scholar writing together; the popular and collective memory of British television becoming increasingly loaded with nostalgia and the nation as we wrote; and the shared, digital and global memory of legacy television finding old and new markets.[1] Any desire to construct objective and accurate stories of British television's past (an aim we did not pursue) was weighed down with the inevitable (and somewhat intended) messiness of our approach: everywhere we looked, everyone we consulted, everything we read and watched, all the participants we interviewed (from those in elite positions to audience members and fans) told us many different stories, tales and anecdotes.

Theory may think through these memories with the help of what is becoming the popular paradigm of 'multi-directional memory' from Michael Rothberg (2009) in his account of post-Holocaust remembering, but this would miss the fact that memory institutions and memory agents have the power of archive, text and resource; that is, to inherit television in very specific ways. Likewise, one could consider concepts of 'travelling memory' of transcultural experiences of television texts, to reference Astrid Erll (2011b), but this might also overplay mobility, openness and pluralism in a national context exporting its television heritage in nation-specific ways for global audiences. In practice, we have found that all these television memories are really anchored in and around places, people, spaces and buildings, homes (and their interiors), as well as clearly defined networks, organizational relationships and professional and familial identities. Subjective and selective stories of television, objective and professional accounts of television, as well as tours of personal collections, national archives and regional exhibitions were precisely the routes to television's memory we followed, and they are more than simply nostalgic. These were/are real places, real people with a real passion for caring for TV. Therefore, we decided that this book was concerned with a need to come to terms with the many ways of telling the stories of British television and the many people with a stake in those stories, regardless of whether their

---

[1]During the writing of this book we were also researching the emergence of television repatriation companies such as Television International Enterprises Archives <(www.tiea.co.uk/)>.

memories and memory work supported contemporary memory studies theories of cosmopolitanism and plurality. The stories are about change, adaptation and resilience, as much as they are about continuity and the past, present and future of television experience.

Understandably, in the background of this book are the many events that interrupted our writing about the ever-dynamic process of what is inheritable about British television. When we started the research in 2013, and shared with each other our intensely regional accounts of television history, we had a sense that 'nation' was becoming increasingly sticky and resilient as a cultural container to more deeply understand current *television as a form of heritage*. One author's work on the Dennis Potter Heritage Project seemed to day-light a deeply emotional connection between landscape, forestry, mining, rivers, community, indigeneity and television drama's legacy in the spaces of its production. Leading up to the 2016 referendum vote to leave the European Union ('Brexit') we had the BBC Charter renewal debated in the public sphere, the departure of Tony Ageh[2] (director of archives and the digital public sphere) to the New York Public Library, the emergence of disruptive digital entrants to television production and distribution (i.e. Netflix and Amazon), the new UK Licence Fee law (2016) legally turning iPlayer into television, and the growing influence of a paratext industry.[3] There were (and are) many popular discourses on national identity and heritage circulating around British television as we write[4] and its impact on audiences at home and abroad, alongside wider explorations of 'European Television Memories'[5] that place 'hybridity' and 'repertoire' as central to negotiating canon/archive and vernacular memory (see Hagerdoorn 2013) in transnational contexts. There have also been seismic shifts within the film and television industry at a national and global level to demand that issues regarding gender and ethnic equality are addressed,[6] alongside movements such as #metoo and #timesup which call for an end to sexual harassment and violence.

---

[2]Tony Ageh was a commissioner for the University of Warwick's commission on the *Future of Cultural Value* (2013–2015) and a participant in our project. See <www.warwick.ac.uk/research/warwickcommission/futureculture/>.

[3]We hosted a Paratextual Memory symposium in July 2016 at the University of Warwick to discuss trans-Atlantic television paratexts and their circulation as legacy television.

[4]The late A.A. Gill references the television inventor John Logie Baird as *remembered* by 'outers' to push the 'Little English drug' of nostalgia in his 'Brexit' article for *The Sunday Times* (Gill 2016). He defined this as 'some point in the foggy past where we achieved *peak Blighty*'.

[5]Jérôme Bourdon and Berber Hagerdoorn edited a special issue of *VIEW: Journal of European Television History and Culture* on 'European Television Memories'. British television is represented by Collie (2013) and Blandford and McElroy (2013) in the issue.

[6]For example, the Brixton, London-based activists Legally Black have extended their re-imaginings of film posters to include a poster of *Doctor Who* replacing the predominantly white, male leads who have played 'The Doctor' with a young, black and female actor, alongside the strapline: *If you're surprised it means you don't see enough black people in major roles.*

We also observed the national integration, devolution or consolidation of media archives by ITV, BBC, BFI, BUFVC, Getty and Pathé, as well as the cessation of activities of key organizations such as ITN Source and the closure of the television exhibition at the National Media Museum part way through the writing of a chapter about this exhibition. Yet, more importantly for our research, which was over a relatively short period of time, we saw the redundancy, retirement and precarious employment of some of our participants that seemed an inevitable part of the working lives of the highly talented, experienced and knowledgeable people who we interviewed in the archive, heritage and television production and creative industries. *Nothing seems to change as fast as British television's past* became our mantra every time a tectonic plate shifted and created ripples. This is where a critical memory studies approach can be most productive; by taking a meta-stance on the remembering of media discourses, forms and practices.

INTRODUCTION

The starting point for this book is *past television* or even 'old TV'.[1] We would suggest that we cannot talk about *old TV* unless we talk about memory. Furthermore, we have discovered in our research process and findings that we cannot talk about memory unless we realize memory is fundamentally social and active (Bartlett 1932), as some form of interaction between individuals and their worlds. 'Remembering is not the re-excitation of innumerable fixed, lifeless and fragmentary traces. It is an imaginative reconstruction, or construction, built out of the relation of our attitude towards a whole active mass of organised past reactions or experience' (Bartlett 1932, 213). Thus, we conjecture that past television becomes realizable as having two mnemonic capacities. Firstly, as a cultural practice of memory, i.e. that memories of past television programmes or memories of experiencing watching television are 'sticky' (de Cesari and Rigney 2014) and shared or shareable. Secondly, past television also becomes a practice of cultural memory, i.e. canons, archives, collections, commemorations, anniversaries, memoirs, exhibitions and artefacts, even inheritable rituals. Television as cultural memories are stored, lost, found, hidden, silent, silenced and re-mediated, selected and circulated to reinforce collective memories in group settings (i.e. of fans, families, producers, creatives, cultural industries and television workers) on subnational, trans-national and national scales.

The national container of British television in and through which we start our exploration of *old TV* (and it is a start rather than a means to an end) is framed by memory studies (rather than history and canon) because this allows us to not only focus on one case study or setting but also to take a contingent meta-stance on the recirculation of memories as a national cultural resource at this juncture. One might argue that television and television scholarship is in a moment of danger. Though, as Amanda Lotz has pointed out: '"The end of television" is a headline

---

[1]Christine Geraghty's keynote lecture 'Old TV' (2015), unpacked why the term 'old TV' is a contradiction in terms considering scholarship's focus on TV as new and ephemeral. We use the term throughout this book and italicize it, mainly to refer to Geraghty's point about a certain impossibility in thinking about TV as 'old' and yet it is ageing.

that's been liberally thrown around for the past 15 years' (Lotz 2015). Not simply threatened by digital media and cultural convergence but also by the absorption of its study into other disciplines of history, film studies, media studies and sociology, for example.

The field of memory studies is then brought into a productive relationship with television studies in this book as they both share a precarious identity as fields of research and, yet, can tell us so much about 'the popular' and its past. They allow us to ask certain questions throughout about the status and function of past television for a particular group or sub-groups, questions that are becoming increasingly important not only to the ontology of the subject position of the television studies scholar or memory studies scholar as a critical (and increasingly interdisciplinary) voice in media research, but also to the status of television itself with its own distinct history from other media forms.[2]

To study television as a technology of memory,[3] then, is to study what the past means in individual-intimate and collective-shared lives at many different scales. In her work on 'affective historiography' in television Anu Koivunen (2016, 5281) draws on Laurent Berlant's work on intimacy to argue that 'archival aesthetics as affective historiography addresses the nation as an "intimate public," foregrounding "affective and emotional attachments located in fantasies of the common, the everyday, and a sense of ordinariness" (Berlant 2008, 11)'. Thus, to make sense of one's past, as and through past television, in the present for the future, has a connection to care and community that may get missed by critiques of structural change or political ideologies.

Memories of television and television as a form of memory also offer some general reflections on time in terms of rupture, continuity, transition, liminality, duration, intermittence, repetition and flashback. There are, then, a few different ways of thinking about time that influence our analysis of television and/as memory. While 'time' has been addressed by scholars distinguishing between film and television[4] it is worth noting that Needham (2009) drawing on Judith

---

[2]While cultural policy questions of cultural value do permeate our research, they do not frame our approach because we think they may miss the value of subjective memories of those working in organizations that deal with the afterlife of television and the lay expertise of those outside institutions. In 'Who are these People?' Toby Miller (2008) spoke of 'bottom feeding neo-liberals' who he saw as destroying the intellectual origins of the BFI. This meta-position misses two key points. Firstly, his 'origins' story of the BFI is one version of the past while Denis Forman's memoir *Persona Granada* (1997) charts his own directorship of the BFI (1948–55) as quite different. Secondly, a focus only on structure misses BFI workers with long careers in curating television and sustaining memories (personal, professional and organizational).

[3]In Steve F. Anderson's (2011) *Technologies of History: Visual Media and the Eccentricity of the Past* he devotes much attention to television as a technology of cultural memory.

[4]See Davis and Needham's useful collection *Queer TV: Theories, Histories, Politics* (2009). In particular, Needham's chapter 'Scheduling Normativity' on television's structuring of time, the rhythms of the everyday, the feeling of being live, and the queering of time in scholarship to imagine time in non-normative ways.

Halberstam (2005, 5) argues that 'Halberstam characterizes normative time by drawing attention to the different categories through which it comes to be organized and given meaning. These include the interconnectedness of family time, reproduction time and *inheritance* time' (2009, 151; our emphasis). Needham continues that these are 'the bases of a normative temporal organization and the backbone of an imagined social, cultural and national future that takes the hetero-patriarchal family as its only model'. Whereas, to *queer* time implies 'asynchrony, discontinuity, belatedness, arrest, coincidence, time wasting, reversal, time travel, the palimpsest, boredom and ennui' in a 'desire for alternative histories and futures, and experiences of the everyday quotidian temporalities' (Needham 2009, 152). While queer theory and texts are not the focus of our research, the queering of normative temporality (i.e. an out of sync-ness of *old TV* or the simultaneous mourning/celebration of repeated *ends of TV*) produces a persistent attention to the afterlives of television and memories of it, which should be considered further by scholars. Here we focus on how '*inheritance* time' is at work in sustaining legacy TV and television's legacy at a range of scales.

We might equally draw upon Aby Warburg's 'cultural studies' approach to art history in his unfinished *Mnemosyne Atlas* (1929) that maps how images of antiquity reappear and have continued symbolic and emotional resonance in contemporary times. His citing of 'afterlife' as central to his thesis has been defined by Schoell-Glass as 'the changing ways in which they [the images] were deployed and the ebbing and flowing energies that they stored, releasing and restraining the emotions and affects' (2008, 6). 'Afterlife' in this sense is a useful way into thinking about past television's (re)new(ed) temporalities. We would suggest that this whole book is concerned with television's afterlife, which, at this *point in time,* is both highly reanimated and markedly in jeopardy. The other idea about time at work in our thinking is, of course, Walter Benjamin's notion that memory, unlike history, is more immediate and that it breaks through chronological time, to create a kind of 'now-time' (*Jetztzeit*) full of subjective experience (see Benjamin 1940: Thesis 14). In this breaking through of historical time, remembering *old TV* moves us. To remember television, then, might mean to be moved once more but it is also to accept that the ways and means by which we are moved (again) are not neutral. As Lindroos (1998, 85) states in *Now-Time/Image-Space*, Benjamin's approach 'emphasises breaks, ruptures, non-synchronised moments and multiple temporal dimensions' and 'qualitative differences in time, as they have the possibility to become actualised through experiences, actions or acknowledgement of the subject in temporally changing situations'.

Therefore, we suggest that to inherit television, (trans or sub) nationally, culturally or intimately is to create and explore the potentialities of old and new memory discourses around television that circulate in four main spaces/places we explore in this book: museums/archives, convergent media, the television industry and families. These are also the meeting places of a nexus of actors: fans, collectors, (re)viewers, scholars, broadcasters, producers, creatives, heritage and archive managers and cultural entrepreneurs. All this requires a great deal of labour. As Matthew Allen has argued in The *Labour of Memory*:

> Remembrance implies work. It requires bodies and objects moving, performing and interacting to achieve a memorial composition. Participants in remembrance practices undertake a material and immaterial work of weaving their emergent experiences as part of the overall composition of the event. A material management of space, objects and bodies structures experiences of participation. The organisers of remembrance practices, memory choreographers, are responsible for designing and assembling these infrastructures of experience.
>
> (Allen 2014, 28)

Memories of British television are, we would argue, being monumentalized, perhaps not always in stone and bronze, though we do have heritage plaques,[5] commemorative events,[6] museum exhibitions as well as other physical manifestations of inheritance (engineering, artefacts, technology and collections). Some of these monuments punctuate the landscape as analogue television aerials, antennas and masts. There are other incarnations through fandom, amateur creativity, memoir and vernacular memory that are practices, things made and crafted, and that ask us to imagine what it means to live in television's time again and again.

Consequently, our experiences of teaching television and working closely with television professionals in our research has led us to consider that the memories in circulation, full of their subjective experience, powerfully shape and inform our understanding of British Television's past, present and future. Memories work to give *us* a sense of inheritance from television's past and to underline *our* past, present and future viewing practices. Therefore, this book is an attempt to think about the role different forms of memory play in understanding British television history from a range of perspectives, and the extent to which these shape inheritances of British television for a range of audiences.

We started our research with questions around the cultural value we place on television as it ages and becomes 'old': that is, how is television remembered and treasured? What criteria are used by archives and museums to store, collect and exhibit television's past? How do viewers' memories affect their feelings

---

[5]There is a blue heritage plaque for John Logie Baird and another 'milestone plaque' was unveiled on 27 January 2017 as part of the IEEE History event 'Evolution of Television from Baird to the Digital Age' (Royal Institution of Great Britain, London). There is also a statue of Baird in his hometown Helensburgh, Scotland, that appears to have his glasses removed. His grandson, Iain Logie Baird (a participant in our research), converted the oldest working television set from 1938 to receive a digital signal during the digital switchover period in Scotland.

[6]One of the authors was involved in two commemorative events during the research, the Dennis Potter season at the BFI dovetailed with the end of the Dennis Potter Heritage Project (see Garde-Hansen and Grist 2014) and *A Beast with Two Backs* (1968) re-screening both in the Forest of Dean in 2015.

about television viewing? And how are these issues related to the story of British television history? As academics, we noticed a scholarly gap in critically using memories as a way of explaining the past and valuing television's role within both tangible and intangible cultural heritage, place heritage, personal identity and life-story. At the same time, we have been wary of simply utilizing memories for filling in the gaps of history or to construct a more cohesive history of British television. We are not offering a 'new' history of British television and we are equally wary of creating anything that attempts this. To do so, would feel like we were placing *old TV* too firmly in the past. As Sue Turnbull states, following on from John Hartley (2008): 'the attempt to render television "historically" has barely begun' (2012, 19).

For this reason, we want to make clear that this is not a book about the history of television genres (this has been well covered by Glen Creeber, Toby Miller and John Tulloch in *The Television Genre Book* [2008] or in *British Television Drama: A History* by Lez Cooke [2003, 2015]). Nor are we documenting television's relationship to other histories (see Edgerton and Rollins's 2001 *Television Histories*, or perhaps *History on British Television: Constructing Nation and Collective Memory* by Robert Dillon [2010]). While Gray and Bell's *History on Television* (2012) covers history programming in terms of the industry's involvement in how the past is constructed, this does not address television as heritage in terms of its industrial self-reflexivity and the ways in which past television has become increasingly valued outside and beyond itself: commercially, nationally, collectively and affectively.

Instead, we focus on the concept of 'inheritance' so as to use memory as a way of thinking about the value and importance television plays in our lives, and in structuring time and the memories we pass on. Inheritance is, we acknowledge, a tricky term to employ in this context. Olick, Vinitzky-Seroussi and Levy (2011) in *The Collective Memory Reader* coalesce the 'often-forgotten debates' within late nineteenth-century theories of cultural inheritance (see Semon 1921, 1923; Warburg 1929). They track through the Durkheimian perspective of 'collective memory' that espoused transmission of cultural heritage as 'shared assumptions', i.e. 'commemoration of certain historical events', 'consensus on the past', and 'a "deep structure" or stored-up legacy of shared culture that binds us together'. They continue: 'in more extreme versions, the "truth" of such accounts is seen as irrelevant in face of the need for them: any myth of belonging, it sometimes seems, even a patently absurd one, is better than none' (Olick, Vinitzky-Seroussi and Levy 2011, 20). To focus squarely on personal memories of British television from a variety of stakeholders and organizational actors at different scales of television's legacy is to unpack this cultural inheritance and expose the individual memories that may confirm or challenge the 'social frameworks' (see Halbwachs 2011) and the national objectives one would expect those individuals to subscribe to.

What is key in our book is to explore the inheritance of British television through, and here we draw on Paul Connerton (2011, 341), a wider focus on the 'custodians' (from elite to non-elite persons) who perform the 'communal memory' of television in their work, leisure and family lives, to 'be repeated to successive generations' wherein their subjective experience of television itself plays such an affective role in their care for the medium. As Bolin (2016, 10) has recently argued in *Media Generations*, people develop 'specific, sometimes, passionate, relationships with reproduction technologies such as vinyl record, music cassette tape, comics and other now dead or near-dead forms'. These passions and performances are, in our research, collected through vernacular accounts of their lives and careers, as well as through discursive memories that circulate around texts both online and through their interviews. We will also consider how the memories of everyday viewers and of those who produced or are producing television make their way into our understanding of past and present television. As Joe Moran points out 'The most banal TV from the past can be wonderfully evocative. Numerous websites exhaustively dedicate themselves to collating and curating the connective tissue of television [...] But most television remains forgotten, and those bits that are remembered are often surrounded by wishful thinking and selective amnesia' (2013, 5–6).

Understanding how the 'connective tissue' of past British television is collated and curated does, we have found, requires a materialist approach wherein we foreground the resources (personal, cultural, social, physical, financial and technical) that circulate in the accounts of the experiences of the many different people with a stake in television's afterlife. This is only possible through speaking with them, taking time to visit their institutions, buildings, exhibitions and workplaces, empathizing with them, tickling stories to the surface, and inviting them to national and local discussions on their sector's approach to past television, as well as being invited to speak with their colleagues. In researching this book we wanted to be part of current debates between cultural workers outside academia concerned with how past television is made public, reused, rebooted and regenerated. The materiality of our approach also shows itself in our attentiveness to memory and its meandering, wherein television becomes the material of memory and remembering, and yet this materialization seems both intimate and public, though never straightforward.

It is worth underscoring at this point, that 'memory studies' as a field has been defined of late by its challenging of bounded identities, of nation, family or religious culture (see Levy and Sznaider 2005; Rothberg 2009; Erll 2011a; de Cesari and Rigney 2014). Why not, then, avoid using the term 'British' in the context of this book? After all, there are limitations to our research, with a lack of examples from Wales (see Medhurst 2010) and Northern Ireland (see Griffin 2014) as key omissions. While we make references to Scotland (through the National Library of Scotland) we had less opportunities to make useful comparisons with Wales, because the scope of the funded research and the methodology we followed (which we describe later) did not afford archival connections with these two countries. This does not mean that the politics of writing the history of subnational 'British' television is outside the scope of our thinking. On the contrary, a glance at the

Amazon reviews of Jamie Medhurst's (2010) history of television in Wales show just how fraught the landscape of writing television history versus collecting television memory really is.[7] Thus, 'British' is already problematic in the title of our book. Welsh-language television (particularly through S4C) in Wales has played a major part in the collective memory of the nation. With one of the authors resident and educated in Wales for many years, and a regular user of the National Library of Wales (NLW), it did not escape our notice that the development of a National Broadcast Archive at the NLW will afford educational and creative hubs in various locations in Wales' that would allow public access to digitized archival material from the BBC and ITV collections.

Therefore, we self-consciously use the term 'British' because our case studies are concerned with intimate experiences with television in key parts of the United Kingdom, while recognizing that other parts (such as Wales and Northern Ireland) will be exploring the interplay of history and memory in future, modelling their television heritage on an example we did research in Glasgow, Scotland (See NLW 2017). While some books drop any notion of the nation in their title when exploring 'television', they may often be speaking to an experience of television within a particular national context, in which the underlying economies of infrastructure, networks and production cultures are hidden beneath discussions of transcultural texts and audiences. We contend that memories of television start with the intimacy of viewing, watching and discussing and those memories may travel and end in different places and at different scales, but we must start television's memory and memories of television from a place: they *belong somewhere*.

The social frameworks of television memory may shift and change, incorporating more frameworks of communities from different nations, cultures and identities, at different scales of global, local and personal. Yet, we make the case in this book that the national scale and the intimate connection of the family on a personal scale are proving remarkably resilient to understanding how we remember television, its texts and our experiences of watching them. We are not saying that *old TV* is a metaphorical black box for the future, to be opened by future scholars to explain what went wrong or what went right with either

---

[7]Beneath the listing of Jamie Medhurst's *A History of Independent Television in Wales* paperback edition published 29 June 2010, there are two customer reviews. The first by Huw Davies (chief executive of HTV Wales) was written a month after publication and totals 3,247 words. It is a very long rebuke of the academic who only focuses on the official archives and ITV's refusal to grant access. Here is an example of producer-ly memory at odds with the academic's approach to historiography, with the Amazon platform providing a space for that debate to play out: 'I happen to believe' writes the reviewer 'the formal documents to which he was refused access would probably not have helped very much. Most, as is ever the case, were not designed to illuminate the historian. However, if he was concerned with getting at the truth there were many other resources both written and human that he could have consulted, which in my view would have been more valid and relevant than those that were denied to him.' (See Amazon 1996–2018). The second customer review posted three years later is a response to the first, championing the book as making the best out of archival restrictions.

television or the nation at any point in time. Rather, the *regenerative milieu*[8] we are currently living in, demands that we acknowledge that television memory matters, its materiality and its materialization, the resources to facilitate these, such that the matter of television memory in our research is specifically locatable in either places or persons.

It goes without saying that British TV and memories of it are both locally, nationally and globally produced and consumed. However, taking an administrative approach to *television's afterlife* and its memories suggests, at least for us, that television memory circulates within specifically resourced and administrative contexts. To only focus on memories of television in relation to identity and the desire for recognition, may miss the underlying organization and governance of memories of television by a wide range of stakeholders and actors, who view memory as a (sub- and trans-) national resource that needs to be managed. It is our contention that the past of British television is being supplied with energy to be kept and stored or to be day-lighted and re-socialized within a national context for wider consumption and recirculation. Assmann (2008) and Erll (2011b) have argued convincingly that memory texts travel (we would say they circulate), and in doing so they produce counter-memories, perhaps even with a focus on forgotten episodes. But who decides what is forgotten needs re-surfacing in the first place? Scouring archives, collections or even foreign broadcasters for *old TV* is not an apolitical 'fannish' or altruistic activity, it resonates with notions of heritage, nation and empire, or new and old concepts of collective memory.[9] For whose benefit are those forgotten memories, texts and media histories day-lighted? What stories do they want to tell, for whom and why? Why remember, commemorate or shine a light on certain aspects of *old TV* and not others? They may be significant to scholars and professionals but what is important about them other than their forgotten-ness, and what of everyday memories of television seem irrelevant to these organizational actors?

A critical memory studies approach to British television's past asks difficult questions about the over- and/or under-playing of differing scales of remembering. In the case of our research, the national and the intimate scales are playing a particularly important part in both a politics of recognition and identity, and a politics of administration and resource. To fund research into or to provide energy for addressing the forgetting of British TV in an increasingly competitive and disrupted global television market is a deeply political, industrial and cultural values project. It is not a neutral act to reactivate television as memory and

---

[8]We are grateful to Charlotte Brunsdon for suggesting this phrase as we described our research during a meeting of The Memory Group at the University of Warwick in November 2016, on the role of cultural heritage agencies in assisting museums in exhibitions of television heritage. We use this phrase as a way of thinking about television, memory and heritage in later chapters.

[9]The search for missing *Doctor Who* episodes has taken Television International Enterprises Archives' (TIEA) archive entrepreneur Philip Morris to locations ranging from 'Aden to Zambia' says Spilsbury (2013, 15).

through remembering practices. How one does this and with which stakeholders can make all the difference to our understanding of what is culturally valuable at any given time. In the meantime, British TV is being stored, collected and remembered under both luxury and austerity conditions of glut and scarcity by corporations (some global) as well as by families, by national media museums and fans, by regional-local institutions and cultural/media entrepreneurs. How should the national scale, frame or container be employed in the legacy of television? This is a question that requires a critical memory studies approach that seeks to explore why the nation and the intimacy of domestic life still matter to producers and publics. This means the television historian cannot only focus on official archives but must engage with memory work.

Drawing on such an approach produces a wide range of questions: is TV an effective vehicle of and for memory and for whom and why? This may begin as a question of scarcity and abundance: how much TV do we really need to remember anyway and can memory be relied upon when TV is so habitually consumed on a day-to-day basis? If other less frequently consumed media or deliberately chosen media are more memorable, rather than part of the flow of daily living, is there something about television's mnemonic quality that means it has less mnemonic significance and as such, needs to be more actively remembered, renewed and regenerated? To actively remember television may be the only way to make it inheritable if archives are inaccessible, closed and incomplete. Is TV always in danger of being forgotten while some of it is timeless, classic and unforgettable? If we were to explore more than simply our memories of interactions with TV (see Bourdon 2003) then what does it mean when we cannot remember fully the programmes we had those interactions with? Certain programmes are remembered and certain experiences of interaction are too, but what are we inheriting here: the texts or the (inter-)generational accounts? 'Because of its historical association with the home, domesticity, and intimacy', states Brunsdon, 'television's implication with notions of generation can be particularly potent, and there is a cluster of work around notions of memory, generation and history that seems to me particularly rich' (2008, 134). It is upon this clustering of memory, generation and history that our book addresses television's inheritability at different operational and affective scales: personal, cultural, professional and institutional.

Television as a technology of social memory

As a medium or technology of social memory, British television has played a pivotal role in preserving and transmitting the energies of previous generations and their cultural, creative, scientific and technical activities. There is extant research and scholarship that has approached some of the questions above from differing angles. Edgerton and Rollins (2001), Wheatley (2007) and Holdsworth

(2011) are excellent interventions, taking the connectivity of television to memory seriously. There are also (re)appraisals of British television archives that have explored the historical impact of popular television (see Holmes 2008) or have rescued British television historiography from privileging the BBC or challenging the BBC mythology (see Johnson and Turnock 2005 and Mills 2016 respectively). There are publications that cover television heritage as produced and inherited in other countries, such as *Remembering Television: Histories, Technologies, Memories* (2012) edited by Kate Darian-Smith and Sue Turnbull, that draws together chapters on Australian television in terms of media and memory studies. While Derek Kompare's *Rerun Nation: How Repeats Invented American Television* (2005) underlines the messiness of repetition, myth, popular memory and (intangible) cultural heritage from the serious business of writing the history of (American) television as a commercial and political form. We would argue that the history of British television continues to be written as a 'history' distinct from 'memory' (for example, Jean Seaton's official history of the BBC published in 2015), while the idea that memory is continuous with history is less well developed.

Our concern, then, is to explore a certain 'located-ness' to the inheritance of television memories (to emphasize Radstone 2000); through the case study we have focused on – the United Kingdom. Yet, we are clearly aware, as a British scholar and an American scholar, that these memories are also transnational and transcultural because British-made television has travelled, is remembered elsewhere, is located elsewhere and may even be returned to the United Kingdom. While television consumed in the United Kingdom has been made in other countries, we would contend that subjectively these are experienced as and archived as memories of 'British television' even though that television may have been produced abroad and be considered 'foreign'.

At the heart of our conceptual framework, then, is the need to understand British television not only from the perspective of elite voices (academic, artistic and institutional) but to address the increasingly emotional, material and visible artefacts of television (as hidden experiences, obsolete technologies, transmission equipment and apparatuses) that accumulate; and the invisible impacts of television (as memories, emotional attachments and feelings) that coalesce into a form of cultural heritage. The energy for remembering British television as both an organic and inorganic resource is coded and transmitted by a range of 'memory-agents', drawing upon Anna Reading's use of this term, who purposefully seek 'to stick or trap memories' so as 'to securitise them in their interests' (Reading 2016, 55). Yet, we are keen to address the more implicit cultural memories and inexplicit afterlives of past television on daily professional and personal lives. In their book *The Collective Memory Reader*, Olick, Vinitzky-Seroussi and Levy (2011, 12) make the point that early understandings of a 'theory of inheritance' (such as in the case of Semon 1921) were keen to 'identify what the mechanism of cultural inheritance might be, rather than hinting at some kind of mystical haunting of the past'.

As noted above, in his 2003 article 'Some Sense of Time: Remembering Television' Bourdon states that: 'What is remembered is not programs but interaction with TV' (2003, 12). Yet, TV programmes *are* remembered, archived, rerun and revisited by fans, audiences, screenwriters, actors, producers, extras, location scouts, studio workers and media museums. Clips of programmes erupt into social media's virality and disrupt cultural understandings, taken out of context and yet providing keys back into that context. Our book addresses this memory agency and the cultural work it does to ensure that more than interaction is remembered. Having said that, interaction with TV is remembered warmly in ways that produce cultural heritage: memories of children's television after school, nostalgia for forms of TV screenwriting that commercial industrial demands preclude, archival exhibitions of TV 'in the home', 'on the set', 'on location' and new articulations of TV 'on demand' and 'on the move'. Again, our book uniquely addresses these forms of cultural inheritance that produce the notion of British television as retransmittable, re-consumable and intangible cultural heritage.

We draw together the broad and multiplying ways in which British television (as inherited and inheritable) is being discursively and practically *passed down* by audiences, archive workers and industry practitioners. We take television as a means of exploring these issues whilst aware that 'British' television is increasingly 'global' television. A series such as Sally Wainwright's *Happy Valley* (BBC One, 2014–), for example, may appear a regional and British programme, yet is also listed as a Netflix Original.[10] Thus, while we are aware of the difficulties in situating our research in national boundaries, we are also aware of their permeability, and yet we use them here to contingently enframe our case studies, to examine how television and memory work together in particular contexts for strategic reasons in the present.

In his work on a 'history on British television', Robert Dillon argues that 'television functions as a visual barometer of what it meant to be English or British, what national characteristics counted, how a national outlook formed. Television organises and motivates how national character has been valued, presented as fact, reality, reconstruction and myth' (2010, 2–3). However, Cooke makes the point that while his book 'has charted the rich and varied history of British television drama, from 1930 to the present, the concept of "national" television drama, already problematic given the make-up of the British Isles, is likely to become even less tenable in future as international co-productions increase and new technology

---

[10]When in doubt, 'heritage' it out, seems to be the order of the day. Natalie Humphreys, controller of BBC Factual and Daytime stated of Netflix: 'Can we compete like for like with that new set of people? Don't know. But we've got a couple of things that they will never have. We have got deep specialism, 50, 60 years of heritage in absolutely knowing how to make things to a particular standard. They can't buy that off the open market' (Plunkett 2015). See also Colin Callender (2014), director of BBC's *Wolf Hall* (2015) in *The Guardian* 'Why we should cherish BBC drama'. Of course, Netflix can indeed buy the cultural heritage of British television off the open market.

such as the internet dissolves national boundaries' (2015, 249). Dillon's use of the past tense concerning what it 'meant to be English or British' and Cooke's certainty that the 'nation' will not stick, may miss the powerful role and significant labour of memory and memory agents in securitizing what gets remembered. What scholars choose to emphasize as important about British television history may contrast markedly with what audiences choose to remember.

Taking on board television's mutability, this book makes a comprehensive and compelling case for reading *old TV* within a framework of the cultural and political economy of memory (i.e. memory conjoined with identity and its management by structures and agents) and less in terms of historical memory (i.e. memory synthesized with epistemology). There are many books that engage with British television history (some of which deal with the relationship between history and memory). For example, Johnson and Turnock (2005) have challenged the prejudice against commercial television in the writing of British television history. Yet, neither in this book nor in Turnock's *Television and Consumer Culture: Britain and the Transformation of Modernity* (2007) is cultural memory and television's inheritability addressed. There are many publications that are based on deeply researched histories of genres. For example, Su Holmes (2008) on quiz shows and entertainment, Christina Baade (2012) on the BBC and popular music in the Second World War, Susan Sydney-Smith (2002) on early British police series, Simon Potter (2012) on broadcasting empire, Lez Cooke (2003) on British television drama, and Ian Jones (2004) on morning breakfast television.

There are also those that have revisited British television history by tracking less well-known producers, developers, inventors and technicians (for example, Mark Aldridge's *The Birth of British Television: A History* 2011). The Arts and Humanities Research Council (AHRC) funded 'A History of Television for Women in Britain, 1947–1989' (Moseley, Wood, Wheatley, Irwin and Collie, 2010–13, see also *Television for Women*, by Moseley, Wheatley and Wood, 2017) has focused attention on the importance of feminist historical research and archiving practice. Reconnecting women with *old TV* goes a long way towards recuperating personal, cultural, social and collective memories in the face of historical absence or silence. We share the drive in these projects to connect history and memory, but our contribution is focused more on the implications of the unpacking of memories of television, for what agendas and with what kinds of impact. Thus, we seek to take a critical memory studies stance on why and how all this *old TV* matters and to whom. While media and memory projects may 'generate friction that may in turn generate the flight of further contested and differentiated memories' (Reading 2016, 55), we wonder how these are being corralled, contained and domesticated by the media, cultural and heritage industries.

The focus of our book, then, is broader and speaks to a wider readership beyond television studies (from cultural studies to history, heritage management, cultural geography and memory studies). This is important because as a part of everyday life, television is historically significant outside itself and memories of it speak critically to and about self, family, nation and globalization. We are also aware that histories of British television have been written from the same starting points that have shaped understanding and perception.[11] In our current research, it is the impact of *past television* into and on the lives of below-the-line television workers, museum and heritage managers, archive managers, and creative practitioners that is contributing as much to an understanding of television history as research into events, texts, genres, broadcasters, producers, directors and audiences. While we consider how histories get written, to set the stage for a close attention to memory and heritage, the main thrust of our book is to present the competing narratives and stories that contribute to how television is made inheritable.

British television heritage (as a concept) is becoming increasingly built upon the technologized ability to self-reflexively produce a history of television inside and outside the industry (e.g. the repurposing of television archives online by broadcasters as well as fans, YouTube playlists, the re-emergence of old idents, or the monumentalization of both popular culture as well as television engineering). Thus, we draw together television theories, audience and archive research and industrial/heritage practices into a discussion about what is being recorded, archived, remembered and exhibited in the production of a *concept of British television heritage*. We achieve this by drawing upon the stories and narratives of those who work and have worked in television in a range of roles: producers, directors, screenwriters, archive managers, production workers and producer-researchers. We also speak to and of those who now seek to construct narratives of TV's history: heritage institutions and cultural actors, television fans and scholars. Importantly, we include audience memories in our case studies where lay knowledge of television contributes to the notion of British television as a more intimate form of inheritance.

A memory studies approach to *old TV*

In John Ellis' book *TV FAQ* one of the common questions 'Why does old TV look so weird?' (2007, 163) is answered in a way that focuses on history (television is simply *of its time*). What we need then is a memory studies approach to television production in a technological, stylistic and resource specific context that

---

[11]For example, one of the authors researched the BBC archive holdings on the Storm Surge of January–February 1953, a catastrophic 'water' event that tested the BBC's broadcasting units in this region, led to massive loss of life, and flooded the Netherlands. The archival holdings revealed material pertinent to the development of TV as a new form of disaster relief programming, the BBC performing a donation receiving function as well as an early warning system. This subnational origin story becomes lost once the coronation of Queen Elizabeth II in June 1953 becomes the starting point and the framework through which the story of TV is told. To reconnect television with its intimate connection with landscape and environment is a new area of research one of the authors is working on.

continues to be (partly) accessible to audiences (if only through their own personal collections) and is increasingly accessible to professional commemorators. It is not wholly surprising that Ellis does not at this point draw upon a media and memory studies framework for addressing questions of past television, nostalgia and remembering. Such a way of thinking about mediating the past was only just emerging (see Kuhn 2002; Grainge 2003; Hoskins 2004, 2005, 2007, 2009, the launch of the journal *Memory Studies* in 2008, Holdsworth's *Television, Memory and Nostalgia* 2011 and Garde-Hansen's *Media and Memory* 2011). We need to approach past television from questions of personal, collective and cultural memory, to think through television's temporality (and visual textures), its spatiality (and locatedness), its materiality (and continued impacts on everyday living) and its continuous change and adaptation (its resilience and durability as an innovative form), to identify continuities and stickiness. Many scholars have been focusing on these areas of late (see Jonathan Gray 2010; Jennifer Gillan 2011; Matt Hills 2014 and Helen Wheatley 2016).

Drawing on Aleida Assmann (2011b) and Jan Assmann (2011), we can apply their memory framework to television as a form of cultural memory and communicative memory. Jan Assmann has argued of the differences evoked through oral history methods of 'informal everyday memory', which knows no limits, fixities and formation, a form of 'communicative memory [that] is characterized by its proximity to the everyday, cultural memory is characterized by its distance from the everyday' (2011, 213). If we were to consider 'cultural memory' in this sense then we might only be focused on the weirdness of old television shows and programmes (their distance from us now) because of our position within a context of choice, market forces and heterogeneity. Jan Assmann has stated that 'through its cultural heritage a society becomes visible to itself and to others. Which past becomes evident in that heritage and which values emerge in its identificatory appropriation tells us much about the constitution and tendencies of society' (2011, 215). While, spectrum scarcity produced a national audience with little choice and with no segmentation this does not mean, as Dayan and Katz predicted, that 'television-as-we-know-it' has disappeared entirely (1992, 23). On the contrary, as the new ruling in September 2016 finds the UK 'TV Licence' fee redefining the iPlayer as 'television', there are increased opportunities in the United Kingdom to treasure television, economically and culturally that tell us much about current tendencies towards the stickiness of the 'national' as a container.

Thus, if we were to widen the approach, as do Brown and Hoskins (2010) in their attention to cultural memory studies, then we would define our approach to TV's treasures as: 'sharing a common view of memory as referring to social practices which orient persons to possible versions of the past in such a way as to make them relevant to ongoing personal, social and political concerns. It is these versions of the past which are propagated through a rich variety of media and which form the object of contestation across diverse cultural domains' (2010, 88).

What looks weird to one person might be the very stuff of ongoing life story and social integration to the next person or forgotten by the next. Moreover, our role as scholars in that ongoingness cannot be forgotten. Aleida Assmann has defined academics as 'shamans at heart, recreating a continuous conversation with ancestral voices and the spirits of the past. We not only work with media in the technical sense [...] but we also *are* media in the occult sense of establishing contact with a transcendent world for a collective benefit' (1996, 123).

To make a distinction between communicative memory (how audiences recall television and what they remember) and cultural memory (how television's texts are remembered and circulated as 'texts' and by whom) is important in this book's focus upon the different scales (and the multi- and inter-scalarity) of treasuring television. Anglo-European theoretical and conceptual frameworks of 'memory studies' have tended to emphasize historical, collective and cultural memory, with less applied research on 'communicative memory' (Assmann 2008), leading to generalization. In a recent edited collection that explores permanence and obsolescence in relation to media and memory, Roberta Pearson (2016, 78) asks the question: 'should we speak of collective memory, national memory, cultural memory, social memory, generational memory, or popular memory?' and answers that 'popular memory' of the character Sherlock Holmes is her chosen term because in its most basic sense it covers what most people remember. Yet, she counters 'this does not negate the value of the evidence, since popular memory has always been skewed by many factors, especially those related to a society's unequal distribution of the power to shape cultural representation' (Pearson 2016, 78).[12]

In this book, we access television's past from the 'communicative memory' of those who have (or are assumed to have) the power to shape popular and cultural memories of British television, and who have worked in television or continue to preserve, curate, commemorate and re-exhibit it. In so doing, they have contributed to the creation of television's cultural memory and legacy. They have shaped how *old TV* is represented, and the more communicative memories we collect the wider that representation could be. Their voices function as a form of personal and professional remembering that day-lights the cultural work undertaken (running parallel to official memorialization) whether they have played a small or large part in the popular memory of television. Our aim is to present communicative memory in its increasingly digital connectivity, as a further contribution to the expanding notions of cultural memory provided by Brown and Hoskins (2010) in their attention to versions of the past and the role of media (personal and public) in reconnecting those pasts. Throughout the book, *old TV* is always potentially shared and shareable beyond more traditional notions of collective memory as defined by Halbwachs (2011). To incorporate into an approach to TV history

---

[12]As the BBC's latest series of *Sherlock Holmes* becomes popular memory in China, we suggest that 'millennial memory' may be an emergent transnational concept that shows up the contested concept that is popular memory.

the idea of scales of memory (multiplying the remembered texts and their remembered contexts), into thinking through the connectivities of the personal and the cultural as two key realms of cultural memory work. We propose increased attention to 'paratextual memory' (which we cover later in this book) produced by those operating in heritage and museum sectors, cultural archives and the creative industries, who make *old TV* not so weird.

'Now' and 'Not Now' nostalgia

Nostalgia, writes Michael Bull, 'is frequently treated as a structural and *contemporary* disease of the present, as a set of ersatz experiences promoted by the culture industry's intent of stealing not just the present, but also the past from consumers' (2009, 91). However, remembering *old TV* can be facilitated by what we will term *now nostalgia*: acceptable, profitable, scalable and responsive to new (global) audiences in new ways. This chimes with Hills's designation of 'an industrial continuum of nostalgic creativity' ('Foreword' for Powers 2016, 5) that interacts closely with fans, servicing them, while reclaiming authorial intent, particularly if those authors are 'fanboy auteurs' (Scott 2013) of a white, male and privileged creative class. *Now nostalgia* refracts Svetlana Boym's 'restorative nostalgia' of nation rebuilding and 'reflective nostalgia' of ironic, self-aware longing-ness by viewing nostalgia through a regenerative medium: the medium of television's past futurity. Boym sees 'restorative nostalgia' as placing emphasis on the *nostos*, she argues that it 'proposes to rebuild the lost home and patch up the memory gaps' whereas 'reflective nostalgia' 'dwells in *algia*, in longing and loss, the imperfect process of remembrance' (2001, 41). We are not attempting to 'patch up the memory gaps' to rebuild a 'lost home' for British television's past, nor are we unnecessarily dwelling in longing and loss. We do not yearn for a past or look back with rose-tinted frames. We are not attempting to construct a 'better' or more 'cohesive' approach to television's history. Instead, our aim is to add to the existing histories and scholarship by highlighting the importance and function of the memory work of remembering and forgetting, and the strategic, commercial and intimate use of regeneration in times of uncertainty.

Now nostalgia emphasizes a sense of place and locatedness (read 'British' in the context of *Doctor Who* in Chapter 7) or a 'golden age'[13] of inventiveness (the 1920s for TV technology or the 1960s for TV drama and 'now' for box-set dramas). It celebrates mainstream culture (popularity or family viewing) and the present moment (social media, transmedia and participatory cultures); and

---

[13]Caughie argues: 'Like "serious drama", the idea of a "Golden Age" of television drama is cloaked in perpetual quotation marks. Golden Ages only exist in retrospect. They are never lived as golden, but can only be constructed in memory from the hindsight of what came after' (2000, 57).

it is spreadable through global capitalist communication networks and locally embedded television communities. In the *BBC Worldwide Annual Review 2012/13*, *Doctor Who* (BBC One, 1963–) is underscored several times (through numbers and commerce) as an example of the BBC's reach and globality: the 200 territories *Doctor Who* (hereafter *DW*) is broadcast in; the 16,144 who attended the *DW* Sydney Symphonic Spectacular; the minting of a Tardis commemorative coin in New Zealand; the 3.1 million *DW* Facebook fans; and the Christmas 2012 range of *DW* homewares, ceramics and stationery sold worldwide.

The creation of new markets (especially in China) is not only concerned with monetizing *old TV* but also borrows some new ways of thinking about nostalgia from these markets. In the global competition for television, the past has become a national and cultural energy resource; as much corporate asset as cultural heritage. Yet, there are different 'entranceways' to such 'regenerative nostalgia' as Amanda Lagerkvist highlights in her exploration of 'embodied performances of memory' (2013) in the westernization of Shanghai (a city with its own golden age). Like the nostalgia industry of many modern cities engaged in regenerative memory work, iconic television texts such as *DW* or *Sherlock Holmes* offer the opportunity to explore the relationship between 'memory and futurity', or to borrow Lakergvist's term '*retromodernity*': a sense in which the new is predicated on memories of the modern' (2013, 25).[14] In the case of *DW*, such *now nostalgia* is able to harness fan-text memorability to produce old and new remembering audiences through digital memories (e.g. Facebook fandom) and archival entrepreneurship (e.g. re-patriating lost episodes).[15] This *now nostalgia* recirculates *old TV* as lost–found, a quest-puzzle-jigsaw, as just tucked away but *now* easily accessible, reusable and reworkable as a rebrand and re-creativity. The rest, can be said to be, *not now* nostalgia, not in and of this present time strategy, stored away in the past, too much of the past. Mundane, messy and routine it forms the real cultural work and graft of making and watching television. Yet, this not now nostalgia is also too much around and in the present, literally hanging around, looming over it with its critique of the nostalgic impulse.[16]

Kenith Trodd (producer of Dennis Potter's plays and series) claimed that when he sought in 2014 to entice Charlotte Moore, then controller of BBC One and now director of BBC Content, to pay tribute to extant (or remake lost) Potter

[14]In the context of literary criticism Frederik J. Solinger also uses the term 'regenerative nostalgia' in the same way as we do here and this chimes with Lakergvist's use of the term: '"nostalgia for the future," a temporally-misoriented concept that is both a nostalgia for that which has yet to happen but feels as though it already has, and a nostalgia utilized for future revolutionary gain' (2013, 25).

[15]Hills and Garde-Hansen (2017) cover this repatriation of *Doctor Who* episodes as an example of paratextual memory work and industry.

[16]Dennis Potter said in a 1979 BBC World Service interview: 'there is in England – and quite understandably – a yearning, a nostalgia, a basically rightwing impulse which is simple in the sense that it wishes things to be as they were: that is, socially, politically impossible' (Potter 2015).

he was met with an inexplicable reaction, at least to him. In his speech at the 2014 *Inheriting British Television Symposium* at the National Media Museum (hereafter NMeM) he exclaimed: "'Dennis Potter!', she said. "That's nostalgia. That could never be BBC1. Not now". Trodd continued: 'Now decoding that remark would be a monstrous task, since practically every bit of dramatic expression on BBC1 currently [...] is backward looking. Nostalgia in a supportive, unconscious and uncreative way.'[17] Amy Holdsworth explored this issue in *Television Memory and Nostalgia* (2011) in her analysis of the BBC's crown jewels of creativity (in the case of Stephen Poliakoff constructed as 'an object of nostalgia' by the BBC and others). Further, Hills asks the important question, 'Why celebrate *Doctor Who* so fulsomely in 2013, yet barely commemorate *The Wednesday Play* in 2014?' (2015, 7).

Unpacked a little further, we would argue that for current television producers, *old TV* is separable into either *now* or *not (right) now (or ever) nostalgia*. *Doctor Who*, we suggest, is *now nostalgia* because it easily reproduces on message (read 'corporate') memories. Its male producer-writers since 2005 (Russel T. Davies, Stephen Moffat, Chris Chibnall) are defined as lifelong fans and trusted inheritors. They have shown their love and devotion to the text, endured the dry times, become showrunners, payed service to the resilient fans while maintaining Hills's 'industrial continuum of nostalgic creativity' cited above. Kompare notes that while 'fan formations are by no means indicative of television viewers in general [...] it is at least plausible to suggest that these groups and their practices have added to the overall historical construction of [...] television heritage [...], helping legitimate television (and particularly past television) in myriad ways as [...] culturally significant' (2005, 124–5).

While much of fan studies has not directly engaged with many of the memory studies theories cited above, there have been some attempts of late to address memory work and cultural memory within television fan scholarship (notably Monaco 2010) and television industries (notably Hills's *Doctor Who: The Unfolding Event* 2015). The rise of vintage gatherings, revivalist shows, reinvention tours, retro-acts, come-back performances and fan memorabilia conventions all speak to a voracious culture of nostalgia which Paul Grainge identified as a hallmark of postmodernism, defined as a yearning for the past (2003). On the other hand, audience nostalgia provides a certain fuel or energy for engaging in more critical appreciations of popular culture's past, as Brabazon argues:

Popular culture is different, being seldom marked as significant or important. The memory of shoulder pads and lip-gloss, Raybans, fingerless gloves and

---

[17]Trodd continued: 'There's better news from another part of the BBC. Radio 3 will do Dennis proud [...] But the supreme news today is that the BFI starting this summer and continuing across two years will show every piece, scrap and glory of his work' (2014). The BFI did indeed celebrate Potter (see Chapter 3).

Wham, grasps an ordinariness and banality that is rarely useful for museum curators or historians. This is the role of Popular Memory Studies – to translate and transform past popular culture into relevant sources in the present.

(Brabazon 2005, 70)

The fan inheritance of British television as a privately and publicly circulating (global) currency and the creation of a new 'public space' for remembering television's value goes some way to challenging John Caughie's (2010) assertion in 'Mourning Television' that there is something to mourn, something lost that is in tension with something to celebrate and rediscover. In his essay, he defines that 'sense of loss' as a loss of the 'object of study', of a sense of the popular, of the public space that social realist drama has created, for example (such as *Cathy Come Home* [1967]), but also a potential loss of, what we would define here as, the disruptive pleasure of enchantment. Recalling a television series that caught him by surprise, Caughie recollects his engagement with television:

> The detail of my memory is fuzzy and impressionistic, and my aesthetic judgment is based on affect and immediacy rather than analysis. But it is worth saying that for most of the final episode I was somewhere beyond speech, beyond judgement and, I guess, beyond aesthetics: taken by surprise by television in a way which is quite distinctive, and quite different to the package of the box-set.

(Caughie 2010, 420)

To be taken by surprise by television, particularly *old TV*, is very much part of its ongoing (personal) memorability and in what follows we address this as a distinct methodological challenge.

Memorability and methodology

In his attempt to think about the creation of a television canon, Ellis reflects on the importance of personal memory to British television history. He explains that his television canon would include the programmes that punctuated his life, from early childhood to the pleasures he took in *Hill Street Blues* (NBC, 1981–7). For Ellis, 'the cultural importance of television lies in the sum of these personal experiences' (2005, 40). How then might broadcasters seek to understand these personal experiences and does memorability feature in their strategic thinking when issues of quality and distinctiveness may overshadow? How can we fully appreciate the impact of *old TV* if the personal memories that circulate implicitly in the writing or British television history may underplay the race, class, gender, age and social status of the author, fan auteur or scholar?

At the time of writing this book, the BBC's director of audiences commissioned a consultancy firm to research and write a report entitled 'Media and Memorability' with the remit to interview ten leading experts on the relationship between media and memory, and to focus on TV, radio and online. The previous year, the same firm, MTM London had completed a report on 'Gender and Media' through a combination of expert interviews, surveys, focus groups and questionnaires. The results of that report had been presented to the BBC senior team with the intention that the data was to be used to reflect upon the BBC's output, audience expectations and sensitivities and the way forward for new developments. 'Media and Memorability' was to follow the same format and the first key expert MTM London interviewed was one of the authors of this book, who was invited to contribute to a 'project [that] is designed to be a comprehensive study on memory and what makes things memorable, with a specific focus on media. The study aims to deliver an industry thought-piece on the role of memory and will also inform future BBC actions in terms of content planning and audience engagement' (Garde-Hansen, pers. comm., 3 March 2016). Once the interview was undertaken, MTM London responded with, we think 'storytelling is an incredibly useful lens through which to think about how we understand memory – understanding the stories the BBC can tell us, and those that we tell each other and ourselves will be a really interesting frame to guide our other interviews' (Garde-Hansen, pers. comm., 9 March 2016).[18]

To shift the focus, then, as we have begun to do in this book from television's history to television's memorability is a strategy the television industry has been focused on during our research and writing, and this chimes with a certain long-standing recognition in the BBC, for example, that what is 'memorable' may be just as important to measure as audience size or cost-per-hour weekly reach. In *TV FAQ* Ellis wrote about the BBC's 2004 policy document – now rather dated in its title *Building Public Value: Renewing the BBC for a Digital World* – in which 'points of impact' through 'memorability' become an indicator to measure (Ellis 2007).[19] While one might measure 'memorability' beyond broadcasting through viewing figures, re-viewing figures, reuse, DVD sales, and production of old and new media paratexts (see Gray 2010), this does not quite give us the longer-term memorability we need to measure. If the BBC's aspiration in 2004 was to 'deliver greater value and memorability beyond the broadcast' (2004, 72) then this may have been achieved when we consider social memory building initiatives such as Capture Wales (2001–08), Telling Lives (2002–05), the Listening Project (2012–) and the Genome Project (2014–). Each of these projects in different ways

---

[18]The BBC's final report for its own uses was to be completed after the publication of this book. A Freedom of Information request would need to be submitted to get access to it.

[19]This requires memory agents (including scholars) to scaffold the narrative. Referring to the previous footnote about the lack of television history writing on the Storm Surge of 1953 suggests that a new history of broadcasting could be written if we started at this point and involved memory agents from environmental studies, geography and hydrology, as well as interviewing those who remember the event. Memorability, then, is not only inside the text or the event (clearly a devastating flood is memorable), but it needs to be worked on continuously by a wide range of stakeholders.

acknowledges that one's memory and media used to scaffold remembering are co-constituted. Van Dijck makes the same point:

> The traditional idea of collective memory is generally grounded in the presumption that the individual and the collective are separate entities that are associated through technological mechanisms, such as media, and through social institutions, such as archives. However, the formation of memory is increasingly structured by digital networks, and memory's constituting agency is both technological and human.
>
> (Van Dijck 2011, 402)

One aspect, then, of our memory studies approach is to think through television not in terms of canon but in terms of memorability-potential. In the literature on cultural memory 'canon' can be understood through Assmann's (1996) definition of those long standing, identity-forming works, around which new cultural memories circulate. However, we are not undertaking research inside television's archival holdings as a television historian would, seeking to day-light forgotten texts, stories and identities that can enhance or challenge the canon. Rather, we want to explore television memorability in order to ask questions about how television archives are already potentialized through the 'ingenuity of memory makers' and 'producers' and 'the subversive interests of memory consumers' of television's past under certain 'conditions' (Kansteiner 2002, 179).

The reasoning, then, behind both the content and structure of this book, stems from our own experiences teaching and researching widely across television studies, media audiences and media history alongside media and memory, digital media, creative media, industry research and audience research. Likewise, our experience of working outside the academy with remembering communities has shown us that many are working in the creative industries and heritage management industries that need to be evaluated for understanding the ways in which television as heritage is being produced, instrumentalized and reworked. We want to understand who has a stake in *old TV*, what is considered important to record, archive and remember, what has been missed in this process and why? Who gets to remember television and who does not? How is television heritage consumed and repurposed? How are identities (fans, communities, media professionals, for example) built upon and around television heritage? Through what new methods is television being remembered? How are the narratives of collective memories of television being challenged by audiences or 'the subversive interests of memory consumers' (noted by Kansteiner above) and by what kinds of memory entrepreneurs?

To address these questions, we bring together interpretations of research material from television production and heritage management (directors, actors, screenwriters, below-the-line production workers, archivists, museum staff, heritage managers and funders) and consumers (fans, museum visitors, heritage volunteers, audiences and online viewers) within the context of historical and theoretical work in cultural studies of television. Bearing in mind the demands upon broadcasters to open their archives to the internet, it is timely to understand television as valuable economically, historically and culturally to a very wide range of stakeholders, who are all invested in making television history meaningful for themselves and future users. The operation of archives in the twenty-first century (their closedness, openness and mutability) is addressed throughout our book's focus upon what it is possible to culturally and personally inherit and re-consume. Our interviews, document analysis, case studies and memory work address current debates surrounding the changes in television's value, viewing practices, technologies, ideologies and content, and contributes toward an understanding of what is considered important to remember. What is remembered and archived are valuable indicators of television's impact upon other media such as film, radio and online media. However, what those outside the archive remember is less well covered and here innovative forms of interviewing are needed.

We undertook our interviews in a participatory and grounded manner, in situ, often on a tour of some kind, in comfortable but actual surroundings of noise, in public, alongside television screens, television sets, archives and tape holdings. Many were interviewed in places of cultural work and operation, while other members of staff may have walked in and out, with one of our participants being interviewed at a university office and then providing a tour of their workplace later. We used a snowballing technique and this works well for researching cultural producers, and especially those at mid-level: 'Snowballing may prove particularly effective since mid-level managers and directors may not be listed on directories or websites' (Herzog and Ali 2015, 43). All our participants were offered anonymity but most were comfortable to have their names used in the published research, were provided with transcripts for redaction, which some opted for, and selections of interview data are herein used to underpin the analysis.

Moreover, we actively encouraged 'anecdote', 'speculation', 'self-reflexivity' and imaginary scenarios as the cornerstone of our narrative-enquiry approach. Interviews were one-to-one, dividing the interviewees between us, using the same open-ended questions, comparing notes afterward and analysing the transcriptions together. We started from questions of personal memory: 'Tell us about your favourite TV?', 'your TV memories', 'your memories of watching television' and 'what value do you place on personal memories of TV?' These were introspective questions for organizational actors but were key to our approach of interweaving for personal memories within professional stories and narratives. These stories may appear to provide 'no data' as Mike Michael defines anecdote:

> Unlike other narratives that can languish in dusty tomes or loiter in the back of one's mind, anecdotes, perhaps because of the nature of the incident, seem to demand to be told, to be put into circulation. Or rather, such narratives become anecdotes by virtue of their telling, because they are deliberately sent out into the world.
>
> (Michael 2012, 25)

Any lack of memory (or rather some memories offered were not the ones the researcher sought) may seem to disrupt the purposes of research that is trying to draw upon non-academic expert knowledge. Yet, taken as successful forgetting it can equally demonstrate the way in which participants anecdotal-ize television as about them, their community, their family, their work or the nation, as well as their professional connections. It also challenges us, as researchers, to shift our theoretical pursuit of verifiable knowledge of television's production and reception (what might be important to a project's rationale and sampling), toward television as lived cultural memory being remade as personal experience for the purposes of intangible and tangible cultural heritage.

Kansteiner (2002, 179) has argued that 'collective memory studies should adopt the methods of communication and media studies, especially with regard to media reception, and continue to use a wide range of interpretive tools from traditional historiography to poststructural approaches'. One such approach might be to consider memory as future-oriented rather than only facing the reconstruction of the past. Many of our participants not only reflected but were in professional positions where anticipatory thinking was required: the future requirements of the medium of television, the skills needed to archive and repurpose, the funding proposals and the development of new technologies for cataloguing and sharing data of *old TV*. They lived and worked in reminders from the future based on having lost so much television in the past. The idea that *this is what you will regret not valuing now responsibilizes* memory agents into taking great care over their memories of television and seeking opportunities to share those memories.

Television's diverse range of content *moves* viewers in so many different ways and directions, and to be cognizant of television's history and the scholarship that surrounds it, while resisting an attempt to write a new narrative, has created several pitfalls to avoid and theoretical mountains to climb. One of the advantages of co-authoring a book is having someone to talk through ideas with and several times we wished that we had recorded our many formal and informal conversations as they probably did a better job of articulating the more complicated aspects of our approach. At a moment when we were both feeling unsure of how to articulate our methodology in this book, we were fortunate enough to come across a description of research in the *Connected Viewing Initiative*, which is a partnership between UC Santa Barbara's Carsey-Wolf Center and Warner Brothers Home Entertainment. In the Introduction to 'the expanded landscape of connected viewing' in *Convergence*, Jennifer Holt, Gregory Steirer and Karen Petruska explain that:

> The *connections* that constitute connected viewing thus take place not only at the level of our research object, but also in our modes of thinking, thus bringing together the perspectives of productions studies, technology studies, economics, the digital humanities, globalization and media flows, regulation and policy studies, consumer behaviour research, cultural studies, and fan studies, among other research paradigms.
>
> (Holt, Steirer and Petruska 2016, 344; our emphasis)

Their flexible, adaptive mode of research, which is inspired in part by John Law's 'mess' research (2004) and Charles Acland's 'dirt research' (2014), means that they let the 'research object itself dictate where the researcher needs to go and how he or she needs to study or view it' (Holt, Steirer and Petruska 2016, 344). The notion of allowing the research object (memories of television or *old TV*) to move the researcher towards other objects, people or texts appeals to us as a way of describing the methodology we have followed in this book. We have allowed the memories of television that are shared with us to lead us to new places in relation to television, to day-light experiences and activities going unnoticed, to encounter new theoretical paradigms and not to limit ourselves either to memory studies or to television studies as disciplinary boundaries. This, of course, does mean that the journeying follows some established routes and networks (see Latour 2005, on actor-network theory), which may have missed key places and persons not plugged into those networks that we have noted already.

As discussed in the beginning, the primary spaces we have been directed towards are the museums/archives, media and cultural industries and the domestic spaces of families. Within these spaces, we have met with a variety of stakeholders: viewers, fans, collectors, (re)viewers, scholars, broadcasters, producers, creatives, heritage/archive managers and entrepreneurs and interviewed them about their own television memories and those integral to the spaces they work in.

The first two chapters focus on the remembering that happens within the study and industry of television. Chapter 1, 'Remembering Television's Past' takes television's history as its focus and explores the way television has been recollected in academic literature, personal memoirs and popular memory. It does so not to offer an alternative history of television but to point to what has been left out from a personal memory perspective. For this reason, it considers the division between 'official' and 'unofficial' histories of British television's history and how these lines have been drawn. Following on from this, and listening closer to voices within the British television industry, Chapter 2, 'Remembering Television Production: Producer-ly Memory', focuses on producers in the widest sense of the term and uses these voices to explore the importance of memories to a broader understanding of television institutions and industries. This chapter draws heavily on interviews conducted with present and former members of the British television industry to consider the ways in which they value their own personal memories working and what sense they have of an 'inheritance' for the next generation. This chapter is inspired by work by John T. Caldwell in *Production Culture* (2008) and Vicki Mayer's *Below the Line* (2011) in terms of its engagement with the people who make up the 'everyday' of the television industry.

The next two chapters move our focus into the museum and archives. What kinds of television treasures reside in or are day-lighted from the archives and how do we make decisions regarding their value? Chapter 3, 'Television's Treasures and Archival Values', draws on interviews with television heritage sector managers and considers the bind they sometimes find themselves in between nostalgia and the economic realities of making *old TV* relevant today with core and new audiences. The chapter considers how a variety of stakeholders, such as the BFI, MACE, Getty, Box of Broadcasts and Kaleidoscope, invest their time, energy and passion into remembering television on behalf of the broadcasters and publics they serve. They are not simply engaged in procuring, protecting and promoting television's treasures, they are involved in surfacing memories that (whether intentionally or not) have the capacity to direct our understanding about television's past and a wider socially shared and shareable past. Chapter 4, 'The End of "Experience TV" at the National Media Museum', explores television as leaving the museum as a case study that draws on interviews with key stakeholders to consider the place of the television set and television technology within museological thinking. It examines a shift within the museum from television as technology to thinking about the ephemera and context to the television experience. The unexpected closure of the 'Experience TV' gallery during our research could be read as a move away from the medium of television during a period when the 'end' of television is frequently prophesized. However, the interviews reveal that precarity lurks more for the cultural labourers in the museum than the box itself.

The subsequent two chapters move our study into families and viewers and to thinking about *old TV* as something that evokes powerful memories and/or is used to pass on to new generations or to attract new audiences. Chapter 5, 'Caring for Past Television: The Case of Children's Television', focuses on the caring evident in discussions of children's television in both Mumsnet and through interviews with mothers who share past television with their children. The chapter reflects on the logic of care that is evoked around the remembering of television in digital media and in people's personal memories. Past television constructs a spatio-temporal locatedness where people can share their memories more freely and feel able to pass them on to their children or loved ones. Mothers are not the only ones who do this kind of legacy work with television, but their voices are often under-represented in research of television custodianship. Often the sharing that happens with past television, as explored in Chapter 5, is embodied by the dolls or objects associated with past television, such as a Bagpuss doll which many of the women interviewed remember or bought for their own children. Following on with the notion of paratexts, Chapter 6, 'Nostalgia and Paratextual Memory: *Cold Feet* (ITV, 1997–2017), Reminiscence Clip Shows and "Vintage" Television Websites' picks up on this sharing across platforms. With a shift within museums to include more ephemera, we consider how this is taking place within television programming, particularly in terms of reboots and the recycling of past television. It uses the reboot of *Cold Feet* as an example and employs textual analysis of both the series and the paratexts that surround it.

The final chapter brings together our study of audiences with that of the museum to consider the structuring of the fan as a paratextual memory agent and maker, whose value to new heritage entrepreneurs creates opportunities for new kinds of memory industries. The caring for past television that is at the heart of Chapters 5 and 6 is explored in Chapter 7 as industrialized and scalable across heritage sectors and considered in terms of the labour that goes into presenting the passion fans have for the texts they love. 'Regenerative Memory?: Crafting *Doctor Who*' explores the crafting of a 'Doctor Who and Me' exhibition held at the National Media Museum and considers the stakeholders involved in the curation and memorialization of television objects.

1 REMEMBERING TELEVISION'S PAST

This chapter addresses how we are called upon to remember television and the various ways in which remembering is made possible – whether through academic research and debate, monographs and textbooks, personal and professional memoirs or popular memory more generally. In so doing, it will consider what sort of official and unofficial histories of television are created and valued, and how this influences our understanding of the ways in which we inherit British television and the experience of television viewing. Johnson and Turnock have pointed out that there are 'absent histories' (2005, 1) of ITV, for example, and there has been a marginalization of histories of other broadcasters due to the dominance of the BBC's corporate and organizational memory. Thus, we may need to consider less the history of television in the epistemological sense and more its memory in the materialized sense. That is, the production of television as 'a certain kind of organized and inferential knowledge' that is distinct from memory seen as 'not organized, not inferential at all' (Collingwood [1946] 1999, 8). While there is a gap, in part addressed by Helen Wheatley's important collection *Re-viewing Television: Critical Issues in Television Historiography* (2007), we are not re-viewing television here. This chapter does not offer an alternative history or a neglected history, rather we suggest an approach that considers the 'question of value [that] has become inescapable' (Johnson and Turnock 2005, 36) because 'broadcast television is both huge and intimate' (40).

Remembering television within the locatedness of a British experience has become an increasingly polarized issue in recent years, with key players writing and rewriting that experience for popular memory purposes and to make statements about the nation, the regions and the relationship of these to a global market economy. There is a sense that a 'bad' cultural inheritance of television may lead to dangerous nostalgia and creative stagnation if left to the whims of the market, an uncritical audience or some global and corporate media company. A scenario which can be rectified if we can only *remember well* such texts as *Cathy*

Come Home (1967) and its television auteur. In a 2016 *Guardian* interview, the British director Ken Loach (referring to programmes such as the highly successful *Downton Abbey*, ITV, 2010–15), hit the headlines by saying: 'This rosy vision of the past, it's a choice broadcasters make [...] "Don't bother your heads with what's going on now, just wallow in fake nostalgia". It's bad history, bad drama. It puts your brain to sleep' (Jackson 2016). Yet, Caughie warned that the 'dangers of such nostalgia' for the period '1965–1975 identified as the Golden Age of television drama' where 'very dull plays and unremarkable evenings' are ignored 'are clear, particularly when an unrecoverable and idealized past is used as a stick with which to beat the all-too-material present' (2000, 57). Suggesting there is a social contract to be had with past television raises important questions in the material present about who now gets to speak about television's past and determine what is important to remember and inherit.

Of 1960s and 1970s British television texts such as *Cathy Come Home* (1967) and the increased broadcast of films and football on television, Ed Buscombe stated some time ago that we must study television because it is *there*, it is influential, and knowledge of its public impact would lend itself to public control over the medium (1974, 8). Furthermore, in the later UNESCO (United Nations Educational, Scientific and Cultural Organization) report *Media Education in the United Kingdom: An Annotated Bibliography* (1983, 13), Len Masterman cited Buscombe's text as 'an early exploration of issues and practice in Television Studies. Sections on "Why Study Television?" and "What should one teach about television?" are followed by descriptions of seven different television courses and a "model" course'. Now that television has transitioned from being *there*, in an identifiable place (toward which furniture is turned and impact has been felt), to being potentially nowhere in particular (mobile and digital) as well as all over the place (ubiquitous),[1] how and why should we study television and its history today when there is so much of it and yet, at the same time, a feeling of scarcity concerning its past? One response is to remind ourselves of the four reasons Masterman used to frame his 1983 UNESCO paper and to reapply these to the new context of something happening to television as it is turned into heritage and memory: '"who" constructs' representations of past television; 'what "techniques" are used which enable' constructions to 'pass themselves as true and authentic'; 'what "values" are implicit' in representations of past television; and 'how are these representations *read* by their audiences?' (Masterman 1983, ii).

This chapter, then, focuses upon key academic texts within television studies and touches on the voices from within the Industry to draw attention to the sources that have been and are being used to officially write that history so

---

[1] It is worth highlighting that the public BBC radio campaign during September 2016 to communicate the TV Licence Fee 'law change' in which BBC iPlayer became officially a form of 'television' is framed by the question: 'To be or not to be' television 'that is the question'.

that we can begin to address how television's past is being presented. In later chapters, we are particularly interested in what has been left out and missed from a 'personal memory' perspective (i.e. production cultures and industry/worker narratives; heritage managers and fans) and what kinds of figures are remembering British television in a digital age and for what reasons. Here, television is not only a form of valuable cultural heritage but is also the intangible heritage of a single person as much as collective or popular memory. 'Why is it popular to remember the past in this way in the first place?' asks Spigel (1995, 23). Perhaps because television gives us legitimate access to ourselves as chroniclers of our own social histories: the small screens of our own lives. As Piper has recently asserted:

> Formal histories of television and broadcasting have attended more assiduously to the 'big picture' than to the micro possibilities of engagement, avoiding the question of what television has meant, if anything, to the successive generations who devoted so many leisure hours watching it. Instead, television historiography has veered upwards towards the epic, the aesthetic, and the political, focusing on nation-states, hegemonies, institutions, advertisers, producers, and, selectively, programmes.
>
> (Piper 2015, 123)

Yet, many television historians (including producers) have declared their own personal passions, small experiences, family lives and micro possibilities of engagement that have never been very far from the page (see, for example, Jane Root's 1986 *Open the Box*).

TV studies and TV history

In *Television Studies* (2012, 119) Gray and Lotz summarize television history research as all-encompassing referring to British and American television studies. In a chapter entitled 'Context' they make the point that 'a great many book length studies of television history transcend these imposed classifications [texts, audiences, industries] so flagrantly as to embody a category all of their own by depicting the environment around programs, audiences, and industries, not just their details'. While, in contrast, it is only in the fourth edition of *The Television Handbook* (2013) – which does not contain a chapter on history – that we have the inclusion of very brief sections on 'History and the MTV debate' and 'Reality TV history', neither of which refer to the extensive histories that have been written on either of these genres (see Inglis 2010 and Holmes and Jermyn 2004 respectively) nor to any specific national framing of television. Television history is then, it seems, either all over the place (touching upon, speaking about and incorporating all aspects of social, cultural, economic, industrial, communicative, creative and common experience) or nowhere, absent from the study of television.[2] To construct a story of television with little reference to television history and memory reproduces mythologies of a medium of ephemerality, flow and forgetting, or leaves the task to the corporations and media companies, who are unlikely to day-light difficult pasts. Therefore, the dominant issue raised within the histories of television focus heavily on the tensions between inclusion/exclusion and materiality/ephemerality. Indeed, one of the difficulties that academic scholars raise in studying television's past is the fact that there is simultaneously too much television and yet so little of its past exists (see *The History of Forgotten Television Drama Project* 2013–16 as addressing this issue).

How, then, does television studies as an area of research and scholarship teach its students about this past? How is this past framed by and positioned within the story of the development of television in the United Kingdom? How do television historians situate this social and cultural past as something worthwhile and pertinent? Equally important, in the light of the 2016 Charter renewal for the BBC where 'Great British' television was used as leverage, is to understand how television's past is selected to make a case to the public about access and engagement to works of art, entertainment and information that they are compelled to pay for. One could argue that television's history has been read as the history of broadcasting, policy, regulation and competition (Briggs 1961–70, 1979, 1985, 1995; Curran and Seaton 2010; Seaton 2015) belying a 'national television' of national texts, genres and auteurs, as one might define a 'national cinema'. As the BBC commissions its latest official history provisionally entitled *The BBC: A Century of British Life* to be written by Professor David Hendy, the focus is not to be on broadcasting, technology or policy but on 'persons'.[3] Who those people will be, how their importance will be determined and whether that 'British Life' will include memories in the widest possible sense of those who have produced television are important issues for scholars of television history and for those critical of how television history has been written in the past.

We cannot escape the sense that while television 'may have become our leading global medium' (today we have new audiences in China, fansubbing their favourites through VPNs, the rise of Netflix or the growth of TV franchises) 'its history is deeply bound up in the identities of nations' (Hilmes 2003, 1). It is on this point that television history overlaps with memory studies, wherein we are required to know about television's history as a form of collective memory that has been controlled 'in the interests of social order, political control and preservation of central cultural and economic hierarchies' (Hilmes 2003, 1; and see Bennett, Mercer and Woolacott 1986). British television in its texts, audiences and industries is, then, as much about the *administration of memory* as it is about

---

[2] See Stephen Lacey (2006) for an engaging account of the place of history in television studies.
[3] His current project is writing *The BBC: A Century in British Life*, an authorized one-volume history of the BBC, which will be published to coincide with the corporation's centenary in 2022.

the *politics of identity*,[4] a key change of emphasis we shall return to. It is timely to consider this, as the BBC has attracted increasing criticism over the perception of its assumed role as 'the chronicler of our time', states Loach (BBC Entertainment New 2016) in his recent news article on 'fake nostalgia', with the resources used to tell its own history again and again and again. Furthermore, and to follow Piper's (2015) perspective cited above, the history of television has been presented in a particular way, and that inevitably leaves gaps. How these gaps are filled, if at all, determines how far television can be measured and valued along different axes for different cultural actors and audiences: women or non-white producers and consumers of television being one such axis.

There are, then, several important texts of the early 2000s that focus on British television history, such as Lez Cooke's *British Television Drama: A History* (2003, 2015), John Caughie's (2000) *Television Drama: Realism, Modernism and British Culture* and Jonathan Bignell and Stephen Lacey's (2005) edited collection titled *British Television Drama: Past, Present and Future*. These not only emphasize the importance within British television history of the dramatic form, but also the way in which this form defines British television history and culture. It also demonstrates that other television, such as factual, news, entertainment and sport, are often overlooked in these kinds of histories. The desire to underscore national monumental television texts and the emergence of *télévision d'auteurs* is not at all surprising when we are reminded that British television began life following 'a pattern established by the late Victorians and the Edwardians for the administration of other national utilities like water, gas, and electricity' (Caughie 2000, 26). We are then back to thinking about television as a (cultural) resource (in need of management, good governance and administration) and, we argue, this accords with the late nineteenth-century concern with 'cultural inheritance', those developing theories of history and early understandings of 'memory' as 'preserving and transmitting energy' (Olick, Vinitzky-Seroussi and Levy 2011, 106). As a symbol of that energy, British television drama, while not quite a national cinema, has been and continues to be considered distinct from cinema, and is a key learning point that distinguishes the cultural value of this developing form.[5]

Lez Cooke's 2015 second edition of *British Television Drama* is divided chronologically – we move from the early developments of television drama in the 1930s, 40s and early 50s, decade by decade, to television drama in the 'digital age 2002–2014'. The decades are loosely marked by sociocultural history, such as the chapter on 'Television drama and Thatcherism' reflects. Caughie's (2000) book takes a similar journey through a chronologically defined past, making reference to certain markers such as the 'golden age' and 'non-naturalism' to

---

[4]See the philosopher Charles Taylor's *Multiculturalism and the Politics of Recognition* (1994) for a discussion on what is at stake in the demand to be recognized.
[5]This point is taken up by Helen Wheatley in her latest book *Spectacular Television* (2016).

signal developments in television's aesthetic landscape. Bignell and Lacey's (2005) collected book is structured as 'Institutions and Technologies', 'Formats and Genres', and 'Representations', which speak in large part to some of the defining approaches to teaching television studies in many countries, and the main pillars of media studies in the United Kingdom and more broadly. All three convey the past-ness of British television as stages of development but the continua of cultural policies of preserving, storing and rebroadcasting television are much less obviously addressed. However, all these books show forth the almost metabolic value of British television drama to the country's resource infrastructure (energy and culture in combination) and something of immense cultural and creative value for heterogeneous and multidirectional reasons (texts and audiences in combination). That the internet now provides new platforms, pathways and transmedia opportunities for British television drama is not lost on these researchers as they update their books to take account of the rapid rise of internet dramas and the new appetite for British television heritage as a high-end commodity to global audiences.

In summary, reviewing some television studies textbooks has shown that there is often a section on television history, such as Bignell's *An Introduction to Television Studies* (2004) which concentrates on the proliferation of histories that can be told in order to encourage the reader to approach the subject critically and not as one cohesive history. Centring on issues such as television's ephemerality, again the 'golden age' the development of technologies and institutions, and a focus on television formats and forms, the chapter/section titles reiterate a certain kind of 'official history' in the demarcation of what is important to learn or study about British television. This can be summarized as a multidirectional approach that locates studying television as being at the intersection of histories (and stories) of industry, policy, audience, aesthetics, society and culture (macro and meso scales of analysis) while offering some potential pathways into micro-analysis of audience taste.

Reviewing television histories

In the introduction to her collection *Re-viewing Television History* (2007) Wheatley reflects on the question of television history and the historiography of television, which at the time was just beginning to flourish. As someone who teaches television, Wheatley recognizes, as do we, that the question of why *do* television history often comes up. Indeed, we are sometimes left wondering what we want our students, who are there to also learn about film and television production, to take from the module. What is it about television's past that they need to know? How will knowing this past enable them to be better television producers or media managers? In part, this is to break through the nostalgia that permeates looking back at television production and expose the real cultural work, sometimes the 'dirty work' underpinning the rise of creativity within the television industry. As Caughie notes: 'the day-to-day experience of the people involved was probably much as professional life always is: a mixture of satisfactions and frustrations, victories and defeats, bureaucratic hassles and creative surprises, moments of excitement punctuated by long stretches of routine' (2000, 57).

For Wheatley, 'an "enriched" sense of television history helps to make sense of television's past as well as its current importance' (2007, 3). But what does an '"enriched" sense of television history' look like, especially when television's past continues to be somewhat ephemeral, difficult to obtain or determinedly forgotten? Moreover, the act of reading about television's past usually means that you begin to construct a sense of that past based on the versions available to you. As Jacobs has argued: 'The danger here is that television history gets reconstructed around what survives for viewing rather than what is actually shown' (2006a, 112), as well as the known pathways to remembering by a creative class. That danger becomes more present when the reconstruction is made around what is readily available online. Spigel argued some time ago that 'television even erases its own past; it selects only a few programmes for syndication and leaves out countless others' (1995, 31), this remains an issue today.

Wheatley (2007, 5) also notes that television studies often 'inherits the industry's propensity for claiming "the next big thing" or "the never before seen"', and this is a point Spigel confirms in her article entitled 'TV's Next Season?' (2005b). The 'new' is often privileged in the television landscape and in our discourse around watching television, to the extent that it seems meaningless to view television historically at all. Yet, Wheatley is keen to challenge 'the new' as an historical concept in itself: 'a discourse of "newness" isn't necessarily a new phenomenon' thus we should 'hold fire on our period of remembrance for the object in historical television studies' (2007, 5). While, this attention to 'newness' has altered slightly in our current context where people are watching 'old' series on Netflix or downloading series from past television, this only serves to underscore the distinction between official histories of television (that canonize or memorialize) and popular memorability and creative mnemonics that find new ways to move old ideas. To be 'tele-literate' as Patricia Holland defined it some time ago, is to think about television as an activity 'that is carried on in many forums, from the pub to the starchiest of academic journals, between tele-people and viewers, students, academics and journalists' (2000, 6), and, of course, online in micro-blogs, fan-sites and media forums.

Thus, some of the literature has been addressing the four key problems Wheatley noted regarding British television history (2007, 8). The first problem of 'national specificity' is being increasingly understood in transnational terms. British television has travelled and continues to travel, and is even being repatriated as valuable lost episodes of, for example, *Doctor Who* are returned *home* (see Hills and Garde-Hansen 2017). The second problem of '(over)privileging institutional histories of television' has been somewhat extended by the production of Jean Seaton's (2015) *Pinkoes and Traitors: The BBC and the Nation 1974–1987*, which unlike those texts of Asa Briggs, was published in a social media landscape of critical reception from audiences and former employees, who remembered the BBC differently to the scholar's evidence. However, many recently funded projects have focused on television producers and their memories, forgotten television drama, women in television, television archives and heritage, fandom and participatory culture, as well as exhibitions on children's television and *Doctor Who* as a key remembered text. These have all brought a much-needed solidity as well as multidirectionality to the study of television outside of broadcaster and institutional histories, and they incorporate or are open to counter-histories and memories.

The third problem of 'nostalgia and the need to confront the connection between popular and academic histories' (Wheatley 2007, 8) has been recently dealt with in Holdsworth's *Television, Memory and Nostalgia* (2011). Yet, as the National Media Museum (a key case study for Holdsworth) closed its television exhibition in 2016 (an issue we focus upon in Chapter 4), the connection between popular memories of television and official histories may have become more fraught than ever. Where will we now see the history of British television and in what kinds of frameworks: scientific, technological, cultural, aesthetic, social or popular? The final problem, 'the question of access to, and survival of, material that shapes our sense of television history' (Wheatley 2007, 8) has come to the fore in the last decade as broadcasters have invested in new platforms and delivery systems for *old TV*. Pathé News, Getty Images, Box of Broadcasts, ITN Source, BFI mediatheques, and more recently Netflix and Amazon, as well as the old hands at Network Releasing, and local archives such as the Media Archive for Central England (MACE), have all invested in past television in its material and digital formats, with different levels of accessibility and consumption. The issue of access is more pressing than ever in a digital age and the *sovereign consumer* (British or otherwise) may well continue to demand the availability of works of television it has financed through a licence fee or seek to purchase now. More than this, such a consumer is bolstered not only by the BBC's Genome Project 1923–2009 but also by pre-Charter renewal aspirational statements such as these from Jake Berger, programme manager of the BBC's Digital Public Space:

> I would like you to imagine that every museum, archive, gallery, library, theatre and studio in the country could all be found next to each other and they each had each item in their collection on display. And imagine if the smallest organisations, archives and objects had the same level of visibility and accessibility as the big nationals. And imagine that all of this material and information were linked together. Now hold that thought for a minute.
>
> (Berger 2011)

All the problems, then, Wheatley highlighted in 2007 continue to dominate how we address British television's history, who we engage in telling its many stories, how the market and the creative class responds, and how these knowledges are connected across and between scales. What is missing from Berger's statement above, in his focus upon memory institutions and the Genome Project with its immense digitized collection of *Radio Times* listings, is *public engagement on a personal and meaningful scale*. Therefore, 'memory' as a concept, practice and form of knowledge, much less showcased in academic television histories, is only accessed by working with audiences and creatives to explore television and its memorability.

It is towards 'popular memory' that we now turn, energized by George Lipsitz's argument that:

> For all their triviality and frivolity, the messages of popular culture circulate in a network of production and reception that is quite serious. At their worst, they perform the dirty work of the economy and the state. At their best, they retain memories of the past and contain hopes for the future that rebuke the injustices and inequities of the present.
>
> (Lipsitz 1990, 20)

Lipsitz adds that it 'might be thought a measure of the inescapable irony of our time that the most profound intellectual questions emerge out of what seem to be ordinary and commonplace objects of study' (20). It is the ordinary personal and communicative memory of working in and with television, as well as watching programmes and recollecting their impact on lives that the literature is beginning to address. Collective memories of television such as can be found in the Granadaland project or in the Alexandra Palace Television Society (APTS) through the work of Sandon (2007), can be added to the fan memories that have been explored by Hills (2014, 2015), as fans take on more of the curatorial responsibility for the 'collected memory' (Olick 1999)[6] of television.

Ryan Lizardi in *Mediated Nostalgia: Individual Memory and Contemporary Mass Media* (2015) has addressed the television collector of American television as one who demonstrates their love through an ordered materialism on a shelf of DVDs; 'what is disabused is any form of collective or critical view of history'. Lizardi addresses in detail this 'nostalgic drive' to 'gain access to one's past and the overarching need to create and maintain those connections' (2015, 39). However, whether collective or collected, there remains much *extra memory*. This memory is expensive to collect, store and preserve, it is from millions of television's viewers or from the proliferating orphan fan websites, or it is the difficult memories of precarious cultural work upon which the industry has depended.[7] What of the glut

---

[6]It is worth highlighting the sociologist Jeffrey Olick's differentiation between 'collected memory … the aggregated individual memories of members of a group' which can be researched through surveys and oral history collection, and 'collective memory', which is the public manifestation as mythology, tradition and heritage (1999, 338, 342).

[7]Such as the late Dave Evan's tribute website *Clenched Fists* to Dennis Potter, not updated since 2005 and without great expense unable to find a home.

of those personal memories of ordinary television viewers who demand anniversary programming, commemorations, collections, memorabilia and new forms of creativity with the original text? How can we account for paratextual memory where the text is absent, lost or rediscovered? How does television's memory emerge not out of a collector's experience of texts – 'creating and monitoring an archive-like access to these texts as a way of staying "up to date" with the past' (Lizardi 2015, 39) – but as paratextual? How can television historians account for the proliferation of paratexts, circulating around the experience of television, its impact and afterlife in a felt and enduring way? What kinds of methodological approaches and interdisciplinary thinking are accounting for memories of working in television where only certain kinds of professional experience have informed the narrative?

Popular memory and television history

Dillon argues that 'when individual, collective or popular memory, popular culture, television and history are combined they become a potent mixture' (2010, 4). No doubt this is because a form of unofficial knowledge is actionable on a mass and highly differentiated scale, and while it is largely mediated by academics and elite persons with their expert credentials and networks of impact, it retains both an inheritability and a demand to be told and shared in and between scales. It is in the liminal space between official and unofficial television histories where much television history scholarship can operate. In the absence of television texts and ephemera, we trust scholars to remember well, while accepting their object of study is part of the living memory of the group. It is important to note that one of the key scholars of popular memory studies, the sociologist Maurice Halbwachs, has argued that the historian 'is not located within the viewpoint of genuine and living groups of past or present', the historian values all details equally, 'all then is on the same level' (2011, 145). But, we argue that the television historian *is located* within the viewpoint of genuine and living groups. Further, these groups consider themselves stakeholders in British television as a part of their cultural heritage and their memories of television are a form of communicative intangible heritage. Halbwachs continues, whereas, 'every collective memory requires the support of a group delimited in space and time' and 'the totality of past events can be put together in a single record', this is only achieved by separating those events 'from the memory of the groups who preserved them and by severing the bonds that held them close to the psychological life of the social milieus where they occurred' (145). Popular memory, then, becomes an important operator in making *old TV* a workable concept for scholars, students, creatives, museum and heritage industries, fans and audiences.

In her reading of the logics of popular memory and academic histories, Spigel considers why students are interested in thinking about the representations of 'past' women to think through the contemporary versions. She argues that they become 'caught between two ways of thinking about the past – one properly "academic" and the other conventionally "popular"' (1995, 21). One of the consequences of this 'potent mixture' as Dillon describes it above, is that the 'histories told in the texts of popular culture simplify the complexity of historical events' (Spigel 1995, 21). As Spigel argues, this simplification is not due to a lack of intellect but rather a desire for other stories about the past. This accords with Pierre Nora's subsequent account of the upsurge in memory studies in Europe: 'unlike history, which has always been in the hands of the public authorities, of scholars and specialized peer groups, memory has acquired all the new privileges and prestige of a popular protest movement' (2002). Thus, Spigel refers to 'popular memory' as a 'form of storytelling through which people make sense of their own lives and culture' (1995, 21). What this kind of storytelling does is to create an 'unofficial' history that is not wholly at odds with the official history but, rather, is connected to and often produces new 'hybrid' histories (22). While this book does not aim to tell a factual story about what has happened in British television, nor address television's absent histories of the personal and the strategic forgetting at the heart of discourses of newness and flow, we do ask as does Christine Geraghty 'what can be said about rescued texts other than their rescue?'[8]

Official and unofficial historians

One of the issues revealed through looking at the way in which television's past is articulated is that there are 'official' and 'unofficial' historians of television. For example, archives or fan collections ('rogue archives' says Abigail De Kosnik 2016), academic and broadcaster histories or retired staff reunion webpages and heritage events of the Society for Motion Picture and Television Engineers (SMPTE). The internet has enabled online spaces to be created, shared and connected, in which the official and unofficial collide and overlap and this is a key reason why we have used it as a primary resource in our own assemblage of thinking about television memory (See Garde-Hansen and Gorton 2013). Such online spaces may be used to thrash out elite debates of vested interests in how British television's history is researched and written, the former television producer and former chief executive of Channel 5, David Elstein's review of Jean Seaton's history of the BBC (Elstein 2015) being a prime example here. As an unofficial-official historian of British television history, expert in policy as well as practice, visiting professor of many universities and publisher of recommendations to various governments, Elstein uses an online platform to discredit Seaton's recent history of broadcasting as an act of 'tunnel vision': 'Yet surely what we need from a professor of media history'

---

[8]Christine Geraghty's keynote lecture 'Old TV' (2015) posed this contentious question of the values being attached to remembering certain television texts.

exclaims Elstein 'is a degree of accuracy, respect for the facts, ability to check detail, detachment and sound judgement, all of which *Pinkoes and Traitors* so lamentably lacks. Let us hope her successor as BBC historian serves us better' (2015). The posted review on the Open Democracy website is long, detailed and scathing, eliciting further posted comments that seek to add more corrections to Seaton's text, with the overall effect of turning television history into an adversarial and elitist game of *who remembers best*, with the only female scholar of BBC history losing the game. This is what Rothberg would define as a 'memory competition' (2009, 11).

Yet, television's resistance to remembrance, what Ellis defined as television programmes as only 'temporarily meaningful, designed to be understood by the contemporary audience' (2007, 154), is an important focus of our research, and not simply the policy documents and key movers and shakers of television governance whose work can be cross-checked in written archives. We think there is a need to shift the focus from a text's meaningfulness in its 'municipal' context (see Jacobs 2011, 506), to its intimate operability as a remembered, forgotten and nostalgic materiality that is brought into the present for agentic purposes. Such remembrance is not easily verifiable but is just as valuable as the 'expert' memories of Elstein: that he pits errors in the presentation of historical evidence with his personal and professional memories (as well as correcting typographical errors) speaks to the power struggle at the heart of researching and writing any popular history. Therefore, how television is remembered and by whom and for what agenda becomes just as important to us as what and how television has been canonized on its different axes: official/unofficial, critical theory/technical practice, producer/audience, academic/fan, to name but a few.

As a springboard for our own research, Wheatley adeptly travels through the key approaches that have been taken in official television history in the United States and the UK – television as an institution, television production histories, what Corner has called 'television as making' (Corner 1991 cited in Wheatley 2007, 7), television as related to a particular sociocultural change; a history that highlights issues of representation, form or aesthetics within a historical period, and histories of technological change (2007, 7). Or, as Spigel puts it: 'Historians tend to isolate periods of television – the "Golden Age", the "Vast Wasteland", the "Turn Towards Relevance", and so forth' (1995, 18). These are, if you like, the official narratives that have been available to us in television studies. Yet, one of the strongest impetuses for this book is to add a new and connective approach through memory studies and to consider what memories have contributed or could add to the story of British television's past and what has been forgotten. Spigel argues that television's 'dual status as entertainment and information places the knowledge it distributes somewhere between fiction and science, between memory and history' (30) and it is in this *in between place* that the following chapters take shape. To evoke memory studies is not to only look backwards (recollect and reconstruct) it is also to think in an anticipatory mode of the future perfect: how will British television have been inherited? An increasingly indistinct space between television as producing collective memories of nationhood, identity and culture to the commodified and commercialized brand logic of television's past in Britain, as having ongoing global and future economic value.

TV studies and archives

As is becoming clearer, one of the through-lines of this book is in the taking stock of the role of elite persons in the production of television as inheritable. This offers a response to Spigel's definition of television archives as producing the 'top-down and "great man"/exceptionalist views of history' that separated good TV from trash, and that was driven by 'public service, art, commerce, and public relations', seeking to produce a canon of TV in the United States in the 1960s (2005a, 69–70).

In his article on the television archive, Jason Jacobs recalls his first trip to the archives filled with 'trepidation and expectation' hoping that they would 'open up and reveal their treasures' and instead was left with feelings of 'incomprehension and disappointment' (2006b, 13). As Spigel argues: 'Historians enter the archive with fantasies and hunches; they search for something they imagine – or hope – was once real. That reality, however, turns out to be at best elusive, accessible mainly through deductions and interpretations of weak, incomplete evidence' (2005a, 68). The archives did not reveal the treasures; rather they exposed the gaps and inadequacies. After some persistence and good academic supervision Jacobs began to uncover what he calls 'the residue of artistic endeavour' which led him to recognize the way in which practitioners 'practically and intellectually' dealt with the new medium of television (2006b, 14). As Jacobs notes, by the time he completed his thesis, which later became his book *The Intimate Screen* (2000), television history had burgeoned into a field of its own and academics were mining the archives in search of television's treasures and revealing new ways of conceptualizing drama (Caughie, *Television Drama*, 2000), adventures serials (Chapman, *Saints and Avengers*, 2002,) and cultures that grow out of particular channels (Johnson and Turnock, *ITV Cultures,* 2005). As he also notes, the growth of archival television research is reflected in successful grant applications, such as the AHRB Centre for British Film and Television History, and in the growing availability of resources for scholars on the internet. In the conclusion to his article, Jacobs reflects on the simultaneous advantages and disadvantages that the internet and its access to archival sources has allowed scholars. On the one hand, it means that academics can read material without having to travel or trawl though mountains of paper to find what they are looking for, and yet on the other hand, as Jacobs' work demonstrates, it is often in the very act of looking and physically being part of those archives that scholars find something they did not know they were looking for and reveal a methodology for uncovering new treasures or ways of telling the story.

When one of the authors first went to the archives in Norwich she experienced very similar feelings of 'trepidation and expectation' only to end up with 'incomprehension and disappointment'. Having gone to view some regional children's television in the hopes of understanding the way in which they became so important to people later, she instead struggled to understand their appeal. She had hoped to understand why certain British programmes, particularly regional ones, made such a lasting impression on the children who watched them (especially as an American researcher viewing British programmes). Instead, she recognized the power of nostalgia to imbue these programmes with interest. It is in the memory of watching them and the context that shapes those memories (watching it after a Sunday roast, watching with siblings or cousins) that added something to the text in the process of recollection. As an outsider and someone with no sentimental attachment to the programmes and yet also a television scholar, someone who is used to analysing the formal qualities of the text – she was able to question the value of what was there and by what means it could be drawing in the remembering audience participants.

Searching for why television is memorable is perhaps not a question that can be answered in the archives but why television forgets requires archives to day-light new evidence. For example, the BBC uses and allows access to its written archives for approved researchers for approved purposes, who will often then produce or contribute to its organizational history or some other official history. Perhaps, the archive will be used to challenge dominant narratives of television history but the BBC archives will still underpin the evidence. In part, this has been assisted by the BBC's arrangement of its internal history based on 'whose papers they are', rather than subject or theme. One could argue that for a certain generation BBC programming is a form of collective memory and that digital technology has, in part, repurposed this for strategic reasons. The making available of old programming online has allowed fans and researchers access to past treasures but it has also created new audiences for old media as the analogue is remade as digitized content for posthumous fandom.

Ellis has argued in 'Why Digitise Historical TV?' (2012) that there is potential for a wide use of data from archival TV: changes to language for language learning, reminiscence therapy for ageing populations, audio-visual data on bodies and performance in the long careers of celebrities, data on physical spaces and lost buildings. All of which 'could then be used for envisioning new uses as well as tracing historical ones' (2012). What is critical, states Ellis, is that bigger data and data mining, which does not yet exist for archival media, emanate from ordinary media outputs rather than exceptional ones. Thus, while it 'does not depend on any belief in TV as a series of cultural objects that might endure' (2012), there may remain a desire to focus on 'quality' and 'the canon', as archivists and scholars preserve, protect, judge and value. *What* is archived and kept will be returned to in more detail in Chapter 3 where we address official archivists in the context of collecting television more informally (see Bjarkman 2004 on video collectors).

The idea, then, that British television is a form of popular cultural inheritance is an important one for thinking through the different business models that now operate in and around its archives.

Conclusion: Capturing television's memorability

The emergence of memory studies has coincided with a period of increasingly democratized media, which engenders risk and opportunity as researchers, professionals, creatives, producers and organizational actors involved in television's memorability realize that television is not *just television* anymore. Memory studies has the capacity to stitch together questions of creativity with questions of digitization as past television is recovered. In *The Collective Memory Reader* (2011) edited by Olick, Vinitzky-Seroussi and Levy, they devote a whole section to 'Media and Modes of Transmission'. They recognize the 'material and technological substrata of individual and social memory' and that 'there is an important interaction between brains and cultures and that brains are not the only or even the most important technologies of memory' (Olick, Vinitzky-Seroussi and Levy 2011, 311). Television is an important technology of memory and as Assmann notes the 'continuous process of forgetting is part of social normality', for 'much must be continually forgotten to make place for new information, new challenges, and new ideas to face the present and future' (Aleida Assmann 2011a, 97). Television has constructed that sense of newness and where and when it has been remembered, a certain group's memory, such as a broadcaster, may have predominated and captured its memorability.

The Popular Memory Group of the late 1970s had characterized the BBC as one of those institutions of cultural memory, 'linked to the national or local state' who operate 'with high-cultural, educational, preservational or archival purposes' (Popular Memory Group 2011, 255). Previously, Halbwachs had argued that collective memory is 'a current of continuous thought' that 'retains from the past only what still lives or is capable of living in the consciousness of the groups keeping the memory alive' (2011, 142–3). While television historians may have focused on television's changes, ruptures, discontinuities, challenges and differences, to pay attention also to collective memory and popular memory shows how these strategies function to produce life 'essentially unaltered'. For the group, 'living first and foremost for its own sake, aims to perpetuate the feelings and images forming the substance of its thought' (146). To focus only on collective memory such as 'when it considers its own past, the group feels strongly that it has remained the same and become conscious of its identity through time' (146), may produce an organizational memory that excludes counter-memories.

Inevitably, television history is no longer entirely reliant on that trusted 'expert' painstakingly appraising archives to which he or she has been granted privileged access. History from below, popular memory research, the growth of the heritage industry, new measurements of audience appreciation, the migration of millions to the internet mean that citizens demand access to archives and expect media's past to be accessible, mobile, context specific and personalized. This creates a great deal of governance and administration, legacy work and cultural labour. Meanwhile, personal memories are gathering credibility and may be challenging the collective and cultural memories of television that foreground corporations and elite persons; to make public their past experiences of television as consumers, fans, extras, below-the-line production workers, or even as victims of historical abuse by television celebrities and within production cultures.[9]

In the context of television this may mean a certain payback for the audience's attention, a kind of restitution wherein television production cultures must give up their gains to the audience who remembers well or differently and wants to reaccess those memories. In a landscape transformed by online media and culture; interactive film, television and radio; and faster, mobile internet, the viewer formerly known as the audience will want the most memorable aspects of their mediated lives available, accessible and possessable. In its reach beyond broadcasting, television's memorability will be determined as much by it personal value as its public value. Unlike Lizardi, we are not melancholy about this transformation. 'The contemporary nostalgic consumer' he claims 'is a collector, not a collectivist' and 'the past acquired through the digital-archive apparatus is based on an individual playlist past' which produces 'a tendency toward rerun mentality and the expansion of this mindset through the digital-archive apparatus' (2015, 62). We think a multi-perspectival approach to the past is required, one that in collecting the memories of archivists, producers, creatives, audiences, fans and television heritage managers we may illuminate not only the consumer, collector or the brand's memory but also the communicative memory of a life story told with, through and in television.

[9]At the time our research began a national uncovering of traumatic memories within television industries was spotlighting gender and power inequalities and a macho culture in television production. The abuse of young females on BBC premises by the entertainer Jimmy Savile and the sexual misconduct of the DJ Stuart Hall culminated in two reviews by Dame Janet Smith published in 2016, see Smith (2016a, 2016b, 2016c). The macho culture extended to many creative and media industries (as well as other workplaces) where there was a predominance of men in power and women or young people in precarious employment conditions. For example, the allegations against the American film producer Harvey Weinstein and actor Kevin Spacey in 2017, led to more memories of abuse being socially mediated through #metoo. Personal memory became powerful.

2 REMEMBERING TELEVISION PRODUCTION: PRODUCER-LY MEMORY

In this chapter, we consider the importance of *producer-ly memories* of television for understanding another key mechanism by which television's history becomes inheritable (or not) as recollection, anecdote and critical reflection. We add to a growing body of research on production cultures (see Ellis 2007, 2014; Caldwell 2008; Mayer, Banks and Caldwell 2009; Mayer 2011) by drawing on a range of interviews with producers and creatives who were at various stages of their careers at the time of the research. In what follows, we address the different modalities of and values attached to their experiences of working in British television. Often, they are strident in their reflections on the industry. As one interviewee defined it, their work no longer 'effectively benchmarks their ability to eat next week' (Interview with Ed Braman 26 June 2014, University of York) and 'because it's really, really expensive to make television [...] there has to be a certain amount of guaranteed box office bums on seats type stuff which strikes me as a real shame in this country' (interview with Lisa Holdsworth 5 May 2014). They are, then, all deeply and critically reflective and self-reflexive about their sense of professional identity, the impact that television has had on their lives and how their memories are shaped by national as well as personal concerns. They often made direct links between their memories of watching TV as a child or teenager and their later work in the industry as well as the programmes they value now, creating a narrative arc for remembering television as a life-work story. This is not a separation of structure and agency but rather by focusing on memory we recognize that personal lives and careers are intra-active, co-constituted and not dualistic.

We have paid attention to producers' and creatives' memories not to identify the heroes or brave agents, nor have we carefully selected those we wished to research based on an agenda around macro issues such as gender politics, technology change, production policy or broadcast history. Those we interviewed and who shared their memories and recollections with us were not working in nor had previously worked in one single genre, nor were they currently considered to be *highly significant* producers or creatives. The distinctiveness of our approach is that it relies upon a level of connectivity across memories of working in television and its creative practices, seeking out continuities rather than only the disruptive, different or divergent. To only focus on the latter misses the powerful narratives at work that shape collective accounts and that make people publicly comply with norms while privately maintaining their critical voice. It offers an approach that is revealing what the participants consider valuable to remember and share, rather than what we as researchers predetermine. We had no set agenda other than for them to share their memories of working in television. This initial exchange between author and interviewee was typical:

> **PT** I worked at the BBC for about twelve years, ITV for about twelve years and then I was freelance for about twelve years.
>
> **KG** Wow, quite a long time. Can you talk me through some of your more significant projects as a producer?
>
> **PT** Okay.
>
> **KG** Or you can choose one or two because I know there's a lot of them.
>
> **PT** I mean it depends what you mean by significant because things that I perceive as really kind of interesting and valuable to me are not necessarily things that anybody else would ever have heard of.
>
> (interview with Patrick Titley 26 June 2014, University of York)

The distinction between communicative and cultural memories that we highlighted in the introduction is important in this chapter. To reiterate, Anglo-European theoretical and conceptual frameworks of 'memory studies' have tended to focus more on historical, collective and cultural memory (i.e. the cultural texts of television for the purposes of this book), with less applied research on 'communicative memory' (Assmann 2008). In this chapter, 'communicative memory' functions as a form of personal remembering in the face of official memorialization, broadcaster celebrations and historical accounts. We started from the assumption that those who have worked in or are working in television production in the United Kingdom have an explicit and implicit sense of media and communication policy, by which we mean they are aware of 'the sum of broad political ideas and guiding principles about the function of the mass media with respect to content, ownership, technical infrastructure and technological development; but also in terms of the relationship to market, state and public' (Sarikakis 2004). They may not express it in this academic language and they may not think about these elements all at the same time but their vernacular memories of producing TV do address in various ways issues of gender, diversity, quality, technological change, heritage, archiving, policy and practice as lived and remembered realities for their careers.

Our twelve interviewees (eight men and four women) were retired from, once worked in the British television industry or were freelance at the time of our interviewing during the period 2014–16, and we allowed one interviewee to lead us to another or approached those who we were connected to through our own networks. While we wanted them to not always take us along *known pathways* we were mindful that their memories may reflect certain viewpoints. Three of the interviewees had left the industry and had become academics, and their memories were particularly interesting for reflecting on how British television's history is being reviewed through *producers-turned-scholars*. Although we knew six of them quite well through our own connections with the television industry, we ensured that we sampled through other methods. Three self-selected and contacted us directly having read about the project launch (we travelled to Glasgow, Sussex and London to interview them); another was a chance meeting at an industry conference in Birmingham, while another was interviewed in a service station in Bristol after we met at a film screening, the final participant was interviewed at the BFI.

We would argue that those we interviewed were not the 'elite persons' of the television industry who 'are used to being asked about their opinions and thoughts' (Brinkmann and Kvale 2014, 171). This point is important because it reflects their willingness to be open and frank, even if some participants altered the final transcripts where they had misremembered. Not being experienced in conveying their thoughts on their careers, it was important to allow participants (who had signed consent forms for their recorded interviews for our research and publications) a second pass on the transcripts. This meant, not looking at 'experiences and memory as separated from their subjects and as things that can be interrogated without them' as Frigga Haug says of 'memory work' within her studies of women's lives (2000, 156). One could argue that allowing our participants to review and edit their memories drew them into the research in such a way as to enable version-ing of different pasts (for them) to emerge: they could rewrite their memories as they went through the process, refining and protecting them.

The opportunity to share memories, to simply have a chance to talk with an interested and focused person about their lives and careers, may be part of the pay-off for involvement alongside the 'happy to help' mode (see Brennan 2008) and the mutual interest in television. Each interview lasted 60–90 minutes in length. Questions were open-ended and framed around memories: childhood memories of watching TV, memories of favourite programmes, recollecting early careers, reflecting on creativity, collaboration and challenges. Our research of memory focused on the person in a way that allowed the interviewees to value television in different ways, interweaving intimate connections with professional and critical thinking. Here is a typical example of an answer to the question of childhood memories of television, to which the interviewee draws upon early memories and builds these into a career story and cultural narrative to make sense of these connected pasts:

I think at that age it was about escapism [...] so *Fame* [dir. Alan Parker 1980] was very much, people I thought I might be like one day, the sort of young teenagers, going off and doing something that I desperately wanted to do. I wanted to sing, dance and be a star. And, I think it almost certainly set me off on the path I ended up on I think. It maybe showed me that things were possible in that crazy TV world.

[...] but later on as you get a bit older things that have a huge emotional impact on you are the things that you remember and it's usually your emotional states as a teenager, something that represents outsiders, I loved *Press Gang* which was written by Stephen Moffat who now writes *Doctor Who* because it was very intelligent children that were, sort of, outside normal, it was very much like that, I loved that show.

(interview with Lisa Holdsworth 5 May 2014)

While those working in the TV industry are not so easy to access, they are often closely connected, one interviewee opens the door to their network of equally insightful and important interviewees. The same can be said of the interviewees from the TV heritage and archive sector for Chapter 3 except that while they are an even smaller and well connected group they are also serving the public in a way that makes them accessible to scrutiny. As Herzog and Ali note of media policy research, the work is often 'steered through by closely connected elites [...] In many instances there are only a small number of key actors involved in these processes' (2015, 38). While this may be a weakness of our approach, we would argue that the use of qualitative interviews with hard-to-reach producers signalled the need to go beyond academic-commissioned and industry accounts of producer histories.

What, then, is the value of researching the memories of 'producers' who Denis Forman defined as 'all the creative people who combine to make television' (Richard Dimbleby Lecture 1987, cited in Forman 1997, 'Foreword'), reiterated by Tony Garnett as television production 'in its widest sense to refer to all creators' (2014, 20)? In what follows we touch upon some of the key published academic research that has utilized producer interviews and consider the value of popular publications of memories of television production, such as memoirs and biographies. Through the interview material, we focus on how producers remember their careers alongside self-reflexive 'narratives' of the heroes of the 'golden age' and the levels of allowable creative risk impact on the memorability of television for them.

Narrative arc of structure and agency

There are several excellent examples of research at differing scales of analysis drawing upon television producer interviews. These may be critical analysis of memoirs and oral histories; critical reflections on work-life story; academic observations of producers remembering; or the incorporation of the researcher's diary entries of producers in their settings. We have the research of, for example, Gras and Cook on Dennis Potter (2000), Irene Shubik about her time at ABC and the BBC (2014) and Georgina Born's social anthropology of a broadcaster during the 1990s in *Uncertain Vision: Birt, Dyke and the Reinvention of the BBC* (2005). What is striking about the producer-ly recollections, reflections, memories and insider stories that have been available for some time (Norden 1985; Neame 2004; McMahon 2007; Aldridge 2011; Ibbotson 2012, for example) is that they are performative of a certain narrative of British television. A through-line of that narrative has seen structure and agency positioned as binary oppositions, with academic texts focusing more on the former and popular memory texts on the latter. It has created a kind of sciences or arts approach to television history, wherein the former deals with verifiable historical facts and the latter matters of meaning, feeling and personality. The historical battle between these two is encapsulated in the titles of books such as *Citizen Greg: The Extraordinary Story of Greg Dyke and how he captured the BBC* (Horrie and Clarke 2000) and is stated neatly by one of our interviewees as: 'I think institutions like to play it safe. I don't think all producers do' (interview with Ed Braman 26 June 2014). This narrative of structure versus agency constructs precarious working conditions for the furtherance of communicative memories of cultural workers, who may, in fact, not see so neat a division between matter and meaning, between the materiality of their working lives and the memories that have become part of who they are.

There are, of course, many examples of writing the history of television by incorporating producer accounts of industry, policy and production (see Bonner and Aston [1998] on ITV; Bonner and Aston [2003] on ITV and Channel 4; Fitzwalter [2008] on ITV; and recently Mills [2016] on the BBC). Yet, in Born's work above, she offers an institutional and policy history through researching people as much as archives and organizations. Born's academic diary reflections on discussions and interviews she had with directors, producers and other creatives at the BBC are illuminating because of their personal recollection and anecdotal qualities. We see 'knowledgeable' human agents engaged in negotiating the tensions between structure and agency (see Giddens 1976) in person-centred ways. In one of those interviews from 2002, Born quotes the interviewee's focus on the 'loss of common memory' lamented by a producer who wanted access to a database of past documentaries, but was not aware of one: 'if you want to know about what was made in the past, it's the memory of the older producers or nobody really knows' (Born 2005, 210).

Born does not reflect on this concern about how organizational, professional or personal memory are enabling structures that are being dismantled, which Richard Sennett (2011, 285) might argue is a direct result of 'de-bureaucratized institutions' that 'instead reward people not prone to institutional attachments'. Rather, she focuses on the important policy impact and institutional changes of a neoliberal agenda of creativity through risk, uncertainty and precarity that pervaded the television industry, and that continues to challenge producers, directors and creatives to this day. The producer cited above really focuses on the importance of 'memory' not only for employment security but for a sense of personal, organizational and professional identity as a producer of television. The producer claims that 'if you lose that common memory' because the staff are temporary, or the production is flexible and distributed, or the workers are all over the place, then why be in one building, why preserve television's past, if new producers and creatives have no 'history of thought' and 'little to draw on creatively' what is the future of television (Born 2005, 210)?

'Memory' is mentioned again in Born's 'Epilogue', in as much as broadcasting constructs 'both our vivid social present and our social memory' and she notes that 'television produces history through a series of heightened media events' while at the same time 'it can desensitise us to the many modes of times passing and can obscure historical understanding' (2005, 513). A producer's perspective on the stickiness or flow of television programming is equally contradictory for one can never be sure (at the time of production) if it will be an event or fade without a second thought. Working on a new television programme with *only the slim possibility of being remembered*, is to work in *retro-memory*, as one of our producers noted: 'you never know when you start working on a show whether it's going to be good or bad [...] the first day in the office everybody thinks it's going to win a BAFTA [...] it's a mystery as to why something works and something doesn't' (interview with Patrick Titley 26 June 2014). Thus, sharing memories between television production workers may be vital to understand the risks and resources in making television. Born's producer reflections above on a 'loss of common memory' are intrinsic not only to understanding how television producers have been sharing (or trying to share) practices, throughout the period of free-market principles and disruptive technologies, but also how this may enable them to make connections across channels, genres and audiences, and between themselves as professionals.

If (corporate and living) memory is being lost and memory work is being devalued (see Worcman and Garde-Hansen 2016), then Sennett's 'Disturbing Memories' provides a useful framework for understanding Born's remembering producer and our producer's sense of television's retro-memory. Sennett homes in on the de-bureaucratization of business and organizations that associate the past and institutional attachments with low productivity. The intense individualizing tendency of the modern economic system, the 'stripping away of collective supports and defences', the isolation of entrepreneurs 'even when they work in large organizations', argues Sennett, means that 'the narrative of a life is no longer a tight, well-made story':

> Institutional, individualizing insecurity makes subjective life itself highly unstable and uncertain. Shoring up a sense of self in a world without reliable institutions thus becomes urgent psychological business, as the economy

deforms the coherence and continuity of lived time. And here, I think, is where the work of memory enters.

(Sennett 2011, 285)

In this context, then, it is important to note that some of the television producers and creatives we interviewed have diversified their income by telling their story and the story of television not only within the industry through training and speaker circuits but also by moving to the security of teaching and higher education. We have worked alongside some of them during our careers in media departments and during the research for this book. This chapter provides the space for sharing a selection of producer memories of working in British television that are always seeking to negotiate and depolarize the narrative arc of structure and agency.

What is producer-ly memory?

John Caldwell's *Production Cultures* (2008), a ten-year ethnographic study of television and film production in the United States, attests to the complexity of the connections within and between television production workers. The revelations about the gendered politics of these cultures does not seem to have had much of an impact on changing sexual politics in these industries in the decade since his publication. His research is important for considering British television production studies because it critiques how television histories have focused on structures far more than agency. Caldwell realized 'academia's penchant for making "industry" one thing, a monolith, rather than acknowledging that "the" industry is comprised of numerous, sometimes conflicted and competing socio-professional communities, held together in a loose and mutating alliance by "willed affinity"' (2009, 200). His research accords with Born's remembering producer above, while incorporating what Vicki Mayer would term the 'entire lexicon of production', which includes people whose labours are 'situated somewhere between the "producers" located at the apex of television studio hierarchies and the "everyperson" implied in the rhetoric of digital production' (Mayer 2011, 1). Like Mayer, we have been drawn in by the people we have interviewed who have 'given life' to television and yet are often seen as replaceable by their own institutions (2). Communal memory is hard work in this context and without the structure of organizational memory, which should offer a narrative arc or mesh for life-work stories, it may be devalued or strategically forgotten.

Inspired by Caldwell (2008), we used our interviews from producers and creatives to understand how memories of the day-to-day 'business' of making TV has come to shape their work-life story when they look back, through the opportunities they take (if they have them) to share this memory as a communal experience. Producer-ly memory is not only concerned with how and why television production workers share their memories of working in the industry but also how their work has been shaped by their own personal memories of television. One of our producer interviewees (now turned academic) marks himself out as of the 'Doctor Who generation', which could be defining if it were not the weirdness, as he described it, of his teenage love for news, current affairs and challenging drama, such as Weekend World (London Weekend Television [LWT], 1972–88) – 'I remember thinking this explained the world in a way that I'd never seen it explained before' – and Play for Today: Penda's Fen (BBC One, 1974) – 'I watched it ever since, it was one of the biggest things, the most important things I've ever seen in terms of thinking of what televisions do. I still believe that' (interview with Ed Braman 26 June 2014).

Such producer-ly memories come to influence not only what he thinks is distinctly British about television but he can also reflect on the contradictory value systems he has experienced throughout his career. A 'certain sense of an idealised British past [...] whether it actually existed on television or whether it was only sort of there because of certain highlights like Doctor Finlay's Casebook [BBC, 1962–71] on the one hand, Brideshead Revisited [ITV, 1981] on the other hand' is held in tension with the drive to be innovative and cutting edge. He continues,

> there's always a sense that the real high points of British television have been these huge cost historical costume series which somehow in a slightly misremembered way, rather like the Six Wives of Henry VIII [BBC, 1970], seem to think that we somehow once had a surer grasp on our history.
>
> (interview with Ed Braman 26 June 2014)

What is interesting about this reflection is his note that 'these things weren't particularly well made' and 'we've got better at making stuff', but 'there is a sort of sense that somehow there was a cosier age' and his concerns are that a *memory* is being played out in British television today, of the 'family gathered around the fireplace' and that watching Keith Mitchell playing Henry VIII with the kids 'translates into some notion of Call the Midwife (BBC, 2012–) and all that sort of stuff. Ecumenical television. People gathering around a hearth' (interview with Ed Braman 26 June 2014).[1]

While the upsurge of television producers-turned-academics may speak to a precarity in television work since the 1990s, where flexibility and free-market principles have had an impact – the long hours and stress, family-unfriendly conditions and rapid technological developments – it also demonstrates a desire to tell their stories of television to the next generation. To find a collegiate space to convey television's history through memory work, finds producer-ly memories of television emerging through interactions with academia or in academic research projects (such as ours) where television producers and creatives take

---

[1] It is noteworthy the interviewee names the very recently departed Janice Hadlow, former Controller of BBC Two, as directly responsible for a neo-Georgian Britishness being inherited through current programming. See a recent *Guardian* article on her departure: Sweney 2016.

some time to step back and remember. Lucy Hooberman (2014), another former producer-turned-academic and a participant in our own research, has noted the value of such memories in her oral history project for the BBC commemorating its 1990s expansion into digital television:

I joined the BBC in 1993 and when I joined it was an organisation that thrived on memos. I'd never seen so much paperwork coming down from on high, 'cascading' commandments, directives leading to much filing and the assumption created in me that such an organised system of internal communications would have its mirror in complete and organised archiving.
(Hooberman 2014)

Yet, she notes that once commissioned to remember the BBC's web innovations she had to rely on producer-ly memories, by undertaking oral histories. Moreover, her own memories as a TV producer of documentaries were sought to make up for the archival absence she experienced in her early career:

I've now had a taste of my own medicine as I'm being interviewed about a couple of films I produced in the mid 1980s which seem to have found some extremely late fanbase nearly 30 years on having been widely ignored at the time. My own archiving as an early Independent Producer sorely tested by moving job, moving house, pre-web days.
(Hooberman 2014)

There is then a different kind of producer-turned-academic reflecting on television's memorability and *retro-memory*, utilizing their own memories that are standing in for organizational forgetting. Television producers as historians are becoming important precisely because of their ability to call upon their memorable experiences and to use that memory work, as well as professional networks of remembered colleagues, as a new form of valuable knowledge for appreciating the complexity of television's history and its impact upon British culture. They also tend to place people rather than texts at the centre of their approach. While their research and publications fall within the academic sphere, the literature they produce is not too distant from memoir-based, autobiographical, anecdotal accounts of working in television, and as such they valorise storytelling as a key mode of engagement and method. For example, Murphy, Aust, Jackson and Ellis (2015), former or current television producer-academics, reflect upon the 'old ways of making television':

Analogue television production has largely given way to digital, and digital technologies are making the heritage of analogue production ever more available. But the meanings and formal habits of archival analogue television are not as obvious and self-evident as they were when originally produced. The old ways of making television were, we can now see, quite specific to their times.
(Murphy et al. 2015)

We are witnessing, then, a growing interest in these producer-ly memories (particularly from British and American television industry workers), all contributing to television's heritage (not only as corporate branding) but as producer-ly memories that extend to television workers who have been only partly involved in the production of key texts (see, for example, Garde-Hansen and Grist's *Remembering Dennis Potter* [2014] on the memories of below-the-line television workers).

My life in television

Very few television historians pay much attention to the memoir genre. Many producer-ly memoirs are presented as 'my life in television' or 'I assisted in the production of this programme or that'. They are wide-ranging and at a variety of scales (from elite to non-elite persons) commissioned or endorsed by a broadcaster, or may incorporate a working life into a broader autobiography, but they are proliferating as those with long careers enter an age of reflection. From histories of administration, governance and decision-making (see *Persona Granada* by Denis Forman [1997] or *Look me in the Eye* by Jeremy Isaacs [2006]) to reflecting on an entire career (see Brockway [2010] or David Attenborough's *A Life on Air* [(2002) 2009]), from the creative side (see television memories in *More Fool Me* by Stephen Fry [2015] or Nat Crosby's A *Cameraman Abroad: From Panorama to Paranoia* [2002]) to the legwork involved in progressing through the industry (for example in *How to Get a Job in Television* 2009, Elsa Sharp draws on reflections from producers). There are many more examples of those involved at all levels of television production (freelancers, waged and unwaged) but frequently those brought to the *top of the mind* are the autobiographies of 'practitioners' (the screenwriters, producers, directors).

There are also many key figures of British television production who have been and are being written into television's past as heroic and brave figures, going into battle with broadcasters over aesthetics (Dennis Potter), or with each other over how sound and image should relate to one another (Philip Donnellan), or with audiences over issues of quality, morality or commercialism (Kenith Trodd). In *British Television Drama: Past, Present and Future* (2nd edition, 2014) the first chapter entitled 'Context' is written by the British film and television producer Tony Garnett. At no point in the collection does 'memory' appear as a concept, framework or action for reflecting upon working in television, even though it is operating in Garnett's chapter as well as others that *look back at television production*. However, the role of 'memory' is taken up by Garnett in his recent autobiography where remembering itself becomes a point of tension.

> What follows is an account of my working life and some of the events that have determined its nature. It is, of course, incomplete and partial. Therefore, it

cannot be the whole truth [...] I have spent my lifetime seeking the truth [...] I've tried to be true to the facts which one checks against documents and other sources, including the memories of others. But facts are not the truth. Facts have to be contextualised in order to achieve meaning. So what I've attempted is an imaginative truth [...] I have often found that what I thought was my memory was actually someone else's. I'd absorbed it and taken ownership of it. I've tried to weight the possibility that these memories were just the gloss and only include those I judge to be credible from other sources.

(Garnett 2016, xi–xii)

Well known for his work on *The Wednesday Play* (BBC One, 1964–70) and collaboration with Ken Loach, director of *Cathy Come Home* (1967), Garnett has continued to make an impact on remembering British social realist drama, and he paints a picture of a landscape of opportunities in television in the 1960s. His narrating of these opportunities acknowledges the lack of women, the overt class politics and the lessons learned about power, money and technical inventiveness.

In an interview with Kenith Trodd in 2013 for *Remembering Dennis Potter through Memories, Archives and Industries* by Garde-Hansen and Grist (2014), Trodd reiterates a similar hero-taking-risks narrative but one that is enabled by the structure. 'We [Loach, Potter, Garnett and others] wanted to make movies in the streets':

You were allowed to do things. I remember describing it long after and that's probably one of the interviews you've seen. You know, you could light a fire. Burn the building down and they'd give you another box of matches. There were opportunities. It was also quite hazardous. Because the BBC was and is a quite fearsome institution and very bureaucratic, or can be.

(interview with Garde-Hansen, 6 February 2013, London)

While Garnett clearly sees himself as an historical agent – wresting 'history from the ruling class and writing working-class history' (Garnett 2014, 17), our interviewees with long careers in television spoke of a structure that was enabling but had become more difficult to find autonomy and diversity in.

Our purpose is not to question Garnett's perspective on television's past, present and future but rather to emphasize his *use of his own memory* in writing and rewriting television production history. How these uses of life story make British television production inheritable as heroic or not creates a narrative that excludes other voices and suggests we need more space for counter-memories. As one of our female screenwriters noted in reflecting on her own career:

There is a severe lack of diversity from different ethnic groups that's for sure. I think there's a challenge to represent the country more as it is, I think, sometimes it doesn't necessarily reflect the real world.
[...] Women, yes women writers – there are a lot of women writers in TV, it's just they don't necessarily all get to the same place but some of them do.

(interview with Lindsay Williams 16 September 2014)

This is reiterated by another female screenwriter:

I mean we're a bit beholden in this country when we talk about nostalgia and the past, we're sort of beholden to the dead white writer and they're usually male [...] and it takes someone with a bit of nerve to start thinking about shaking up the casting of those. Your first line of defence is the posh, rather white male actor and it all needs shaking up a bit.

(interview with Lisa Holdsworth 5 May 2014)[2]

In the background, and referred to by our interviewees, were the 'symbols' of the golden age of television (see Corner 1991) carrying the meanings of working-class realism; the 'heroes' (the directors, writers, producers) and the young men pioneering and protesting (overseen by older men such as Sydney Newman[3] or Sidney Bernstein[4]). This narrative of heroism was locatable in our own interviews with those who had worked their way up from the very bottom within the BBC:

So I got the job. I met a lot of my lifelong friends in a room at Ealing Studios on 4th January 1964 [...] I was given a lot of responsibility very quickly [...] I became a Film Editor I think after a year and a bit which I think was a record speed. They put me on the *Tonight* [1957–65] programme as an Assistant Film Editor [...] it was fire-fighting the whole time. I loved it. I absolutely loved it, it was tremendous fun and we worked on the 7th floor, which was ours, and you could get hold of something happening and make it your own.

(interview with Peter Ceresole 8 September 2014)

There are the 'rituals' seen to show through in the creative collaboration television production staff enjoyed that the system may or may not have encouraged. Peter Ceresole effused about working with Michael Bunce on *The Money Programme* (1966–), who went on to make *Nationwide* (BBC One, 1969–83), acknowledging that he was laughed at by others for being too 'tabloidish'. At the centre of these practices (or rather unconsciously underlying them) Hofstede would argue are the 'values', 'the core of culture' that are 'often unconscious and rarely discussable, that cannot be observed as such but are manifested in alternatives of behaviour' (Hofstede et al. 1990, 291). The dominant narrative of the golden age as creating

---

[2]In 2018, (after this book was written), more than seventy female TV writers, including Lisa Holdsworth, signed an open letter to British TV Commissioners accusing them of unfair practices in terms of writing for primetime programmes. The letter points towards the success of female-penned dramas, such as *Call the Midwife*, and yet the reality that only a small number of programmes have a female lead writer. See Khomami 2018.

[3]Sydney Newman headed up BBC Drama from 1963 to 1970. Described by Tony Garnett as 'a big influence because he was a heavyweight [...] I was influenced by Sydney and we were protected by him' (see MacMumraugh-Kavanagh n.d.).

[4]Sidney Bernstein headed up Granada Television from 1954 to 1969. Often referred to as the founding father of independent and ground-breaking television, Denis Forman notes his tendency to write himself into history as a 'hero' (1997, 4–6).

a 'common culture' through producer-ly risk and innovation is well remembered. Ed Braman readily lists an eclectic mix of texts that speak of his (or his inherited) idea of that golden age: Dennis Potter's work, *Cathy Come Home* (1967), Trevor Griffith, *Bill Brand* (Thames/ITV, 1976) for ITV, *This Week: Death on the Rock* (Thames TV,1988), *World in Action* (Granada, 1963–98), *The Wednesday Play* (1964–70), *Play for Today: Dreams of Leaving* (BBC One, 1980), *Compact* (BBC, 1962–5) and *The Newcomers* (BBC One, 1965–9). Yet, he also reflects upon how that creativity of television has been stretched and worn out. He notes that pulling *Big Brother* (Channel 4, 2000–10; E4, 2001–10; Channel 5, 2011–) in 2009–10, which he says was five years past its best, the audience had drifted and producers were bored, was considered 'creative renewal' for Channel 4:

> what it tells you is that innovation is only useful if you can market it at a particular time otherwise television is a conservative business, an incredibly conservative business. And also historically, again when do we remember television coming up with a lot of its innovative ideas? Well, early days of Channel 4 perhaps but we also have to allow for the *Minipops* [Channel 4, 1983]. And *Union World* [Granada/Channel 4, 1985], you know, one of the most obscene and one of the most bizarre programmes ever made. But when was the Golden Age of television when all of the innovation took place? Late 60s, early 70s.
>
> (interview with Ed Braman 26 June 2014)

This conservativism, which is the opposite of the intentions of independent producers and free-market principles, is considered entirely economic for screenwriter Lisa Holdsworth, not only in that *Midsomer Murders* (ITV, 1997–) pays her mortgage, it also does 'very well in Scandinavia [...] and in Australia [...] because they think it's a representation of what actually happens in British villages and everybody is terribly nice and speaks to the Vicar. When I think that's probably a very small percentage of British people that is their experience of British life' (interview with Lisa Holdsworth 5 May 2014).

(Dis)organizational memory and producing television

To access one's past in being a television producer and creative is an active process of personal preservation, critical reflection and social inheritance that speaks to and against television's characterization as flow and fleetingness. One of our interviewees distinguishes between what is considered historically important (to academics and industry) as opposed what is memorable to produce and watch, using a prop from a game show (that he has preserved) to make his point:

> I mean there are lots of series that I had fun making that I wouldn't particularly now. The one that won the BAFTA was a show called *The Scoop* [YTV, 1996–9]

but it wasn't an important series in any sense you know, we just happened to make one really good episode that won a BAFTA. I wouldn't claim it was a particularly good series or anything you know, just again it was washing up [...] I think it's more about the fact, the historical perspective makes you think actually that show affected people in a way that that show didn't. None of the kids, if you ask any of the students now if they've ever heard of *The Scoop* they'd never have heard of it. If you ask them if they've ever heard of *Jungle Run* [CITV, 1999] they would have heard of it because *Jungle Run*, this is my best prop when I'm doing lectures. When I do the game show lecture I let them pass this round and they all take selfies of each other with it. Because they are all fans of *Jungle Run* because it went out on CITV [...] It was a very well designed game show and it ran for 8 series. *That's what the kids remember.*

(interview with Patrick Titley 26 June 2014; our emphases)

His concern is with the way television (in this example children's TV) programmes 'are' remembered and 'not' remembered and yet there is the sense that he works through this problem by inserting himself into the narrative of television's memorability, knowing that others will judge what is 'good' and what is 'average'. So, while he can see within his lifetime and experience a way in which something aesthetically good is forgotten, he also cultivates the concept within his reflections that a show that simply bombarded viewers through its practices of memorability, is where stickiness really lies, for himself as producer and the remembering audience. Recognizing these practices suggests children's television should not only be inherited in terms of cultural value or historical development, an area we return to later in this book.

Three of our interviewees had not only worked in television but had also produced television programmes about television's own history by using archival content. Their memories of this process of creating new TV from old TV offers an insight into the economies of freshness involved in producing television that remembers itself. As one archive researcher for the BBC defined it:

If they say 'can you show me 60s psychedelia' what they mean is 'please don't bring me that Alan Whicker [*Whicker's World*, BBC/ITV, 1958–94] shot of hippies with the love sign on their face' because every single programme uses that. 'I want to see something new.' I want to be the one with new archive. Directors want it as well. I want to show them something new. And people go 'wow!'

(interview with Mhairi Brennan 23 June 2014)

Another interviewee, a freelance producer, noted also that: 'It is a challenge to find new material which is deemed as new' and 'commissioners like to see material that has recently been found or rediscovered. It creates an air of excitement in that their programme is showing something that's not been seen since first tx [transmission] many decades ago, or forgotten about' (interview with freelance female TV producer 16 July 2015). Moreover, this new marketability for 'lost and found TV' has an emotional impact that is afforded by the television producer having access to and approaching the archive in a critically informed way. The freelancer continued:

> I found some footage [at the BBC's Perivale archive] that had been forgotten about and was not even known to be there. It was an American company making a programme about the *Sunday Night at The Palladium* [ITV, 1955–] show and used footage from some of the shows at the time. You could call it the first archive show utilising clips from a programme to show in another. Anyway, there was a great *Morecambe and Wise* [BBC/ITV, 1968–83] sketch which had been wiped but was used in this new show. We reunited the footage with Eric Morecambe's son who had never before seen the sketch and was very emotional about it.
>
> (interview with freelance female TV producer 16 July 2015)

Thus, while it is important to note that academics have played a key role in turning fragments of television's past into a coherent and evidence-based history (see Wheatley and Moseley 2008), and have explored nostalgia and emotion in exploring past television's pull on the audience (Holdsworth 2011; Piper 2011), as well as addressed past television technology and archives as operative in determining what knowledge can be passed down to the next generation (Miller on the BFI, 2008; Griffin on Ulster TV archives 2015), television producers have also been doing this within their own practice.

In an interview with TV producer Mark Helsby we noted an interesting tension between the planned obsolescence built into his experience of TV production (especially nostalgia programming) that produced ephemera, props, scenery and materials, and the perception of real hard work undertaken to craft the objects that TV left behind. He came to value them for their not-throw-away-able-ness, rather than for any commercial or cultural value. To go to the skip (where everything normally goes) was a shame, to salvage that item was to value the craft and labour of another person, and to preserve a small part of television's material production:

MH   If you're making an archive programme I think you want to show people things they haven't seen for a long long time or things they would never ordinarily be given the chance to see [...] A lot of the props and sets and stuff like that, they are still seen as being just disposable and they just go. There are some things that when we worked on those 'I Love ... ' things we used to commission some props to be made and I can't bring myself to chuck them away.

KG   What do you have?

MH   I can't remember what they're called, those puzzles that are 9 cubes on a tray but with one missing and you can move them around to make a picture. We had one of those made. It's about 2-feet square with 'I Love '75' and a props company made it out of wood and built it and we had it. I think it's still in the garage, I can't bring myself to throw it away. I know it has no value to anybody, even me, but someone put a lot of work into that, you know, it's wrong just to chuck it into a skip! But a lot of stuff went when we moved to Media City, a lot of stuff had to go. A lot of stuff was just propped up in corners in the office and just couldn't be taken over.

(interview with Mark Helsby 24 June 2014)

Remembering the materiality of television production is not, then, only concerned with technology, institutions or labour but it also covers the materials and cultural work that producers have recognized and continue to recognize as memorable that researchers and industries may not. If 'remembrance [also] involves work', and by this we mean 'any activity that involves the direction and application of material and immaterial resources and capacities to the production and reproduction of conditions achieving remembrance' (Allen 2014, 5), then to what extent are producer-ly memories (self-)organizing to address the failures of the television archive and television historiography?

It is on this issue of organizational memory that television as a form of cultural heritage is integrated with personal memories of those who have worked in television and have first-hand experience of production equipment, locations, collaboration, personalities, policy and practice, as well as alongside a wider appreciation of television producer-ly memories extending well beyond the text, the studio, the equipment, and transmission (see Panos 2014). Emma Sandon (2007) notes this in her research of the Alexandra Palace Television Society (APTS) of retired staff members whose professional pride, their roles in the BBC and other loyalties, created strong identities that ensured oral history work revealed those shared values. In reflecting on their technical work from 1936 to 1952, Sandon noted 'a nostalgia expressed about the collective spirit' (2007, 105). Such producer-ly memories acknowledge the role of organizational memory in telling the story of British television and 'the specific conception of memory as property' which 'is the basis of certain humanist ideals that frame widespread reverence for remembrance that has often distracted academic research from the underlying work that goes into remembrance' (Allen 2014, 13).

Addressing television's organizational memory through producer-ly memory presents opportunities for 'inventive methods' (Lury and Wakeford 2011). Of the ADAPT[5] project, the team defines the research activities of reconstructing production techniques with retired producers on old equipment as neither 'reconstructions' nor nostalgia:

ADAPT's simulations are acts of memory for the participants, but they are memory events which are quite unlike those which take place in an interview. The participants are asked to demonstrate what they used to do regularly: how

[5]See the European Research Council funded ADAPT project 2013–18 at Royal Holloway University London (see ADAPT n.d.).

their machines worked, how they worked together, what their routines once were. They are active collaborators in the research, living again their physical and emotional encounters with machinery that they used to use on a daily basis [...] The gamble of the ADAPT project is that this technique will be able to produce a number of generalizable insights into the normal everyday production techniques which lay behind the thousands of hours of television material now becoming available from the archives.

(Murphy et al. 2015, 8)

Producer-ly memory in this new research not only conveys social and professional histories through the architectural heritage of television production (a kind of media and memory archaeology) but the machines produce tangible encounters with one's work-story through scaffolding a remembering capacity not only through others (retired workers' shared stories) but via the materiality and the matter of production. Collecting memories of producers might allow researchers of television history unique access to a different form of critique of the collective memory of British television hitherto inherited as cultural narratives.[6]

One of those cultural narratives concerns the concept of 'narrative' itself as a form of organizational memory in its powerful shaping not only television's past but of how television is made from other people's pasts. One of the interviewees, who is an archive researcher recounted a project in which footage from the 1970s in Scotland was to be used. Her proximity to the factual archive, the people it depicted and the detail she conveyed to demonstrate the power of television memory had prompted an audience member to write to her about his memories of the footage, which she recounted to us but later redacted on reading her transcript (reminding us that the methodology that respects multiple layers of memory is important). She annotated her transcript with: 'I'd feel a bit uncomfortable about so much of this person's story being printed without their permission, sorry, I didn't really think about it when I was talking' (interview with Mhairi Brennan 23 June 2014). This gatekeeping of professional/personal stories is increasingly at the mercy of narrative as one producer replied when asked to reflect on the ways that making television had changed. His response began with the obvious reference to technology (disc space, cheap cameras and 'the ability to shoot for ever and ever and ever and ever has obviated the need for making serious editorial judgements early and creates a convoluted editing process'). He continued:

One of the other maligned features [...] particularly in Factual [...] is the rise of the so-called series producer, the edit room producer, you know, loads of little working ants go out all over a housing estate, shoot the living shit out of whatever it is and then somebody comes along and fashions narratives in the edit suite with no primary relationship with the people and only an investment

---

[6]A recent example is the AHRC funded 'A History of Women in the British Film and Television Industries, 1933–89' led by Melanie Bell-Williams (2014–17).

in apparent narrative [...] creating high-level narratives out of precarious factual material [...] And it's one of the big failures of British television [...] when we talk nostalgically that's, generally speaking, a lot of what we talk about as professionals. And, that we've created *terms of production* which do see the schedule as a supermarket shelf.

(interview with Ed Braman 26 June 2014; our emphasis)

Narrative as organizational memory emerges again in the interview with screenwriter Lisa Holdsworth, wherein the mythology of the writer as central to the script is reorganized into a memory of how the writer's role is shifting due to the underlying economies of television production. 'I think because of the speed and the leanness of television, budgets have come down, it means there is a lot less indulgence of writers and sometimes that's a good thing and sometimes the whip's cracked and you need to get on with it and stop being so precious.' She continues:

but sometimes it means that the writer is de-valued in the process and there has been the rise of the Script Editor who previously was someone who was a facilitator of notes between people and was on the writer's side, and I would say in the last 5 years it's gone the wrong way, they're not on your side, they're there to get you to do what the producer wants you to do.

(interview with Lisa Holdsworth 5 May 2014)

Conclusion: Glut and scarcity – 'you transmit it and it's gone forever'

The concept of a 'supermarket shelf' noted above and yet the scarcity of resources that rewrites the role of the screenwriter are clearly inscribed with a critique of the glut-like production culture wrought by technological change and disengagement from people who are the cultural resource of television's texts and practices. Producers are caught between their own personal and connective memories of working across channels, platforms, programmes, genres and places, and the new digital connective memories that are associated with risks to creativity, cultural value and professional identity. Precarious material (whether freshly filmed, rediscovered or transcoded from the archive) poses another risk to their work and sense of identity. In their recent book *Risk and Hyperconnectivity: Media and Memories of Neo-Liberalism,* Hoskins and Tulloch (2016) hold in tension the bottom-up possibilities for new cultural and media workers with the flexible labour markets pervading all industries that disconnect life stories from more certain futures. For 'whereas connectivity/memory theorists speak of the "postscarcity" *glut* of new media forms, risk sociologists and neoliberalization theorists discuss the increasing economic *scarcity* of populations during the era of neoliberalism' (2016, 95).

Our older producer-ly memories did speak of a heyday of collective identity, autonomy and longed-for security of 1950s and 1960s television production, which chimes with cultural narratives, but this period was not without risk and uncertainty. Well before the neoliberal agenda took hold, our retired producers reflected on the precarity of television work and the desire for any kind of security. Told he would make 'a good floor manager', Chris Hodson asked 'what the hell does a Floor Manager do?' on hearing

I thought gosh if I was doing that job on the staff I would have a regular salary, probably get paid holidays, this is just right for a married man, yes, I'll give it a go. So I got lucky and I got a job as Floor Manager with Associated Rediffusion which was one of the first four television companies to go on the air. I think 22nd September 1955 was the date.

(interview with Chris Hodson 10 July 2014)

Moreover, remembering the risk of that early television work is deeply associated with the medium's relationship to its own memory, as scarcity:

So this was live television and of course as you know I'm sure, live television has to be rehearsed. It's just like a play really. You rehearse a play for 2 or 3 weeks maybe more. You had to rehearse a television play for about the same length of time. And then you transmit it and it's gone forever.

(interview with Chris Hodson 10 July 2014)

We wish to suggest, through only a brief selection of material above, that interviewing television producers, creatives and workers of different ages, from different genres, channels and communities could be an important multi-modal approach for understanding how British television has played a pivotal role in preserving and transmitting the energies of previous generations and their cultural values and activities. That is, as a form of constructing a television heritage out of the memories of producers, directors, screenwriters and technicians in a way that interrogates two key problems. Firstly, that there is too much TV archive, what Hoskins and Tulloch (2016, 4) term the 'glut of emergent media possibilities' in a digital age, too many texts, too many collections, too many TV sets going to the dump, and so we should be glad some of it is lost, forgotten, trash-able or too trivial and ubiquitous to be important. Programme makers may assume abundance 'everything is on YouTube' says the screenwriter Lindsay Williams: 'It's almost like, you know I spent years of keeping videos of stuff that I've written [...] I think as far as I know, everything I know about, everything I've got an interest in I can find on the Internet' (interview with Lindsay Williams 16 September 2014). Secondly, that if the text is lost, forgotten or scarce the cultural value of that part of television is negligible until memories create marketable value in the present: *what you do not know you do not have, you do not miss.* If memories and archives create value in the present from *old TV* then today's television producers and creatives might assume that there is abundance and so out-source their own collecting of their own cultural work:

> I don't tend to go and watch anything that is on that's been catalogued in libraries or media museums. I know that it's there though. I just don't tend to get round to doing that. However, somebody I know, yesterday, literally had an hour to kill yesterday and went to a library and decided to watch a programme online because they knew it was there. So I think it's getting, I think we're living in an age where things are very accessible.
>
> (interview with Lindsay Williams 16 September 2014)

What we wish to demonstrate is that producer-ly memories show that television's cultural value lies parallel to the text and to the archive. Producers' memories operate in a paratextual way and they produce 'paratexts' (see Gray 2010) as a new afterlife of television, which can be used to reanimate, rekindle and re-collect dormant audiences for the original, lost or rebooted programmes. We need to explore producer-ly memories as more than simply nostalgia recuperating lost practice and consider their ability to speak frankly of memory cultures in and around television. For Lisa Holdsworth 'the re-boot is definitely the king of them and it's about money, it's recognisable territory, the instant pitch [...] it's beginning to bleed into TV and so what's it about? It's about vampires, it's about someone's bought the books up and particularly with detective dramas. Adaptations of books that people have really loved, they've got a readymade audience' (interview with Lisa Holdsworth 5 May 2014). These kinds of producer-ly stories, memories of innovation and creativity and reflections on how television's creativity regenerates memory or forgets innovation, can be used by television historians to understand histories of precarious cultural labour over time and in time.

As Wheatley has argued the 'micro-histories of television production' have focused upon 'quotidian production cultures and examine production practices in relation to key periods or genres (e.g. Skutch 1998; Born 2000; Cottle 2004)' (2007, 7). Yet, at the centre of these micro-histories are even more creative 'persons' with personal memories that may conflict with cultural memories of past television as produced by 'above the line' producer accounts, producer-turned-academic histories or scholarly and archival research. In this chapter, we have made a first step toward a wider sense of producer-ly memory from the perspective of the personal and the professional. Their perspectives both do and do not reify a collective memory of past television as an ongoing battle between creativity and economics to become a tension between the producer (artistic impulse) and the consumer (market forces, viewer pleasure). Their reflections on practices are entirely personal and show forth 'symbols', 'heroes' and 'rituals' that offer a deeper insight into 'values', that is, a richer sense of television existing outside its own flow, of its own historical account of itself, a looking back that seeks to make narrative sense of messy experiences. The memories of working in British television from the 1950s to the present day that we have collected and sampled here show that personal risk has often been a part of the culture of television production, that organizations and networks have sought to mitigate this through conservative interpretations of creativity, innovation and renewal and that a communal memory of television production is in danger of becoming scarce if researchers do not seek to collect it and support it, while producers assume it is archived elsewhere.

3 TELEVISION'S TREASURES AND ARCHIVAL VALUES

There has been a certain shame, urgency as well as opportunity gathering momentum in recent years, generating much creative, cultural and heritage entrepreneurship around *old TV*. Several TV history projects have been funded by UK research councils and the Heritage Lottery Fund.[1] British television may not have been cherished and treasured enough it seems, at least not as much as cinema, and now there is significant activity addressing the lacunae. While the archives may not have been fully mined for the many gems that are buried there, and important works and key creatives have not been celebrated and commemorated with the respect they may deserve, there is still vital material lost forever. What is not lost forever are the dormant and core audiences who remember television and who will find ways to access and share those memories. While the BBC has been admonished for its 'trashing' policy of the 1950s to 1970s (it reused expensive tape or was live), ITV has been considered careless with its paper archive and disorganized with its multiple copies of tapes in the regions. Joe Moran in *Armchair Nation* taps into this popular lament by referencing Dudley Moore in 1970 on the *Parkinson* talk show (BBC One/ITV, 1971–2007) in a way that confirms Dennis Potter's 'sense of paralysing anti-climax as the end credits rolled on each of his television plays' (2013, 225); knowing they were gone, ephemeral, lost and used up. If *The Wednesday Play* of 1964 is not worth celebrating in 2014, a fiftieth anniversary for challenging British drama, this is because the plays are largely forgotten by the public, too difficult to commemorate for a globally-facing BBC in the twenty-first century, or off message and not on brand.

---

[1]For example, ERC funded ADAPT (2013–18); HLF (2015) funded 'The Story of Children's Television from 1946 to Today'; AHRC (2013–17) 'History of Forgotten Television Drama'; AHRC Collaborative Doctoral Award (2011) 'Writing the History of Southern Television: 1958–1982'; AHRC (2010–15); 'Spaces of Television: Production, Site and Style'; and AHRC (2010–13) 'A History of Television for Women in Britain, 1947–1989'.

Previous interviews with BBC Information and Archive managers (see Garde-Hansen 2015) corroborated the contention that British television has only been seriously collected, preserved, archived and made accessible in the last forty years (since 1978 the archive policy for preserving BBC television output has been in operation), with BBC archive managers only recently working through uncertainty in order to create what is to be treasured. The position of archives in the minds of producers, broadcasters and audiences was and perhaps still is relatively 'back of the mind', as a function that happens at the end of the process. One of the producer-archive researchers we interviewed recalled:

My first job actually at [the] BBC after doing my work experience was sorting out the archive for the department I now work in and their archive system was just a big, literally a pile of tapes in the corner of the room like leaves that had blown into the corner, and I was getting them all laid out on the floor in this basement storeroom in the old BBC building in Manchester, I got them into some sort of order and then started watching them because the idea was, 'Well some of these things people might want to buy.' [...] What do we keep and what do we chuck? What might have an ongoing value?

(interview with Mark Helsby 24 June 2014)

Thus, even our producer interviews corroborated the economics of memory for anyone interested in television archives, creating scarcity from plenty or potentially new value from detritus (literally tapes swept into a corner). As the BBC archive managers below state, increased governance over what has ongoing value is resource-intensive: 'if your building is full you can't just run out and build another one' for 'digital storage is starting to create those kinds of problems' as the '"management of a digital service requires the same infrastructures and people around it"' (interview with BBC Information and Archives 27 September 2012, London, cited in Garde-Hansen 2015, 588). At the creative end, another television archive researcher we interviewed noted how, restricted by budgets, she does not have the time to 'look for that nugget. You don't get the time to really shovel into the archive and really dig through it.' She gave the following example: 'I worked on a one-hour archive-based programme for the BBC. It was 90% archive and we were only originally given three weeks in the edit which is just no time to put something together, and a couple of weeks to research it' (interview with Mhairi Brennan 23 June 2014).

Promoting British television and protecting and preserving British television are different attitudes requiring different economies. Searching for TV treasures (see Fiddy's 2001 book *Missing Believe Wiped: Searching for the Lost Treasures of British Television*) must be worth the effort and time to re-present it to a contemporary audience and there should be a pay-off in the present. It also needs old and new kinds of skills and cultural workers who can make that bridge between television archives and contemporary television production, as Mhairi Brennan explained of her own role as archive producer (freelance for the BBC at the time of interview):

nobody really gets trained how to do it anymore [television archive research]. So, knowing a bit about copyright law, knowing how to use the archive companies, being able to say, 'here's a visual presentation pack' stood me in good stead and particularly when I moved back to Glasgow. I found I was getting more and more work doing that and that I really loved it. I really enjoy the process because it just combines so many things – you're like an historian, a social commentator, a storyteller, you're a librarian, curator, you get to choose the piece of film and present it and say, 'actually I think this would fit the story that you're trying to tell'.

(interview with Mhairi Brennan 23 June 2014)

With this in mind, some television heritage sector managers can find themselves caught between the lament of a lost past, infilled with nostalgia, and the real economics of making *old TV* relevant today to old and new audiences alike: 'One of the bugbears of this job is that if you're not careful every single discussion that you ever put together about any single season from the archive can end up being a backward looking discussion about the so-called Golden Age of television' states Marcus Prince, television programmer of the BFI (interview 19 March 2014).

Any momentum of collective guilt has now culminated in a growing waged and unwaged industry to find (Missing Believe Wiped Campaign), to restage (BBC Lost Sitcoms season), to repatriate (*Doctor Who* missing episodes, see Molesworth 2013), and even to reanimate (*Dad's Army* [1968–77] missing episode animation) what has been lost, thought used up, or considered *out of sync* at the time of broadcast. All this new creative industry and endeavour is built upon and demonstrates the power of remembering television, the afterlife of a medium that refuses to be fully de-materialized and the new kinds of precarious labour that materialzes as television-specific memory work. The case of documentarist Philip Donnellan (1924–99) is an excellent example of this memorial labour and such archival values at work. His collection of over 200 cans containing film rolls, as well as 16mm film, programme notes and research files was transferred from his own possession (not stored in preservation conditions) to the Wolverhampton Borough Archives, then in 1996 to the Birmingham Archives and Heritage collection. Assessed by Ieuen Franklin (2014) for its condition, value and outreach use, the legacy and inheritability will depend on transfer cost, whether duplicates exist, if it is material that has never been broadcast and how 'at-risk' of further degradation it is.

The recent attempts to better account for the work of Donnellan, for example, whose documentary films for television from the 1950s to 1970s were innovative, revealing and controversial on topics of black and minority ethnic communities have been in this vein: 'Donnellan [at the BBC] was allowed to develop styles of production and to experiment with the documentary aesthetic with a freedom that is unimaginable today' says Franklin (2014). Similarly, Paul Long (2011b) laments Donnellan's absence from history, even the BBC's history, and the Pebble Mill Project is enabled through interviews, reviews and critique to reveal memories of other heroes who worked with or against Donnellan. Interviews with the retired cameraman John Williams, for example, provide evidence of bringing Donnellan's vision to the screen despite the difficulties (see Long 2011a; Poole 2012; Williams 2014).

While Franklin focuses on 'Donnellan's films' that 'persistently convey a sense of the weight of history, exploring memory and archival evidence to pose difficult questions about the construction of history' (2014), the Pebble Mill Project addresses the weight of Donnellan's 'at-risk' archive by harnessing production memories of working with him. It is a holistic approach (a space for academic critique, critical review, archive reports, video recollections, photographs and postings from remembering audiences) that helps off-set any intellectual elitism of the academic or esteemed person, but it is not at all the same as the 'rogue archives' (De Kosnik 2016) cropping up all over the web. Some of which may be considered more trustworthy than those produced by 'elite organizations' such as universities and museums.

For example, the freelance television lighting director Martin Kempton has diligently covered the history of British television studios at <www.tvstudiohistory. co.uk> for the last ten years, and acknowledges how much his collection of information and images is based upon a relationship between himself and the producer-ly memory work of those who interact with his site.

> There are still gaps and no doubt a number of errors – although hopefully these will be relatively minor by now. I am still very much welcoming any comments and, of course, corrections and additions. Around 240 people have contributed so far and I am very much in their debt for taking the trouble to write or talk to me. In fact, I have received well over 2,500 email messages in total – some with corrections or additional information, others simply saying thanks.
>
> (TV Studio History n.d.)

We would argue, and we will return to this point later, that academic entrepreneurship for remembering television taps into a *regenerative milieu* of heritage funding and subnational regeneration policy, in which Donnellan's legacy as an example could be nurtured and grown through the real and affective labour of academics, fans, enthusiasts, archivists, libraries and museums, universities, students and local historians. The added layer of members of the public sharing their own memories of being Black and poor in Birmingham attaches itself to the production memories on the Pebble Mill Studios site, and demonstrates public engagement with how TV has been made. Thus, salvaging television history through producer collections and memories has become a significant resource of social and cultural capital-building for a wide range of stakeholders, and reveals much about how archival values are being played out. To some extent such projects open up the possibility for other kinds of memories of TV to surface or to be day-lighted, as they circulate and recirculate the television producer/creative/text as cultural or social (anti-)hero or iconic.

Television collections and archives (distributed widely) present problems that have begun to create solutions in the form of increased collaboration between a wide range of organizational actors, from universities to libraries to enthusiastic collectors. One even has Sony Technology Centre, based in South Wales, UK, offering its afterlife service 'Media Lifecycle Solutions' recognizing on its landing page that 'many of today's media and broadcast companies have vast archives on video cassette, and these old tapes are deteriorating rapidly. At Sony UK Technology Centre (UK TEC), we aim to give your archive media a new lease of life' (SONY 2016).[2] This cross-industry, cross-disciplinary and cross-sector effort often runs parallel to television production itself and contributes to television's wider paratextual memory, as we shall show in Chapter 6.

There is a growing industry of archive strategists, heritage entrepreneurs and new cultural value makers who (as we shall explore in Chapters 4 and 7) reactivate dormant memories and inheritable core audiences, to create new kinds of viewers, users and visitors. They tap into an *always already* transmedia memory of television through the medium's past connectedness to print media (i.e. *The Radio Times* Genome Project 1923–2009), to sequential art (see Colin Harvey's 2015 *Fantastic Transmedia* on *Doctor Who* comic strips), or to a celebration of TV's audio, visual and design ingredients. As TVARK defines such trans-mediality at the heart of *old TV*, visualized through its web banners as idents (see Figure 1):

FIGURE 1 Screen grab of ARKTV homepage at <www.tv-ark.org.uk/>. (Accessed 24 October 2016.)

---

[2]The webpage continues: 'As inventors of the VCR way back in 1964 there's nobody that understands video technology better than Sony. As the pressure to digitise content before it is lost forever increases, we have extended our offer to provide digitising and archiving solutions, helping you to future-proof your content' (SONY 2016).

TVARK is an online TV museum. The site is intended as a tribute to the work of television presentation and graphics, and to preserve a slice of our social history. Through images and video clips, we present those modest little chunks of television that are never repeated: idents, programme promotions, opening title sequences, public information films, commercials, daily start-ups and closedowns, break bumpers and station clocks.

('About Us' page of TVARK <www.tv-ark.org.uk>)

Yet, before we get to this stage of increasingly digitized, connective and data-driven inheritance, displayed as transnational and trans-medial, it is worth returning to those key people who have quietly worked behind the scenes of TV archiving and preservation to ensure there are multiple collections of British TV to protect and repurpose. Steeped in the cultural values of television history (British or otherwise), some of these people were made redundant, retired or left their roles during our research.

While those interested in television history – and the list of stakeholders is growing – seek to engage the public in past TV treasures for a range of academic, impact, educational and heritage purposes, organizations such as the BFI (formerly the National Film Archive) and MACE (the Media Archive of Central England) have focused on the technical and curatorial demands of capturing, storing and making accessible *old TV* at a national and regional level respectively. This focus has been facilitated, managed and driven by key individuals with a passion both for television and the technical challenges of making it inheritable. As Charles Fairall of the BFI stated in interview:

The management of the physical collection is really not to be underestimated. The National Television Archive amounts to a really vast amount of physical collections, so if you unpack that, there's a considerable amount of real estate involved in storing and keeping everything in the right climate – and also a massive collections and management place. So, the technical database information on television has to be as comprehensive as the database information for film in so far as you need to know what format the tape is, what the technical issues are around it, where it's located on a shelf, in a vault and because it's master material you have to make sure that it's treated properly. And of course, most importantly that the programmes themselves are researchable, that you can find the content not only internally at the BFI but from an external perspective too. So I think, perhaps the slightly less visible aspects of managing a huge heritage collection have to be appreciated. That means good storage, good logistics, good practices and a powerful database.

(interview with Charles Fairall 12 December 2014)

When libraries, museums, universities and TV enthusiasts take on a collection they may see TV treasure and its cultural historical value. Yet, for those who work in TV preservation, they see cost, challenge and the ethics of sustainability. This chapter draws on their experiences and recollections as they work in these areas and face the tension between the treasure and the technicity of *old TV* everyday, as an ongoing challenge in terms of media archaeology, cultural value and remaining employed.

On method

There is, undeniably, a 'national' boundary to place around these findings. Firstly, we focused on UK institutions, our participants work in British organizations funded by government and/or broadcasters with some commercial aspects. Because we used a 'snowballing technique' (which made professional/relational connectivity tangible) there was a geographical limit to what we could achieve in the twelve months of interviewing during 2014 to 2015. Therefore, this is not a comprehensive account of the voices from the widest spectrum of spaces where past television produces inheritable 'content' from its archives. We have few voices from commercial footage houses, such as Index Stock Shots (n.d.) a privately-owned provider in the market, but we do have a contribution from Getty to our symposium, which during our research struck a deal with BBC Motion Picture Gallery. While our 'organizational actors' are mostly in England (primarily London, the Midlands and Yorkshire), we were referred to Scottish counterparts in Glasgow which led to some interesting insights as archives between London and Glasgow worked together to move material from the south to the north. While the clear majority of those interviewed were white, male and between forty and sixty years old, we view this as a reflection of the demographic of those working in these senior (technical or managerial) positions in this sector.

The original scope of our research was to undertake 1–2 hour interviews with ten key 'organizational actors',[3] and this was added to two interviews with BBC Information and Archives undertaken the previous year as a pilot. To generate interest in the research we kicked off with a series of papers delivered by TV archivists at the *Inheriting British Television Symposium* held in February 2014 at the National Media Museum. However, three limitations emerged. Firstly, although we undertook fourteen interviews (largely due to changes of staff during the research project) our approach meant that Wales and Northern Ireland emerged

---

[3] The final fourteen organizational actors were: one senior staff from the National Library of Scotland (NLS), three senior staff from the British Film Institute (BFI), two senior staff from BBC Information and Archives, three senior staff from National Media Museum (NMeM), one independent archive manager, one commercial archive manager, one regional television archive manager, and two producer-archive researchers. Some of these participants were involved in the Kick-Off Symposium of our research held at the NMeM, Bradford, where they were joined by Tony Ageh (then BBC director of archives) and Matthew Butson (manager of Getty Images). Previously, we had interviewed two BBC Information and Archives managers in a pilot project, and some of the findings of these interviews were published in Garde-Hansen (2015). Our analysis here focuses on the transcripts from the twelve interviews we undertook in 2014 to 2015, and is supported by findings from the symposium papers and videos.

as unintentional blackspots (our interviewees simply did not lead us to further relational contacts in these regions). This leaves them ripe for further research, perhaps around a *devolution of television memory* through archives/collections held there. Some of this research is already underway through the determination of media archaeologist Ken Griffin (2015) at the University of Ulster who has been researching and finding missing television programmes from and about Northern Ireland in the Ulster TV Archive (UTV).[4] Moreover, the emerging project at the National Library of Wales (noted in our introduction) suggests a growing attention to *old TV* from Wales. We know that small projects on TV archives such as Elinor Groom's on the Southern TV Archive have produced important insights into the infrastructure of the British television regional franchise from the 1950s to the 80s (see Groom 2014).

Secondly, as became apparent from our interviewing, there are real and tangible legal boundaries around television's archival inheritability that means past 'British Television' is preserved and protected as a national resource, increasingly circumscribed by the preservation of territorial rights in the face of global demands.[5] As one archivist researcher pointed out to us in an interview wherein we discussed the cost implications for contemporary programme makers keen to explore and reuse the widest and freshest archival television footage: 'one of the things that might change that's just happened for programme making is the BBC has just signed a blanket agreement with the BFI, ITN Source, Associated Press Archive which covers Movietone, British Pathé and the Imperial War Museum' (interview with TV archive researcher 23 June 2014). Which, on the face of it could be considered 'transnational' in nature and extending beyond national framings. However, she later added (once shown her interview transcript for signing off) that:

> the Blanket Agreement can only be used for programmes to be transmitted in the UK – UK tx – it doesn't apply to programmes which will be broadcast around the world. Although Getty are not part of the Blanket Agreement, they are now offering the same terms as the Blanket Agreement for footage used in UK tx [transmission] programmes.
> (interview with TV archive researcher 23 June 2014)

Thus, what is easily accessible of past television in the market remains determined by territorial and legal considerations, and this is constantly evolving. It is worth adding that the former director of BBC Archives and the Public Sphere, Tony

---

[4]For example, programmes such as *Counterpoint* (UTV, 1978–96) 'a long-running current affairs series produced by Ulster Television (UTV) [...] which became renowned for its hard-hitting political coverage and its investigations into controversial social issues such as abortion, divorce and AIDS' (Griffin 2015, 13).
[5]See Auslander's (1999) *Liveness: Performance in a Mediatized Culture* for a detailed discussion of memory and law (i.e. copyright, testimony and legal memory).

Ageh, was keen to spread the BBC archive beyond the 'national' for the creative use of the world. Ageh is, from 2016, at the New York Public Library and has publicly lamented the national constraints he was working within while at the BBC.[6]

Thirdly, those we interviewed have personal and family memories of television and these are framed by and deeply connected to local, regional and national memories (cultural, social and communicative) as well as to their generation. They are emplaced and enmeshed, with affective roots in television, continually remaking their role in the present through the cultural resources available to them. Many are working in TV preservation, archive and heritage because they love TV (technology and texts) and their first encounters with TV are described as 'exciting' involving a 'bigger conversation' around good TV, which was 'celebrated and talked about endlessly' (interview with Charles Fairall, head of conservation, BFI, 12 December 2014). They are also aware of the precarity of their position and their work. If one follows FootageInfo. com – whose strapline is 'the footage industry's talking shop, the first with its news and the best footage site listing anywhere' – we can see change, risk and redundancy as new archival agreements are signed or footage archives monetized. For example, at the time of writing this chapter ITN Source would cease to exist from 2017:

> ITN Source, the archive licensing division of UK news broadcaster Independent Television News and one of the busiest of news footage houses with a world news collection going back to 1955, is to cease operations from mid next year. It is handing over licensing to Getty Images and dropping third party archive representations, including that of Reuters TV news footage. The thirty staffers in the archive division are, according to ITN, 'at risk of redundancy' and 'have been informed and a consultation period is underway.'
>
> (Flewin 2016)

Therefore, talking shop with all our organizational actors was inflected by a set of cultural values around the purpose of preserving and reusing past British television in risky times, alongside a set of personal and childhood memories of British television that they shared with their own generation of audience members and wanted to share with younger audiences. As one interviewee stated:

---

[6]Tony Ageh, who we have consulted many times on the status of British television archives, provided an exit interview to *The Guardian* (Kiss 2016) newspaper explaining his reason for heading up the digital strategy at New York Public Library. It is useful to note the implicit 'national' versus 'global' dichotomy at work in his discourse around moving from one 'memory institution' to another: 'I believe in universal and equal access for all of British culture. It should not be the case that anyone gets better service because of their wealth, sex or religion. We should bring the best of our culture to as many people as possible.'

I was a fan of all kinds of stuff in the '60s, *The Man From U.N.C.L.E* [NBC, Arena Productions, 1964–8] was my favourite at one particular time but I also watched all the news, as I became more aware, I remember vividly following the moon shots almost obsessively, and watching hours upon hours of *Countdown* [Channel 4, Granada/ITV Studios, 1982–] things like that. And then in the '70s *Doctor Who* [BBC One, 1963–] of course, you can't fail to mention *Doctor Who* having seen the first episode as it went out and ignored the Kennedy assassination being obsessed by *Doctor Who* [laughs].

(interview with Steve Bryant 19 March 2014)

Thus, methodologically challenging for the study of television's archives is the inclusion of these personal memories into professional life stories of managing to maintain television's value as a cultural resource balanced with the financial pressures of storage and monetization. 'Organizational memory', that is, an institution's or corporation's accumulated knowledge and data is really only a metaphorical concept for how such a structure manages knowledge. In reality, there is no 'organizational memory' (where say a TV company stores, retrieves and recollects its past as if the company were a person).[7] There is, though, a distinct and key group of interconnected agentic individuals who remember or forget how an organization (its processes and practices) come into being, how challenges are overcome and how to maintain the cultural value of television for a wide range of audiences. We were interested in the micro scale of inheriting British television operating within meso scales of national organizations and macro scales of global and digital challenges. How they treasured television was key. As one archive entrepreneur noted:

I have this kind of view which may be true or not I don't know, that you associate TV programmes, certain music, certain times of your life with the things that go on with them. So, if you're having a particularly good time in your life you often remember those TV programmes and there's a happy memory associated with those times. And when I look back I watched a lot of television when I was younger, with my parents, *The Gentle Touch* [ITV, London Weekend Television, 1980–4] on a Friday night eating fish and chips. *Multi-Coloured Swap Shop* [BBC One, 1976–82] on a Saturday morning. Having to switch between *Doctor Who* and *Buck Rogers in the 25th Century* [NBC, Glen A. Larson Productions, 1979–81] because my sister wanted *Doctor Who* and I wanted *Buck Rogers*, you know, little things like that.

(interview with Chris Perry from Kaleidoscope 14 July 2014)

---

[7]Numerous data management policy documents make a note of 'corporate memory', such as Channel 4's (2013) and the BBC's (2013), which they will define as determined by the uniformity of the record keeping process so as to ensure a narrative of continuity despite change. In reality that corporate memory is also very much elsewhere (i.e. in the National Library of Records as well as in retired staff members' heads or distributed storage spaces).

It was this level of personal meaningfulness of television in the lives of those we interviewed that provided the backstory for their enthusiasm for working through the storage, accessibility and exhibition challenges of making as much past television available to the public as possible. They sought to not only record, store, transfer, digitize and preserve *old TV* but interpret, curate and make it meaningful again. They wanted to share a feeling they had always had with and for television.

In what follows we offer an analysis of the stories our archivists told us and the narratives these stories create around material issues of storage, access, preservation, availability as well as the use of new discourses and practices for digitally 'remembering' television for new audiences. We do not subscribe to a position that the internet per se is archiving and making accessible past television. That is not its role. As Taylor has argued:

> The owners [of websites] may or may not commit to preserving these materials long term. Further, there is no selection process for materials uploaded online. No one vouches as to its sources or veracity. Expertise is irrelevant. The materials seem free and available to anyone with Internet access – avoiding the rituals of participation governing traditional archives.
>
> (Taylor 2011, 8)

While one producer in chapter two relied on the internet for *old TV*, we suggest the real work of storage and exhibition goes generally unnoticed.

Making space for *old TV*

Without spaces in which to store, preserve, access and view past television there would be no past television (on a widely-distributed scale) to research, view and enjoy, no written and document archives to substantiate the production of those texts and no paratexts (ephemera, merchandise and memorabilia) to display to or from fans and audiences. In terms of British TV there is a fairly unique and wide variety of different and 'relatively accessible' national and local spaces for keeping and reusing old television (permanent, temporary and emerging). We say relatively accessible in quotation marks as many TV scholars would argue that access to television's history is limited to an elite few, is (increasingly) behind pay-per-view walls, may require freedom of information requests in some cases, is complicated by multiple rights clearance and historical mergers of media companies, or is only available to the industry itself. Nevertheless, initiatives such as the Box of Broadcasts through which broadcasters and institutions can make hundreds of thousands of hours of television available for re-viewing are essential innovations for the public service broadcaster as custodians of a nation's TV heritage. In comparison to other countries, and here we draw on the work of Spigel (2005a) on American TV archives and the slow work of the Library of Congress, and Darian-Smith and Turnbull (2012) on the lack of non-serious programme archives in Australia, we find that British television has had enough of a national and transnational impact that a substantial amount of it is preserved.

Compared to a fully commercial system (as in the USA) there is an enviable expectation in UK public circulation (however unfulfilled) that British television 'belongs' to the people if produced through public funding and hence such broadcasters are the 'custodians', thus making the possibility of access more a logistical and resource issue than an ideological one. This does not mean that members of the public routinely demand access to past TV archives but if the recent upsurge in interest in children's television and the work of network releasing are indicators of public appreciation, then it is not surprising that the past of British television is having something of a resurgence. Television itself offers a space for its own treasure and is treasured by the public (particularly on YouTube) for creating a space for personal and generational remembering (which we shall focus on in Chapters 5, 6 and 7). Popular criticism[8] may lament TV memory as a throwback, as producing an uncreative and nostalgic mindset, but to return past TV to the present allows for reappraisal of past cultural values and an exploration of how far it has travelled (or not as the case may be). This return comes as much from YouTube as it does from official archives. As Darian-Smith and Turnbull note in their reflection on this issue:

> In these official and alternative histories of television, it is important to consider what gets remembered, by whom and for what purposes. Even more importantly, we need to consider what narrative and histories of television and its content, audience reception and boarder cultural meanings may be marginalised or even forgotten. In this way, the role of the television archive can function as a technology of memory – or, perhaps specifically, as a means of collecting and preserving particular stories.
>
> (Darian-Smith and Turnbull 2012, 7)

In terms of physical and internet enabled archival spaces relating to television, the UK has the BBC Written Archives, the BBC Archive Centre at Perivale, the British Universities Film and Video Council (BUFVC) with its Television and Radio Index for Learning and Teaching (TRILT) and a database of listings (1995–), Channel 4 document archives are held at The National Archives, the BFI archives are at London's Southbank, the BFI Reuben Library is in London and the BFI large film and video storage facility at Gaydon ensures more facilities are available. The BFI has nine Mediatheques (at the time of writing) in UK libraries and museums ensuring an extensive collection of film and television holdings are viewable by the public. It would be interesting to explore the data on viewing at these Mediatheques (what kinds of programmes, by whom, for how long, in what location) to learn

---

[8]See, for example, Frankie Boyle's (2016) 'TV comedy has gone back to the 70s'.

more about audience memory and interaction with television's afterlife. We say this because one of our interviewees (a freelance archive researcher in Glasgow) recalled the following as a striking memory of connection:

> I remember going down to the opening of the BFI Mediatheque in Bridgeton in the East End of Glasgow [...] There was a care worker in with [an] old guy in a wheelchair and she didn't really want to come into the booth: 'I don't think I'll fit him in.' The guy from the BFI said, 'Oh no, come on in, I'll make room.' He clicked on a show reel of *Glasgow Belongs to Me* [British Transport Films, 1965], 'I think your guy will recognise this' and the guy would recognise stuff and he was singing along and he was so happy and she was like, 'I've never seen him like this. I've never seen him this happy.' You know, that power to connect.
>
> (interview with Mhairi Brennan 23 June 2014)

The power to connect can also be discovered at the National Media Museum in Bradford, the National Library of Scotland, as well as Ulster TV archives mentioned above. We have ITN Source (until 2017), Getty Images (ever expanding), British Pathé and Kaleidoscope (regional to the Midlands), as well as more recent sources of publicly available and free content from Box of Broadcasts (BoB). All of which have the power to connect at a range of scales for different kinds of audiences and users. We have no doubt missed off other key physical and online storage and distribution gateways to accessing past British television (some established and some emerging), affording transmedia storytelling for broadcasters, researchers, teachers and the public. There are also several collections based on programme series or a particular screenwriter in need of new homes, as space becomes an issue or the creative person passes away and leaves their collection for their family.

The creation and sustainability of any significant spaces for remembering such television may seem to be driven by media archivists, media historians, cultural policymakers and cultural and creative industries who value television (its texts and more recently its paratexts) when many of those around them do not. Yet, it is also driven by singularly passionate individuals who simply love television and see it as an indispensable technology of memory, when often it is described as 'a struggle' to 'have television taken seriously as an art form' where cinema is 'the top thing and television is somewhere below it' (interview with Steve Bryant 19 March 2014). This view is corroborated by the BFI freelance TV consultant Dick Fiddy who defined his changing role in the organization with the growing view of *old TV* as valuable (a view he had been instrumental in developing): 'When I first joined here there were lots and lots of people who knew a fantastic amount about film. Rather fewer that knew or cared about television. That seems to have changed over the years, television has become sexier, to use the parlance, and lots more people are interested now' (interview with Dick Fiddy 10 July 2014). However, the 'long period of time where it's been quite difficult to have television taken completely seriously' (interview with Steve Bryant 19 March 2014)[9] may not be at an end. Even within the spaces being made for *old TV*, a description that still feels difficult to imagine considering our memories of its futurity, it may be struggling to be taken seriously as a form of cultural heritage.

In fact, however young television is claimed to be (not quite assignable to a history) and still in the immediacy of family memory and an everyday leveller of audience differences, there is still this *old TV*, much of which has gone *out of sync* very quickly, *out of date* sometime later or *out of mind* completely. It may even run *out of time* to be re-viewed if it is not salvaged or the equipment for its transference and transcoding is not procured from ebay or broadcasters in other countries. As important to the *history* of British television as this *old TV* might be (especially to academics, those with cultural capital and taste, the monetizers of assets or the many more with an enthusiasm for the medium) it may be just too complex and costly to regenerate despite the demands. There is also a talent and skills gap in the mass engineering solutions needed for the move from analogue to digital. Nevertheless, legacy demand is there and comes from remembering audiences as well as enthusiastic collectors and new creative ideas on repurposing. As Steve Bryant, at the BFI, made clear:

> In terms of the fans, again, when we deal with people like Kaleidoscope, they're always saying, 'I remember this and I remember that.' Titles that may have completely slipped our memory or not been regarded as particularly important, I mean maybe they are just important to those individuals. The fact that somebody, the fact that programme has made a bit of impact on somebody makes it worth investigation and making sure that something of it is kept.
>
> (interview with Steve Bryant 19 March 2014)

The *out of sync* demand is also coming from broadcasters themselves who archivists seek to work with and alongside, but who deposit in a variety of formats that makes impossible material demands on their resources and skills.

> And, of course, with the digital material, we're now receiving, we don't receive television programmes on digital files, even the likes of BBC Scotland who are allegedly tapeless still supply to us on tape. How long that will last goodness only knows so we have to be prepared for the day when that ceases to happen.
>
> (interview with Alan Mackay from the National Library of Scotland 23 June 2014)

---

[9]In the 1970s and 1980s the Wider Television Access (WTVA) group in Australia made the same point. As Sue Castrique declared in 1987 WTVA 'believes that preservation of television archives must become a national priority. Television constitutes one of the most important archival resources for filmmakers and is essential to the development of a television history [...]. Thirty years of Australian culture should not lie locked away in film and television storerooms. [...] It is the view of WTVA that "old TV" is an important part of our cinematic and cultural history' (1987, i).

Our point here is to draw on these interviews to set the scene for how a concept of *regenerative television memory* that frames our later chapters on nostalgia, heritage, the museum and childhood memories, is underpinned by significant material challenges, cultural and digital labour, and the uncertainty that technological change will bring. As a response to this uncertainty, we have witnessed in our research a complexity of trans-memory work being performed and negotiated by industrial, archival, heritage and creative industry actor-stakeholders, drawing in fans, audiences and former producers, directors and screenwriters. In some respects, this challenges Boym's definition: 'nostalgia is a sentiment of loss and displacement, but it is also a romance with one's own fantasy. Nostalgic love can only survive in a long-distance relationship' (2007, 7). In many cases, the *old TV* is not lost but is found, cared for, treasured and lifecycled, due to the efforts of actor-stakeholders, such as those we interviewed in our research. Where there is loss and misplacement there is also the immediacy of memory, oral history, unofficial collectors and archives. The displacement of *old TV* and the memories of home that television carries are addressed by those archiving television as a precarious affection 'no less deep, yet aware of its transience' (Boym 2007, 16).

Yet, this *old TV* is becoming as much in place as displaced, much less transient as the material conditions for making space for it become top of the mind in regenerating not only past television but the new sites that television archives occupy. Making space for *old TV* is technically and strategically challenging but for the television archivist in the region it is a cultural and political necessity. The Gaelic and acquisitions officer, Alan Mackay, at the National Library of Scotland stated, when asked has anyone been collecting Gaelic television:

No one was collecting it at all. I mean television didn't really feature, the organisation was always called the Scottish Film Archive which tells the story, and the little Scottish television output that was being preserved was being done by the BFI, they do preserve a small amount of Scottish output but they also have, I believe, some significant collections of Scottish material which it acquired through its broadcasters.

(interview with Alan Mackay 23 June 2014)

Some of this output has been slowly moving from London to Glasgow, as new spaces are made for *old TV* in politically and cultural important places, which challenges the notion that for some key actors, *old TV* is not leaves swept in a corner.

The underlying economy of 'fresh uses'

Although we began our interviews by prompting personal memories of television, the focus of our questions was designed to explore 'trade talk' (as Caldwell [2008] defines it). That is, in our context of the more invisible spaces of archiving television, the critical and self-reflexive understanding of working in archive media and heritage, and the real economic restraints on creativity. The nitty-gritty costs of 'fresh archive' can determine how much a programme (e.g. a new historical documentary or drama) reuses what is cheap and readily available over the interesting, never-seen-before, and not-yet-transcoded. As Mhairi Brennan notes in detail (and this interview exchange is worth quoting at length):

JGH   What's a 'screener'?

MB   A low-res version of the programme you want to see, so some companies, even to see a DVD, just to see what's on it, you might have to pay £50. So, you've got to be thinking about, 'well, is it worth my time?' Fortunately, a lot of companies are digitised now so for example, if I was working on a history programme about the Suffragettes, I could go to Pathé and everything is digitised. You can log in to their website and watch all their footage online. It's fantastic. You choose the clips you want and store them in an online workspace that the website provides, which you can share with other users, so your director can go in and see what you've collected. Then you order up your high res version that you're going to use in your programme. You can view footage in the same way on the Getty website, and Scottish Screen Archive, AP Archive and ITN source have a lot of digital content as well. More and more archive suppliers are making their content digitally available. But it's about having a good relationship actually with the archive suppliers. [...] You find with archive suppliers like Scottish Screen Archive, AP Archive, ITN Source, Pathé, Getty and the BBC, there are archivists who can advise you and help you and get that bit of research as well.

(interview with Mhairi Brennan 23 June 2014)

Storage, working across organizations and in multidisciplinary teams has been essential to the preservation of television which has had to be far more concerned with weaving together relationships, partnerships and shared resources in order to build a television treasury. It has been reliant upon key actors working cross-organizationally to enmesh, sift, catch and collect the television treasures as they fell into their possession, sometimes literally as they tumbled off the conveyor belt of television production lines, out of the back of vehicles or left in wills.

In some respects, this enmeshing of organizations chimes with Allen and Brown's (2016) recent exploration of 'memorial meshwork' which replaces a concept of memory as 'preservation' by focusing on organizational space, relationships and ongoing memory building. The National Library of Scotland (NLS), for example, preserves Gaelic television in a partnership that has evolved not only in organizational terms but also in physical building requirements (a brownfield site, away from the pollution of the city where they grapple with 'storage conditions' that 'are kind of changing all the time you know'). We are, says the Gaelic and acquisitions curator,[10] 'constantly looking at how you can develop […] in the way we work with the material, we're now able to do our own transfer from film to video in-house which we haven't been able to do in the past' (interview with Alan Mackay 23 June 2014). From the Gaelic Television Project of the mid-1990s to the Scottish Film and Television Archive, later the 'Scottish Film Council ceased to exist and it merged with an organisation called Scottish Screen Locations and another organisation, the Scottish Film Production Fund. A few years later these three organisations came together under the name Scottish Screen so we then became Scottish Screen Archive' (interview with Alan Mackay 23 June 2014). The partnership with the NLS serves the purpose of ensuring that 'production' of television does not dominate the agenda:

> I think somebody once said, 'Oh archive is not sexy, production is the bees' knees!' And the archive was just something that might or might not happen at the end of a production. So, I think there are certain benefits with joining up to the National Library and of course our colleagues were very helpful in securing the finance available to buy all this equipment.
>
> (interview with Alan Mackay 23 June 2014)

This interviewee was not alone in citing resource issues as the key challenge. In fact, the answer from the different stakeholders (despite their different roles in organizations at publicly funded national and regional or entrepreneurial-commercial scales) to our question 'what are the challenges facing your institution/organization?' was invariably 'financial'. Just as material costs had meant television was too expensive to save before the 1980s, so too the high cost of storage, preservation, transfer, access and exhibition continue to dominate what is achievable, with a necessary optimism in the face of adversity:

> Always financial. That's the number one. If we could sort that out, the financial. If our grant was reinstated to its full level or if we got a billionaire backer then I think things would be different, but to tell the truth, for the money we've got, the resources we've got, I'm really proud of what they do with it, and because, I think they're doing the best they can at the moment.
>
> (interview with Dick Fiddy 10 July 2014)

---

[10]Working in this kind of role since 1994, he defines it as being created out of necessity as 'the material was being deposited and there was some immediate problem because there was no Archivist capable of speaking Gaelic. So the tapes were coming in, nobody could deal with them so then our parent organisation at the time was the Scottish Film Council. They reached an agreement with the Gaelic Media Service that Gaelic Media Service would provide some of the funding for the post so they created a Gaelic Television Officer post. A grand title I had initially of Gaelic Television Officer, and the job title has changed now to Gaelic and Acquisitions Curator because we're responsible for some other collections as well. But the Gaelic Media Service continues to this day to provide probably about 70% to 75% of the funding for the project' (interview with Alan Mackay 23 June 2014).

Likewise, a regional archive manager[11] noted the *precarious permanency* of storing film and television at a university:[12]

> The agreement that we have with the university runs for an initial 10 years. It's about as permanent as anything we're ever going to be given. This is an impermanent place and funding, it's like saying, 'you're funding is permanent' no, our funding is fragile of course but it's like all these things, it's as permanent as can be I think.
>
> (interview with James Patterson 22 September 2014)

While archiving television had brought funding from 'TV companies under the terms of the broadcasting legislation' there was a sense of change on two fronts. Firstly, TV companies consolidating and rationalizing their archives as ITV has done in Leeds with a view to taking stock of what they have and what is of value. Secondly,

> we face the challenge of the technology. Because what we used to be able to do and have the expertise to do is now much, much more widespread, and that's a good thing, we're not the only people making television accessible and it already is a good thing, we'll have to rely upon the areas of expertise that we do have particularly in obsolete technologies and knowledge of content to take our place amongst many.
>
> (interview with Steve Bryant 19 March 2014)

Yet, this knowledge and these skills are precariously tipped toward material change in formats and the diminishment of technical skills:

> Formats are a nightmare, video formats are changing and have been changing at a great rate of knots and now in this new digital world it's a very expensive digital world I have to say [...] So, finance will always be a problem, equipment will always be a problem, even video tape formats now are becoming obsolete and just having the equipment that is going to be able to play back your collections is a big problem.
>
> (interview with Alan Mackay 23 June 2014)

While Ellis makes the point that digital processes 'now mean that it is easier for anyone to cut and paste pieces of footage from one text to another' and this is 'no longer the province of a professional elite' and that those 'who simply regret this

---

[11]It is worth noting that during the writing of this chapter, the management role of this archive was advertised.

[12]Such arrangements are not unusual if the film and/or television archive benefits the university (especially in a context where public engagement and impact are key). A good example being the Bill Douglas Archive at the University of Exeter. However, these agreements are complex and resource-intensive. During the writing of this book, universities were in discussions with Kaleidoscope and ITV about housing collections as their massive stockpile of tapes outstripped their spaces and resources. Space is at a premium everywhere.

process are regretting the decline in importance of an elite' (Ellis 2014, 19), this may undervalue the television archivist, the public-funding challenges and the monetization of an asset already paid for through a licence fee in many cases. While digital 'establishes fresh uses' the underlying economies cannot be strategically forgotten and the impact fresh use has on archivists as custodians of materials produced in particular aspect ratios, for example, must also be rethought. As Bryant (2015) argues in his warning to television historians who ought to rethink archival television footage as illustrative rather than evidential: 'Much the same also applies to the use of reconstruction. Once frowned upon by the makers of "serious" history documentaries, it is now commonplace.'

Conclusion: 'Causing ripples beyond the moment of their transmission'

The increasing connections being made between archives, universities, the commercial sector, the television industry and the public (facilitated by shared online services) is an indicator not of the value of specific television texts necessarily nor of particular types of national televisual content (as in a 'national cinema'), but as Steve Bryant noted: 'we are now concentrating on what is called the "art, history and impact" of television. So, looking at it more as a medium than in terms of content' (interview with Steve Bryant 19 March 2014). Impact (a term used across the public, academic and third sectors) finds past TV texts exhibited with this intention, TV programmes 'that cause ripples beyond the moment of their transmission' as Bryant defined it (interview 19 March 2014). For example, the Pebble Mill Project, *Doctor Who and Me: 50 Years of Doctor Who Fans* at the National Media Museum (2013–14) (covered in Chapter 7), the *Children's TV Exhibition* that toured from 2015 and started in Coventry, the photographic display of *Faces of BBC Comedy* at Compton Verney during 2016 and numerous smaller, private collections of fans, producers and enthusiasts, which may or may not be made public, or produce wider ripples beyond national boundaries.

Connections between television archives and spaces where past TV can be viewed (off and online) are now (at least at the time of writing) more readily available due to the collaborations between the BBC, BFI, ITV, ITN Source, the National Media Museum (NMeM) and the NLS, for example, with new collaborations, as in Wales, emerging. In fact, the nine BFI Mediatheques (at the time of publication) generally retread these economic and spatial pathways (housed in London, Birmingham, Bradford, Cambridge, Derby, Glasgow, Manchester, Newcastle, with the first venue in Wales at Wrexham Library). Television historians themselves have taken up an important role in demonstrating the cultural value of past television and identifying how public engagement with television's history reveals most starkly the lacunae in our understanding and appreciation of different voices and memories (for example, black and minority ethnic communities, the role of women in television production, the representation of class, region and identity in television research, the role the environment and landscape has played in shaping television's development). Our interviews with those who work in the sector address the simple but constant issue of accessibility to past television and how life-changing this can be and illuminating for the present and future. For those collecting and curating television in and about Scotland, for example, accessibility affords a different experience of 'the national', which is played out in the discourse of the Gaelic Media Service and the NLS:

> When you see it in front of your eyes on a screen, you know, and when you talk to some young children today and you talk about things like mobile phones, iPads, computer games and things, they don't understand that these things weren't around in your day. So, it's really, it's a history of the country. It's a history of the country at work, at rest, at play, it shows all the various elements of what happens throughout the nation and it's there for people to actually see.
> (interview with Alan Mackay 23 June 2014)

Television programmes and their viewing not only remain in one's memory but become a part of one's life as a resource for identity, personal and collective storytelling and social relations. This begs the question of whether generalized remembering of television (Ellis 2007, 164) has a value or not. Without it, we would not have the necessary fertile soil in which to trigger and scaffold more specifically remembered television texts, and the BFI or Kaleidoscope would not have an audience. While in this chapter we have explored how a variety of stakeholders invest their time, energy and enthusiasm into remembering television on behalf of the broadcasters and publics they serve, for them the *textural memories* of past television are the productive growing conditions for developing new social practices of remembering through archives. However, we must be cautious if we privilege the internet as some sort of democratizing force or even as a 'digital archive'.

Vanessa Jackson in her case study of the Pebble Mill Project sees the opening-up of:

> previously untapped possibilities that can both change and enrich the television historian's view. What is worth preserving and discussing is no longer at the institutional archivist's discretion, but is now under the control of a collaborative online community. The relationship between personal memory and television history comes into effect here.
> (Jackson 2014, 245)

By taking a meta-stance from a critical memory studies perspective we have sought to day-light the memory work, cultural labour and deep thinking about television and personal memory already operating in the institutional archivist's theory and practice. To leave television's treasures to competitive remembering enabled by local, national and global online memory agents cannot assume a cosmo-optimistic 'collaborative online community' will have the most to gain nor that history and memory are easy bedfellows. There is an ethics to reading the television archive deeply and this relies on types of people passionate about television's meaning-making operating as a collective.

Organizations such as the BFI, MACE, Getty, BoB and Kaleidoscope are not simply engaged in procuring, protecting and promoting television's treasures, they are involved in curating memory that (whether intentionally or not) has the capacity to, say Brown and Hoskins (noted in the introduction), 'orient persons to possible versions of the past in such a way as to make them relevant to ongoing personal, social and political concerns' (2010, 88). The 'online collaborative community' is not separable from these institutional archivists (public and commercial). In other words, to rephrase Merrin's exploration of media ecologies, we would argue that remembering British television in a digital media ecology of archives, creative industries, increasing accessibility and newly connected audiences 'implies a *world view*: it *evokes a world*' (Merrin 2014, 47; our emphases). How far this worldview smooths over the precarious archive, the free labour of fans, the profits to be made in servicing the 'collaborative online community', the powerful role of academic institutions, broadcasters and archives as they work together, the risks associated with organizational change and the necessary and sometimes dying skills of creating heritage from television should not be forgotten. This requires the arts and humanities to be at the table where discussions about the future of *old TV* are made.

4 THE END OF 'EXPERIENCE TV' AT THE NATIONAL MEDIA MUSEUM

Introduction: The television set with *nothing on the screen*[1]

Derek Kompare begins his chapter on television heritage with the opening of the Museum of Broadcasting in Manhattan and *New York Times* critic John O'Connor's question in 1978: 'Has the time arrived for serious television retrospectives?' (2005, 101). As Kompare argues, this moment was to crystallize the importance and significance of television as a cultural art form with a 'greater acknowledgement of the everyday culture of modernity' along with the beginning of 'television's historicity, that is, its articulation into discourses of history and memory' (2005, 102). The fact that the museum offers a sense of acknowledgement of television's importance within culture highlights the museum as a space of inheritance. Yet, what of the museum of television wherein the collection has nothing on the screen? As Michael Terwey, head of collections and exhibitions at the National Media Museum (NMeM) explains of the materiality of television as museum object:

> A television set which doesn't have anything on the screen is not the same as sitting watching something on a television set. So, the experience of watching television is not the same thing as looking at a television set in the museum even though you will be able to. When you see a television set you might have had when you were younger, you are able to connect with that memory potentially, whereas a museum, we're not necessarily providing you with that experience.
> (interview with Michael Terwey 22 June 2016)

During the writing-up phase of our research the NMeM rebranded as the National Science and Media Museum. We will continue to use NMeM throughout this book as that is how our participants referred to it and such brand names remain in the collective memory for some time.
[1]Maeve Connolly raises the point that it is 'relatively unusual to encounter functioning television receivers in gallery or museum spaces' (2014, 29).

How then, can a museum of television's technological history explain the cultural value of the materiality of the television set which does not have anything on the screen? How can a museum circulate the spectacular cultural value of everyday objects when so many of these sets remain in our homes, inching one step closer to a household waste or recycling centre?[2] While the cover of our book is a photograph that captures the care and curation of the television sets in the store at the NMeM (at least until the room is repurposed), this should be contrasted with the many stacks of television sets discarded as waste and encountered daily at refuse sites.

The connective museum

Academic scholars, such as Amy Holdsworth (2011), Maeve Connolly (2014) and Helen Wheatley (2016), offer insightful work on the place of television within the museum and exhibition space. They reflect, as will this chapter, on the way television continues to be a medium in change and yet a consistent archive for memories. *Old TV* and the way it is curated and exhibited in museums is crucial to interrogate when thinking about the memories we have and how they intersect with heritage and institutions. This intersection, between museum and television, materiality and meaning-making, is also a fertile landscape to explore issues concerning cultural policy and government intervention around television, as this chapter will go on to explore. Methodologically, we used the same interview in situ methods for focusing on the NMeM and its three senior staff members who worked in the precarious area of curating television's history during the short period of our research. We wanted to focus squarely on the museum as a key thinker and doer on issues of memory work, cultural memory transfer, remembering and forgetting because we think museum workers offer 'bold self-critical narratives' and 'we need to seek out and study more of them, and to understand the processes of intellectual exchange and commissioning which help give birth to them' (Chalcraft and Delanty 2016). We cannot assume that only academics of media and memory are asking and investigating the most critically-informed questions about popular cultural pasts, and the materials and feelings on which these pasts are based. If, as the latest report on transcultural memory from The Cultural Base Project suggests, 'common ground today in contexts of complexity and pluralisation can only consist of zones of intersection' then *old TV* in the museum is one example that 'requires a rethinking of the notion of unity and the idea of a shared culture' (Chalcraft and Delanty 2016). What kind of

---

[2] In one author's home, the cathode ray tube set has now taken pride of place in a teenager's room as the only set that can connect to two early 1990s Nintendo game consoles and thus allow at-home play of 'retro' games that belonged to the parents, and give access to a gaming experience that was being exhibited at the NMeM's Games Lounge.

shared experience of television can the NMeM *afford* to provide and what happens when that *experience* ends?

Our research strategy of focusing on the cultural workers' recollections and memories of television and its place in the museum as a ubiquitous technology of the past, present and future revealed to us that those grappling with the challenges of resources, museum audience development, a changing media landscape, organizational change, branding and marketing were best placed to inform us of the impossibility of thinking through collective memory in a national container. They helped us more concretely place the 'British' of *Remembering British television* in scare quotes because their work is so connective and (as shall be explored in Chapter 7) transnational. As a national museum in the region, at the heart of a *regenerative milieu* of much needed urban renewal (Bradford), a city with a history of immigration and post-industrial challenges, the NMeM may be considered an outpost to collective memories of elite narratives. De Cesari and Rigney note in their critique of the nation state as the natural container, curator and telos of collective memory that globalized communication and time-space compression, post-coloniality, transnational capitalism, large-scale migration and regional integration: 'all these mean that national frames are no longer the self-evident ones they used to be in daily life and identity formation' (2014, 1). Thus, a museum that seeks to collect, curate and interpret its material collection of television technologies, revealing its connections to international manufacturing, global consumerism and the transcultural consumption of television as a travelling technology of memory, is well placed to teach 'scholars in the field of memory studies to develop new theoretical frameworks, invent new methodological tools, and identify new sites and archival resources for studying collective remembrance beyond the nation-state' (1).

Having stated this rather grand objective, the reality of working in a museum where television's history is precariously balanced on its ability to be relevant in policy, practical and people terms needs to be addressed head-on when cinema and photography are its much-lauded bedfellows. Drawing on interviews with the current and former employees of the NMeM in Bradford, West Yorkshire and with material offered to us by the museum regarding the closure of the 'Experience TV' gallery, this chapter will explore the way television has been curated, exhibited and valued to consider the ways in which this effects policy and creates wider ripples within the way we inherit television.

In her work on the TV museum, Maeve Connolly (2014) points towards the way in which the televisual has often been eclipsed by the cinematic in theorizations of the moving image, suggesting that 'this relative occlusion speaks to a specific difficulty around television in the art museum, which may be linked to its indeterminate status as simultaneously a material thing, medium, institution and cultural form' (2014, 6). This chapter will return later to television's mutability, but what is so pertinent here is the way in which Connolly recognizes this as a potential threat to television's place within the museum space. Moreover, writing in a context where *old TV* is being simultaneously valued and devalued, it is necessary to spend more time on this claim and its implications. Indeed, in the time we have spent writing this book two major television experiences announced their closures, and surely by the time this book is in print they will be closed.[3]

Case study: The end of TV?

The NMeM in West Yorkshire, formerly known as the National Museum of Photography, Film and Television (and rebranded as the National Science and Media Museum during the writing of this book) was founded in 1983 and is now part of the National Museums of Science and Industry (the Science Museum Group). The NMeM is at the centre of Holdsworth's (2011) exploration of the role of museums in television memory, especially the NMeM's Experience TV gallery. Her work usefully explores the curatorial practices within the museum and the way in which television is exhibited. It is a personally meaningful space to one of the authors of this book, the NMeM is the place in which one of us encountered the spectacular screens of Imax on the opening day in 1983 and then visited more or less monthly for the next ten years. As a free museum, wherein technologies of photography, cinema and television were brought under one roof in a display that focused inwards on the domestic home and outwards with rooftop viewing of the city beyond, the NMeM had a direct impact on the future direction of one of the author's education and career. No other museum in Bradford during the 1980s and 1990s seemed more about the future than the past, and about the potential of domestic technologies to engage visitors and change the way we see the world through multiple viewpoints and screens. On reflection, to spend time in the NMeM was to walk into a place that made sense through its performance of connectivity and vision. To experience television, for example, as a technology with an infrastructure of cables, materials and engineering, and a production of spaces, jobs and skills, was to reveal the underlying economies of the everyday in a way that shaped one of the author's future thinking.

At the time of our research and writing this book, the NMeM had two key spaces for television, Experience TV and 'TV Heaven'. However, as our interviews unveiled, Experience TV was soon to be decommissioned. As Holdsworth acknowledges in her work, 'There is a clear difficulty in writing about the constantly evolving practices of the NMeM determined, as it is, not only by technological innovation but also financial constraints' (2011, 147). Indeed, aside from this acknowledgement, Holdsworth also identifies some of the challenges the gallery faces in her analysis – highlighting the way in which visitors come to the exhibition with a knowledge of the medium that constructs a puzzle to the curator

---

[3] As well as the closure of the Experience TV gallery in the NMeM, the *Doctor Who* Experience in Cardiff Bay will close (Prince 2016).

as to how to 'add value' to the visit – to extend the visitor's knowledge and sense of enchantment with the medium – or re-enchantment as Holdsworth (2011) describes it, drawing on work by Huyssen (1995). Holdsworth's work demonstrates the changing nature of how television is valued within the museum space and the challenges curators face in exhibiting television, which, in our analysis below, is precarious.

Exhibiting television

The first television exhibition took place at the Science Museum between 10 June and 20 September 1937. Images and layouts from the event speak to the obsession at the time around the technology and to the male audience it attracted. As Helen Wheatley explains in *Spectacular Television: Exploring Televisual Pleasure* (2016), the exhibition was the space that many people in mid-twentieth-century Britain would first encounter television or new developments in television technology (2016, 24). Because of this, the exhibition space also became a site of contestation for the meaning of television. As Wheatley argues: 'the large-scale public exhibition played a vital role in the early negotiation of the ontological status of television: what it was or is, what it would be, what it offered for a particular group or group of viewers' (24). This assertion leads Wheatley to suggest the medium of television as a 'spectacular attraction', which counters more recent arguments regarding television as the 'new' cinema or new area of interest for the spectacular. Indeed, Wheatley (2016) makes a convincing case through her exploration of the 'spectacular', that television has always drawn interest from its audience which troubles previous understandings of television as something in the background or as wallpaper. Thus, whilst television as a material object has changed and continues to change, our fascination with it does not.

Wheatley notes a shift away from the technological aspects of television towards a focus on celebrity in the latter years of the 1950s (44). In her analysis of the Ideal Home Show in March 2015, Wheatley makes some important observations regarding the role of television in contemporary society. Although television and its personalities were still very visible, the actual material box was absent. There were no televisions on display in the three show homes in the exhibition (53). In considering this absence, Wheatley suggests that perhaps our screens have become more personalized and that 'rather than being a spectacle of modernity in itself, the television set has receded into the background, hidden out of sight' (53). The material absence of television is an important thing to consider further, particularly within the space of the exhibition. What does it mean to exhibit the domestic without television? What does this suggest about television's place in everyday life and in contemporary society? Does the personalized space of the iPad or laptop become a more preferable way to consume television? Does the absence of the television set in the domestic space signal a retro move away from technology? And what does this move away from technology suggest about the inheritance of television in future generations?

Connolly argues that 'television's status as public cultural form is presented as open to question and subject to continual redefinition' (2014, 152). As discussed earlier, television, as a medium and object of study, has often been the subject of speculations about its end. As we write, distributors such as Netflix and Amazon are seen to be questioning the nature of television and the future of how we watch it given their lack of schedule and adhesion to episode length and the way in which their programming has affected viewing and created binge watchers (see Matrix 2014; Jenner 2016b). Many viewers now watch television on ipads, tablets and laptops, while others, including us, continue to watch on the box in the corner of the room. Indeed, a programme such as *Gogglebox* (Channel 4, 2013–) reiterates the *experience* of TV as one of being in a room, on a couch, looking at a box – a simple and yet reassuring formulation while revealing the very mixed demographics of the audience. Drawing on Ien Ang's (2011) work, this familiar-unfamiliarity 'cracks open the nationalist narrative of seamless national unity, highlighting the fact that nations today inevitably harbour populations with multiple pasts, bringing memories and identities into circulation that often transcend or undercut the homogenising image of nationhood and national heritage' (Ang 2011, 82). Thus, while the medium is often seen as changing and in flux, it is clearly also seen as something that can be both fixed and moved aside for other experiences or as something that can be wrapped into broader mediums.

Connolly raises the issue of television's lifespan and argues that 'television's status as the dominant medium of contemporary culture is no longer secure' (2014, 13), a claim that has been visited and revisited by television scholars. For instance, over a decade ago, in the introduction to *Television After TV: Essays on a Medium in Transition*, Lynn Spigel considers the way in which television has had to reinvent itself and suggests that we may be entering into 'the phase which comes after "TV"' (Spigel 2004, 2). Noting changes around advertising, the rise of reality television, notions of 'quality,' 'stand-alone' and 'appointment' television, traditional routes of sponsorship and television's convergence with the internet, Spigel sees television as it has been known and as it was known at the turn of the twenty-first century, changing enough to question its future and its role within the cultural sphere. These claims may seem prophetic now but also dated in relation to more recent work on 'connected viewing' that not only refers to the 'multiple ways viewers engage with media in a multiscreen, socially networked, digital entertainment experience' (Holt, Steirer and Petruska 2016, 342), but also reflects a new way of researching and thinking about 'actors and processes normally studied separately' (343). Research on connected viewing reminds us of the ever-shifting platform of television and its programmes and content – it is indicative of television's insecurity, mutabilty and continual state of flux, and yet also its adaptability, spectacularity and its endurance. Television is at once ephemeral and uncertain and yet, as this book hopes to demonstrate, a medium that engenders deep, affective memories that tie people to its materiality and to their experiences making and watching it.[4] Where better, then, than the museum to explain these complexities to us?

Important to the work of any museum of television is the notion that television's 'abundance', noted by Ellis in his categorization of television's history (age of scarcity, growth and abundance) is 'accompanied by a relative scarcity of content' that requires 'extensive recourse to archive material and old television to feed [...] the voracious appetite' (2014, 13) – which Milly Buonanno (2008, 21) sees as creating a 'living museum of itself' (cited in Connolly 2014, 13).[5] In this sense, as Connolly follows from Buonanno (2008), 'the museum – even though it precedes television – has become part of the imaginary of the televisual' (2014, 13). Furthermore, to take this a step further, past television becomes intimately woven with contemporary television. For Connolly, the art museum is a 'space in which the history and future of television, as a once-dominant cultural form, can be reassessed' and part of that reassessment leads her to argue for television (in the museum space) as an object that is framed by 'cultural memory' (2014, 52).

Wheatley notes the way in which television's ontology is challenged by early exhibitions and yet, we suggest, this is still the case with contemporary exhibitions. Connolly raises issues of representation and audience as a means of explaining the inherent difficulties in exhibiting television. Trying to exhibit television ultimately raises questions about what television *is* and what its audience *does* when watching it – and even how they watch it and on what device or platform (2014, 6). She draws on Caldwell's (1995) work to illustrate the shifts that have taken place theoretically in terms of seeing the television audience as a temporary, unfocused horde towards appreciating and rewarding a more faithful, dedicated crew (2014, 6). Alongside these considerations, she also asks us to think about what a television monitor is meant to signify within an exhibition. Is the monitor a television at all, given that there is nothing being broadcast through it or is it an empty receptacle used for cinematic or artistic purposes? Returning to the issues raised at the start of the chapter, the question of whether something is or is not a television seems in part to depend on the experience of the viewer, and how television meaning has become de-materialized. There is a difference between the television set that broadcasts something else (a film or display in a museum); the old television set that reminds you of your past and the memories associated with it, and the television (here thought of as content) you watch, whether that be on a laptop, mobile device or a box in the corner. In other words, thinking about television's materiality in the museum, the way in which it is exhibited and what it exhibits on the screen, reminds us of the importance of what we, as viewers, bring

---

[4]See Kristyn Gorton, Media Audiences: Television, Meaning and Emotion, Edinburgh: University of Edinburgh Press, 2009

[5]Charlotte Brunsdon (2010, 64) made the same point also drawing on Ellis and Buonanno, concerning the abundance/scarcity dialectic and the rise of the DVD box set. While it may be a case of the remembering and forgetting audience, the box set 'can be treated as a methodological palimpsest', she says, which 'embodies some of the current challenges to the founding national and textual assumptions of television studies' (64).

to it and what it brings to us. Thus, it is our television viewing memories that attach themselves to the material objects and immaterial meanings and give value and importance to it.

The TV as material and memorial object

To pursue these ideas further, this chapter will draw extensively on three interviews from primary stakeholders associated with the NMeM: Paul Goodman, former head of collections projects, Iain Logie Baird, former head of television archives (and grandson of John Logie Baird, the leading British player in the development of television), and Michael Terwey, current head of collections and exhibitions (at the time of writing). Their interviews reveal issues around the television as material object, the insecurity of their own working positions within the museum, the mutability of the museum space and its storage rooms, and around key shifts that have taken place in terms of the visitor experience and Science Museum organizational and policy alignment. Indeed, despite the shift discussed above, all three interviews referenced the television as a material object and discussed the significance of the medium itself. As Paul Goodman explains:

> I've found that nothing in our collection, bar none, has the capacity to engender discussion, reminiscence or nostalgia like a television set. So, we take people into the Large Object Store [...] and almost immediately people are drawn on the right hand side of the room, to the television receivers. And I wish I had a pound for every time someone has said, 'we used to have a television set like that.' Straightaway you've got a connection with people.
>
> (interview with Paul Goodman 5 October 2014)

Those same sets (photographed on the cover of this book) may also evoke surprise when they consider their recollections of seeing similar sets at their local dump or recycling centre (see Figure 2).

The materiality of the television set often speaks for itself and in and of itself, it has the power to provoke powerful memories and associations, particularly insofar as it is linked to people's personal memories and to their concerns for the future. Yet, as McCarthy noted some time ago we have not quite come to terms with the material object of television's places (outside the domestic paradigm). Focusing on its contemporaneous siting in the home, through video walls, at airports, in streets and public squares, McCarthy notes that the 'language of placelessness makes us forget television is an object and, like all objects, it shapes its immediate space material form' (2001, 96). The two other places the same material object of the television set may now find itself in are the museum and the rubbish bin: in both cases switched off, but in the former governed by preservation policies.

FIGURE 2 Dumped 'TVs and Monitors' fairly carefully stacked at Stratford-upon-Avon Household Waste site in 2015. (Photograph by Joanne Garde-Hansen.)

The surprising sadness we may feel as we drive past the growing stacks of *old TV* sets at our local waste and recycling centre is as indicative of our excessive consumption of technology and the detritus this creates, the disconnected television industries of manufacturing, infrastructure and production, and the recognition that these screens have nothing on them. Such sets are not the polished wood furniture of the 1950s to 1970s but the mass plastic production of cathode ray tube boxes of the 1970s to 2000s. They are so ubiquitous not even a museum of technology can justify the space, but that does not mean that their ubiquity forgets their materiality, rather, it forgets ubiquitous memories. As Iain Logie Baird explains:

> We've been offered 30 of the same type of TV set and you know, there are certain memories that we don't value with the TV sets because it's just not unique. Everyone remembers where they were I think at certain times when they got their set and you do feel sad throwing out your TV set. There's a sort of phantom pain that you feel because it is your technological extension. So, we understand it but because it's commonly felt by everyone it's nothing that a museum needs to document because it's true of almost every single TV set we have.

> (interview with Iain Logie Baird 25 September 2014)

As Baird describes, the television set becomes a kind of 'technological extension' for most people (implicitly referencing McLuhan 1964), and because of that, it becomes very difficult to part with old sets. The idea of having their old television memorialized in a museum sounds like a kinder fate and yet, as Baird explains, the museum can only keep so many and the memories attached to particular sets are 'not unique'. Here Baird points to the parameters both of the museum and its ability to collect and preserve, but also of the value placed on memories of television and the growing sense of the public that their memories matter. If they are all the same, they are not seen as valuable and yet, in different places in this book, we have come to understand the 'collective memory' of *old TV* as something very powerful in our memories of programmes.

Of course, many people will have parted with their sets or their parents will have done that for them, and so the museum becomes a place where they can resurrect these memories, possible through the box itself. Michael Terwey explains that the data they received from the exit surveys revealed a higher than expected desire on the part of visitors to see past objects:

> we ask people for the key reasons why they visit the museum and they can pick a number of different kinds of options and one of the options they can pick is 'to see objects from when I was younger' which is distinct from 'to see important objects from the past' or 'a chance to see interesting objects'. So, how does this relate to people's personal experiences of things they saw when they were younger? So, last year [...] 25% of all people who we interviewed chose that as one of the options, which is higher than I thought actually.
> (interview with Michael Terwey 22 June 2016)

What the NMeM see this data as uncovering is a desire to see past objects that are linked to individuals' pasts, rather than to learn about new objects or objects that are not linked in some way with an individual's memories of television. In this sense, many visitors arrive wanting a nostalgic experience with television. They desire a connection to their past through their interaction with the object, and they want the museum to move on from presenting only elite persons and history. They might also want the past object to serve as a physical intermediary with the past. So, for example, older visitors such as grandparents might take their grandchildren and show them these objects as a means to evoke the past and as permission to narrate stories about their childhood. Used in this way the *old TV* provides an experience to its visitors, but one that is highly personalized, contextualized and narrated.

Though the technology has changed markedly, the emphasis on technology remains within the NMeM. As Goodman explains:

> We collect television technology, both broadcast and reception, so what goes on behind the camera and in front of the camera basically. And we also have a responsibility for the cultural interpretation of television, for example, *Doctor Who* and the exhibition that we did there. We don't have a collection of every single *Doctor Who* programme that was made, somebody else does

that whether it's the BBC or whatever, so we have to look at a different way of telling the story.

(interview with Paul Goodman 3 October 2014)

In this sense, the NMeM is telling the story of television in a different way to other archives or museums that may have more resources at their disposal. It primarily reflects not only the technology and science behind broadcasting but also how this technological development relates to culture. As Michael Terwey states:

we care for and we're responsible for collecting television technologies in this museum, so our role is in relation to the BFI in their role of collecting television programmes and archiving television programmes. So, our area of interest is on how those things are produced, how they are broadcast, how they are received and how people view them.

(interview with Michael Terwey 22 June 2016)

The caring and collecting that is inherent to the museum practice is articulated here by Terwey, and offers another entry point into researching the 'site-specificity' (McCarthy 2001, 109) of television's afterlife in the museum collection, as a fourth place of television (to expand upon McCarthy's exploration of the places and sites of television). However, Terwey also notes a shift in the priority of the collecting practice:

I think one of the other changes in collecting practice for us has been around [...] meta-data, the intangible stories and things around the objects themselves, as a kind of museum of technology. I think in the past we have acquired types of things as a type of camera because it fits this kind of technological story [...] and now I would say we are as interested in who used it, why they used it, where it was used and those kind of stories. The provenance, that information is equally important because they speak to the significance of the object more broadly and not just as a piece of, kind of, kit, not just as a piece of equipment. [...] And that requires curators to think slightly differently about things and not just make a case for 'there's a gap in the collection, this fits that gap. We want to have one of these things because we don't already have one of these things' towards a kind of we can't collect everything and actually we should only collect things that are of significance. But how one defines that significance is something. That becomes a more complex thing.

(interview with Michael Terwey 22 June 2016)

The interviews reveal a significant shift from a focus on a history of technology per se (a topic of great interest to early television scholarship) to an interest on the cultural and material ephemera that surrounds that technology (the impact of which has become more fascinating to recent researchers as materiality and meaning become *intra-connected*). As Terwey argues,

the provenance of an object provides the context *and* the interest for visitors. A piece of technology with facts associated with it is just that, but reflections on what it meant to peoples' lives and bits of ephemera that went with the technology, that collection of material creates a more complex and more interesting thing to exhibit and to draw visitors in.

(interview with Michael Terwey 22 June 2016)

In this way, curators have learned from the past and inherited a sense of the significance that ephemera plays within the exhibition space. From exhibiting the TV sets themselves, to a much broader understanding of how this box functions in peoples' lives, is a shift that reflects a growing understanding of the role memory plays within our appreciation of television's technological impact. A recognition that the sciences and the arts will need to work together to understand more deeply how these materials and technologies become emotionally and memorably interwoven with lived experience. It also suggests that memory institutions, such as museums, are thinking widely and deeply about their roles and responsibilities within television history.

As Iain Logie Baird reflects: 'I think the purpose of the collection [...] is to extend the human sense of memory and therefore we do want to optimise that and when we're thinking about "how much information does this object convey and ask if there's associated metadata that goes with that?"' (interview with Iain Logie Baird 25 September 2014). Here, Baird explains the curatorial process of weighing up how much the object itself 'conveys' and what 'metadata' is needed to broaden out the interest and understanding for visitors. It also speaks to the importance of metadata and the role of museums to collect and preserve this material. As Goodman explains: 'the ephemera that we've got – children's annuals, scripts and that kind of cultural interpretation or contextualisation – we see acquiring that as one of our roles, along with the preservation of artefacts. That material source preservation is hugely important' (interview with Paul Goodman 25 September 2014).

'Affective labour' and the precarity of *old TV*

The shift towards ephemera is a shift towards vernacular memory, popular culture and increasingly amateur craft and creativity and the role it plays in the exhibition space. It is not as expensive to collect, curate and seek rights permissions for, and it is a recognition of how context affects the experience visitors have while going through the exhibition. The ephemera operates in this sense as affective cues (memory triggers), reminding its visitors of what the old technology meant to people and the role it may have played in their lives. It is concerned with fixing an object to a certain extent, imbuing it with significance so it's stake within the exhibition is more secure. We explore these issues in more depth in Chapter 7 where we consider the cultural work that materializes the commemoration of television fandom.

At the start of all our interviews, we asked participants to tell us about their role within their museum work. The lengthiest response we received came from Iain Logie Baird who discussed his transition from curator of television (until 2011) to creator of boadcast culture. The shift from curator to creator is a shift in museological discourse that was not lost on us, and signals a general shift within the cultural industries toward 'experiences' of the past rather than transactions with or translations of the past. Since the interview, Baird has now been made redundant, following further cuts in the Science Museum Group. The change in his roles, which he details at length below, demonstrate a shift away from the medium specificity of television towards a broader understanding of broadcasting and the integration and importance of culture in the understanding of technology, as articulated by Terwey earlier. His memories of his career path also tell a story about precarity within the curation of British television, even for someone so symbolically connected to television's origin story:

> We were known as the TV Team and we were a close group and we were doing a lot of interesting outputs including exhibitions and events. We used to do regular TV history talks in TV Heaven before the public [...] We did an event about the 75th anniversary of the BBC television studios at Alexandra Palace, in fact, that was one of the last really good things we did. Then there was the restructure in 2011, and a job share resulted called Creator of Broadcast Culture and I was doing that for about a year and a half with the former Assistant Curator of Television. Yes, we basically maintained the television outputs for the entire museum between the two of us. Each two and a half days a week, then there was another restructure when I was put back to full time and I became one of the Associate Curators at the Museum of which there are four, I was the Associate Curator that was presumably covering television. This was much more collections-based work, virtually no exhibitions work, and a lot of research.
>
> (interview with Iain Logie Baird 25 September 2014)

Baird's description of his time at the museum, which has now ended, reveals a sense of disappointment and insecurity in his roles from curator to creator at the museum. From a sense of collegiality and involvement, of achievement at creating landmark events around television, to an uncertainty about what the work focused on, and that the work had become 'a lot of research' and balanced now between two instead of four people. This suggests both a shift in the way television was being valued by the Science Museum Group (focused on STEM with less space for Arts) and of cuts that meant that more work was being done by fewer people.

The latter issue that Baird raises, of two people doing the work of four, ties in with coverage on austerity Britain at the time of our interviews and a feeling of precarity, a concept that is often linked to the consequences of neoliberalism. Precarity returns again and again as a central concept to unpick and consider in relation to television's afterlife as stated in the Preface. More research on memories of precarious cultural work are needed in order to understand how precarity is dangerous to *remembering well* and how *strategic forgetting* (to paraphrase Connerton 2008) maintains the uncertainty and thus the conditions necessary for significant change and entrepreneurship.[6] But what also lurks in Baird's career description is a story about 'affective labour' and 'immaterial labour'. Baird's narration of his career at the NMeM begins with examples of public-facing events and exhibitions. His account of this time is suffused with hard but rewarding work in which he feels part of a 'close team'. There is a sense of collegiality and belonging that slowly fades as people are made redundant and outward-facing activities are closed-down in favour of in-house research or distributed knowledge.

Such knowledge, of course, comes cheaper from fans of *old TV*. Melissa Gregg (2009) draws on fan studies' to demonstrate the way in which fans will offer free labour to the projects they love in an attempt to reveal academics' participation in a similar dynamic. She argues that: 'For academics in particular, affective labour explains how the university draws on the psychological lives of staff to exploit and disguise the "immaterial" dimensions of working life' (2009, 212). This 'immaterial labour' is also recognized in the role of the museum curator and indeed, Rosalind Gill and Andy Pratt note the way in which cultural labourers become 'poster boys and girls for the new "precariat"' ([2008] 2009, 26). Not only is the role precarious because of the way in which museums are funded but the vision of the job and what it entails has shifted and becomes more precarious over time.

There is another, important dimension to be explored here that is specific to Baird. As the grandson of John Logie Baird, a significant British player in the development of television, he seeks to embody an authentic sense of cultural heritage in relation to television. In an article in *Yorkshire Life* he is pictured standing in front of a collection of old television sets with the caption: 'Iain Logie Baird, appropriately the curator of Television' (Haywood 2010). The word 'appropriately' speaks volumes as it is used here. As the caption suggests it is appropriate that he become *the* curator of Television precisely because of his family heritage, he is the *proper person* who can lay claim to owning (through his genetic inheritance) a certain sense of personally inventing television (even though he did not and nor did his grandfather on his own). It is not his intellectual achievements or experiences (though he has many) but, rather, his name and affiliation with a major player in the development of British television in 1926, according to Wikipedia, even if that inventor is presented by the BBC as only precariously part of the origin story.[7]

---

[6]John Logie Baird's experiments with television transmission in the late 1920s and early 1930s were determined by the precarious working conditions of his attic, the resources available and the power of Marconi-EMI.

[7]'Nevertheless, a BBC committee of inquiry in 1935 prompted a side-by-side trial between Marconi-EMI's all-electronic television system, which worked on 405 lines to Baird's 240. Marconi-EMI won, and in 1937 Baird's system was dropped' (BBC History 2014).

The article begins by explaining that most family photographs feature grandfathers with a child balancing on their knee, whereas in the Baird family album, Iain is 'cradling a cathode ray tube' (Haywood 2010). The article goes on to tell us much about Baird the inventor and very little about Baird the curator. This is a piece that advertises the museum by highlighting the cultural legacy of those working in it as inheritors of television. The 'inherited cultural capital', as Bourdieu imagines it, works to ensure, and is sanctioned as Iain Logie Baird's authority, not as a man who has been a curator elsewhere or as highly educated, having acquired cultural capital of his own (though this is mentioned briefly), but as the grandchild of the man who played a significant role in the development of television. Yet, Baird's cultural legacy was ultimately not enough to ensure his place within the curation of television at the NMeM. The sanctioning of his 'inherited cultural capital', however socially profitable would, to draw upon Bourdieu, have had to have come from the 'educational system, by its monopoly of certification' and its governance of one form of cultural capital into a more securitized form (Bourdieu 1984, 80–1). Now more than ever it seems museums and archives need universities, sponsors, public support and diverse funding streams and not just cultural capital. Perhaps the proximity to television, a medium that is continually changing, evolving and redefining itself, results in a more precarious position for the people working within it or with it, as is the case with the curators and producers we have interviewed. There is a sense that their roles are being redefined with the medium itself – as it changes so too does their relationship to it and the claims they can lay and resources they can call upon as its inheritors.

End of Experience TV

One of the biggest and most distinct exhibition spaces within the NMeM is (or rather was) the Experience TV gallery. For the purposes of the next section we will contingently use the present tense as it may no longer be there once this book is published. It is located on the first floor and is, for many, the first substantial exhibition space visitors will explore when they arrive. The gallery features old television sets, cameras and memorabilia. The museum often runs workshops for children asking them to find various objects, and on a visit with one of our children, we found ourselves looking for the 'coffin camera' which is a very large, coffin-shaped camera used in early broadcasting.

The spooky name – redolent of the superstition and sorcery that McCarthy (2001) notes of how television is often imagined as it materializes and de-materializes – and the size of the relic intrigues visitors. It draws them into thinking about how past technology functioned and was used to create television, its ghostliness and distance and yet it being conjured up as very present. The gallery also features a mock set for a newsroom and the camera relays live images for people to experience television in 'real' time. They get to either use the camera or sit behind it, which provides them with a tactile experience of television. Connolly raises Caldwell's (1995) work on television 'presentness' in her reading of television in the museum and the way it is used to relay 'live' images to create a sense of immediacy (2014, 9). This accords with Jeff Sconce's reading in *Haunted Media* (2000) of television's 'now-ness' and intimacy though he is not particularly site-specific in his thinking about television and the afterlife. The museum has locked into this haunting of the present by old and traditional ways of making television. Seeing their own faces mapped out on and in the technology allows visitors a 'real' sense of what television is and does, at least in the site-specificity of the continua of analogue modes of production. However, it is not clear whether this particular experience, this use of live and present television, will carry on now that the gallery is set for closure.

Following a freedom of information request, we received documents regarding the NMeM's decision to decant the Experience TV gallery to make way for a new 'Interactive Gallery'.[8] The paperwork we received which included minutes from a senior management meeting and cost breakdowns and analysis of three different options suggested that closing the gallery was primarily a financial decision as it was the most cost-effective solution. The Experience TV gallery is the most accessible and well-located gallery and closing others would have meant significant restructuring of the museum and follow-on costs. The afterlife of television's afterlife is mutable, and its seeming ability to always haunt the present may make it the most disposable medium on the cultural heritage of popular media.

Closing it down also impacts greatly on the way in which television appears as a real and present medium. The new Interactive Gallery will focus more broadly on the experience of broadcasting, in all its different guises, instead of the medium specificity of television as a unique form. As Terwey explains, people do not come to the museum to see objects from their past, they are also coming to experience their past: 'So when people are talking about objects from when they were younger [...] they are also more likely to want these kind of vintage experiences' (interview with Michael Terwey 22 June 2016). Here Terwey is talking in particular about the Games Lounge in the museum that houses video games (the actual objects) that people can use and then experience the pleasure of video games from their past. Not a switched off television set.

The use of the expression 'vintage experience' is interesting here in relation to Helen Piper's work on 'vintage television'. In her work, Piper is in pursuit

---

[8]See 'My Message to Bradford' by Jo Quinton-Tulloch (2016), director of the NMeM (and former 'science explainer' at the Science Museum), on the changes, and the many disgruntled replies from Bradfordians and visitors. The very long message from a former 'Cameraman' dated 24 May 2016 is particularly illuminating for his critique of the television collection. Most local and national column inches are on the movement of the photography collection to London as the main loss (Quinton-Tulloch 2016).

of what she describes as the 'felt, lived and remembered experience of regular viewing' and suggests that her 'somewhat fluid notion' of the term vintage means that 'vintage may well be to heritage as memory is to history' (2015, 2). Piper argues that 'engaging with archive television by re-viewing it is therefore problematic because it plunges the viewer into a new state that may efface the original experience through re-observation, causing "knowledge" to be readjusted and the text to be reinterpreted' (6). For Piper, the act of re-experiencing vintage programmes means that the past is readjusted and the lens through which we see them can alter them to such an extent that we might misread or misunderstand. As she goes on to suggest, 'shifts in technical, social and aesthetic expectations mean it is simply no longer possible or rewarding to watch these shows as they would have been viewed. As artefacts they are, to some extent, already lost to us' (6).

There are two things to consider here: firstly, even though things might not be rewarding in re-viewing, we do need to properly account for why are they so often on offer for commemoration, reconstruction and re-experience? Why do we have events, such as the eightieth anniversary of the first television programme aired in Britain (BBC, 2 November 1936; Dowell (2016)) and what drew over fifty members of the public to a small memorial hall in Lydbrook, Forest of Dean, in the summer of 2015 to watch for the first time, since its broadcast in 1968, Dennis Potter's *A Beast with Two Backs* (BBC One, 1968). Secondly, how does this logic extend to objects, such as the television set in a museum? One of the implicit ideas explored in this chapter through the interviews is that a second viewing of old objects allows visitors to 'plunge into a new state', but not one that effaces the original, rather one that evokes and returns the original to a position of materiality and meaning. The television set stands there as both a matter of fact and as materializing the care, intimacy and emotions that the set evoked in one's memory. The wood, plastic, cables, wires, engineering and technicity are re-encountered and re-membered. The ephemera 'causes knowledge to be readjusted' but in such a way as to allow for a better understanding and further appreciation of television's afterlife as real and material. In other words, the same logic that Piper (2015) sees as detrimental to vintage television programmes works in an opposite fashion to vintage television objects, according to museum curators. The 'vintage experience' is precisely what draws visitors in, as the exit surveys suggest, because it provides a return to the original moment that the user first encountered the object. Unlike the programme, there is no risk of interpretation or anachronistic judgements that might cloud understanding, rather a chance to re-explore and re-experience the joy, fear or excitement that the object originally incited, or to see it afresh as an object of weight, size, texture and tactility. Indeed, this desire to re-experience becomes central to our exploration of children's TV in the following chapter where box sets are purchased and passed down to the next generation and viewing experiences are reconstructed as intra-connections of bodies in living rooms.

Terwey, the current head of collections and exhibitions, believes that the NMeM needs to move into being 'a museum of experiences rather than as a museum of objects'. As he explains: 'a television set which doesn't have anything on the screen is not the same as sitting watching something on a television set' (interview with Michael Terwey 22 June 2016). The notion of a 'museum of experiences' versus one of objects is interesting in terms of our theorization of memory and television, and remembering or forgetting television's site-specificity in its afterlife and the resources and spaces it needs for its remembrance. It accords with a general experiential tendency in a wide range of creative and cultural industries from fashion and shopping to gaming and social media. The emphasis on experiences, on actively taking part (or interaction), where even the routine of everyday TV watching is turned into an experience reflects, on the one hand, a growing appreciation of the role that affective memorability plays within our understanding of television. On the other hand, it strategically forgets the mundane and the work, energy, time, skills, expertise, space and logistics needed to properly inherit television in a time of austerity.

Thinking about the television in the museum reminds us of the various ways in which we engage with television – whether as object, memory or content. Are we thinking about the programmes as Piper (2015) does in her figuration of the television experience or are we thinking about the box itself and the memories it evokes about a different time, place and resources? The television set and televisual infrastructure that has been exhibited in the NMeM, to tell visitors something about its technology and its development, clearly also tells them something about themselves as consumers and the materiality of living with television in changing times. They see the way they have changed in relation to the object itself and the way that object has both changed and not changed in response to their lives. Television (and the material object of the set) can date individuals, it can place you in a particular time and space based upon both what you remember watching (the content) and what kind of box (or device) you watched it on.

Switched off and in the museum the television set is a rather haunting object, it reminds us of those Derridean ghostly qualities that inspired McCarthy's reading of television's 'sorcery' noted earlier as 'a piece of furniture endowed with frightening conjuring powers' (2001, 109), and yet is no longer 'animated by an unseen force' but must find new commodity-chains to be re-materialized into. Amanda Lotz has argued that televisual 'events requiring immediate viewing will be on individual workplace computers; while coffee shops and other public venues may fill with people watching pocket-sized screen devices such as phones and PDAs' (2007, 65). As she suggests, television's immediacy becomes 'unshackled from the home' but also from the collective experience – the proximity to others is replaced with the proximity to technology (65), and yet we are doubly haunted. The ghost of the ghost of the set in the corner of the room continues to circulate in site-specific ways (from the museum to the landfill to the upcycling centres of developing economies and life cycle solutions of media companies who serve the transcoding sectors). It is not quite dead yet and many have typed into Google: 'where do all the old TV sets go?' To store it in an archive or a museum may be, as Connerton argues in 'Seven Types of Forgetting' (2008), 'tantamount to saying that, though it is in principle always retrievable, we can afford to forget it'. Yet, it is also a reminder, not that we have too much television memory and need to discard it, as Connerton argues, but that we cannot afford to store and archive what we need to remember of television, even when we care, or have cared, for it so much.

5 CARING FOR PAST TELEVISION: THE CASE OF CHILDREN'S TELEVISION

When my wife told me she was pregnant with our first child, over seven years ago, the next morning I went on Amazon and ordered Dangermouse, SuperTed, Bananaman, The Wind in the Willows, Rainbow, Button Moon, Dungeons & Dragons, Mysterious Cities of Gold, Dogtanian, Ulysses 31, Bagpuss, Pingu, Willo' the Wisp, Mr. Benn, Ivor the Engine, Sooty *… and a whole bunch more. I also bought books by the absolute boatload, but I knew I really, really wanted to pass on the classic TV series to all my children.*

> (user comment contributed in response to Anita Singh's 'Super Ted, Pingu and Humpty from Playschool could rival Peter Pan', Daily Telegraph, 16 May 2015)[1]

The television set and the ephemera around it prompts memories of childhood, a 'vintage experience' that is both evocative and individual and yet also something visitors can communicate to the next generation. As the exit data in the last chapter suggested, many visitors hope to be reacquainted with past objects as a means of explaining the past, both their own and a collective one, to their children

---

[1] The texts cited are most likely the following versions, though it is a guessing game as they are relational to one another in terms of constructing a personal 'canon'. While they could be said to demonstrate transnational viewing pleasure in British children's television viewing during the 1970s to 90s, the texts do not give us direct access to this viewer's preferred episodes, or which versions of long running texts. If these texts were short run they were generally repeated over a long period of time and so very memorable: *Danger Mouse* (Thames TV, 1981–92), *Super Ted* (BBC One/S4C, 1983–6), *Bananaman* (BBC, 1983–6), *The Wind in the Willows* (ITV, 1983–90), *Rainbow* (ITV, Thames Television, 1972–97), *Button Moon* (ITV, 1980–8), *Dungeons & Dragons* (CBS, 1983–5), *Mysterious Cities of Gold* (BBC, 1982–3), *Dogtanian and Three Muskehounds* (BRB Internacional [Spain], Nippon Animation [Japan] and MBS [Japan], 1981–2), *Ulysses 31* (FR3, 1981–2), *Bagpuss* (BBC, 1974), *Pingu* (SF DRS/BBC Two, 1986–2006), *Willo' the Wisp* (BBC One, 1981–2005), *Mr. Benn* (BBC, 1971–2005), *Ivor the Engine* (BBC, 1975–7) and *The Sooty Show* (BBC/Thames, 1955–75, 1976–92).

or grandchildren. With the rebooting of children's television through the reissue of box sets of episodes and extras, the content's recirculation on YouTube and rebooting on platforms such as Netflix,[2] adult audiences can introduce their children to the television they watched as a child. The YouTube phenomenon of 'American's watching British TV' also extends this inheritance transnationally as *out of sync* shows and *out of context* clips recirculate on social media creating *estrangement* for contemporary British and non-British audiences alike.[3]

They consider this the selected inheritance of a cultural economy that they value and remember as important to their personal media heritage. As one of our screenwriter interviewees recalls of her own childhood (an interviewee of the same generation as the parents in this chapter):

> I think like most kids that grew up in the 1970s, 80s, the first experiences are the one television set you sit and watch with your family in the living room, and we watched a lot of television. We were a television viewing family definitely. So *Coronation Street* [ITV, 1960–], *EastEnders* [BBC One, 1985–] when it came on in the '80s. And mum and dad I think were quietly passionate about their television. There were things that they really loved like *Upstairs Downstairs* [ITV, 1971–5], *The Forsyth Saga* [BBC Two, 1967], that kind of thing, but my early memories are very much about the shows that were aimed at me, *The A Team* [NBC, 1983–7] I loved that, *Knight Rider* [NBC, 1982–6] I would sit and watch that with my brother, and *Fame* [NBC, 1982–3] as well was my absolute obsession as a child.
>
> (interview with Lisa Holdsworth 5 May 2014)

Focusing upon British children's television, this chapter draws upon interviews with mothers and a netnography of Mumsnet 'talk', to understand how and why memories of children's television are so important for appreciating television's overlooked 'unofficial histories'. What is it that parents want their children to learn and how does this learning root television in intergenerational memories that inform children's historically inflected media literacy? What are the memories these parents have of past children's television? How are those memories impacted by rewatching episodes? How does social media allow these memories to 'travel' within and beyond cultural containers?[4]

---

[2]For example, Netflix recently rebooted *Full House* (2016–) as a way not only for parents to share their past television with their children, but also to prepare new viewers for *Fuller House*.

[3]See Jackson-Edwards (2016) "'What the f*** did I just watch?" Bizarre clip from old British children's TV show confuses Twitter after going viral (completely baffling US viewers)' which covers a clip from the BBC programme *Stupid* (2004) featuring a 'devil finger' scene in which a boy and a girl bend each others fingers.

[4]One of the authors has continued this research in terms of television archives of children's geography programming in the UK. How do children as 'agents' or a concept of 'childhood' emerge, perhaps unexpectedly, in *old TV*? What concepts of childhood are being reaccessed by contemporary audiences through the TV archive? It is particularly important to address this as children are gaining increasing responsibility as the future consumers who will need to (a) remember well, and (b) clean up the mess of past generations.

This chapter also considers how the practice of introducing children to past television constructs a logic of care for the past as well as the future. Following theoretical work on mothering and the discourse of care, this chapter addresses the moral implications that are bound up in the choices parents make about what television to show (and not to show) their children and in what extra socio-historical contexts to frame it. Early findings suggest that these viewers feel that they are not only passing down their own childhood and generational experiences (which may be national, sub- or transnational) but also offering their children a 'better' television diet than anything currently on air (potentially reaffirming an older national context of viewing in the current context of viewing), while reaccessing a concept of 'childhood' they very much value.

In the process of writing this book and conducting interviews with industry practitioners, museum curators, archive managers and television viewers, we always began by asking our participants about their own childhood television memories. The question prompted remembering and reflection and provided us with compelling insights on the role of television in marking childhood memories. For example, British screenwriter, Lisa Holdsworth responded by saying:

> I said something [...] about the emotion memory, the physical memory of sitting down and eating fish and chips watching something. Watching Saturday afternoon wrestling. And I probably didn't watch that much but it's very keyed in to visiting my grandma and those kinds of things and you can't re-create that. You can't be 8 years old again sadly, and so some of it will be very much valued.
> (interview with Lisa Holdsworth 12 October 2014)

Holdsworth's phrase 'emotion memory' gestures towards the way in which emotion binds and surrounds certain memories we have from this kind of childhood, and, in this case, the role television plays within them as a carrier of this experiential memory as both a 'matters of fact' and a 'matters of concern' and care (to paraphrase Latour 2004). As she points out, she 'probably didn't watch that much', but television is a conduit for recalling and taking pleasure in the physical and emotional memories of visiting her grandmother, in cementing a concept of childhood in the mind. Very similar memories are retrieved by Mark Helsby, producer of *Mastermind* (BBC One, 1972–1997; BBC Two, 2003–), as he explains:

> Some of those memories of watching telly then are [...] vivid and really dear. I was saying about watching my grandpa watching wrestling, that's one of my fondest memories of my grandpa. He was a lovely, lovely man and was really kind and I think like most boys, my grandpa [...] was my hero in the same way my dad was my hero. He served in the Second World War, he had been injured at the end of the Second World War and still bore the result of that, a really pronounced limp and suffered for that all the time but, so that kind of thing. That memory of my grandpa is a really fond one.
> (interview with Mark Helsby 24 June 2014)

What comes through in both accounts is the way in which these participants value their memories and the importance they hold in their lives, and importantly for our research, the role television plays within these memories as intergenerational experiences, with television playing a key role in connecting. In each case, television focuses the travel back into the people, places and experiences they care about and in this sense, the retrieval of the *experience* of watching television becomes more important than the actual programmes watched.

Caring for children's television

This chapter is not able to fully address the wide and expansive field of children's television,[5] nor can it discuss its policies, directions for research or future projects. Instead, this chapter dips into the established literature to pull out salient aspects for us to consider in terms of how children's television is remembered and used by parents who are anxious to ensure that their children have access to the memories they had and continue to have about past television. This is important because normally 'childhood' is conceptualized as an elision of hope with futurity (see the work of Peter Kraftl 2008 on 'childhood-hope') rather than as drawing children into the past fears, regrets and enjoyments of parents. Childhood is made thinkable through a parental version of *childhood as past television watching*, to be passed into the future, and placed alongside other competing media for children's attention.

In her seminal work on children and television, Dafna Lemish argues that television 'is part of the taken-for-granted everyday experience of most children' (2006, 2). One of the significant aspects here is to consider the 'everydayness' of children's television. It is often part of the morning hum drum in homes along with shouts to 'brush hair (and teeth)' and to 'get dressed'. Many homes have 'rules' about how much television watching can be done (if at all) and even what channels or programmes can be watched. Part of what we will go on to discuss in this chapter is this 'mundane' aspect of children's television and its role within the ordinary routine of households.

However, what also comes with this 'taken-for-granted' experience are the hopes and anxieties parents have about their children watching television, producing the 'nagging question: "What is television doing to our children?"' (2007, 2), what impact will it have on their futures?[6] As parents ourselves, we are very familiar with the recurrent guilt and concerns about what our children are watching and

---

[5]Davies 2001, 2010; Drotner and Livingstone 2008; Singer and Singer 2012; McAleer and Gunter 1990; Buckingham 1999; see also Lury 1995; Woods 2016.
[6]As Lemish points out, countries that can afford to do so allocate public funds to try and answer this question (2006, 2).

how often they are watching it, and with its increasing mobility, where else in the home are they watching it and what kinds of devices. Therefore, part of the reason that parents care what their children watch comes from an anxiety that there are morally good and bad things that their children could watch if not monitored and supervised. In this sense, caring becomes an inherent part of the television watching experience for many parents who worry about the effects of television and the influence programmes have on their children. As Lemish argues: 'children are active consumers of television. They react to, think, feel, create meanings. They bring to television encounters a host of predispositions, abilities, desires, and experiences' (2007, 3). She also points out that most of children's television viewing happens in the home and within the context of the family (2007, 11).[7] The fact that children are mostly watching television at home means that it is very difficult to separate out the 'study' of children and television from the 'context' in which they are watching it (2007, 11).[8] One of the interesting issues that comes out of thinking about the context is the 'talk' that happens in the room whilst children are watching television. Lemish argues that even the most passive form of parental involvement (just sitting in the room and watching but not commenting) 'encourages the child to pay more close attention to the program, thus increasing the chances for better learning' (2007, 27).

Writing in the mid-1990s, David Buckingham explains that 'psychological research on children's relationship with television has implicitly assumed that [children] are passive victims of an all-powerful medium' (1996, 7). He goes on to state that very little research has been done on the ways in which children 'make sense' of television, let alone how they emotionally respond to what they watch. Although television audience research has moved on in terms of our understanding of the audience and its activity, as reflected in Lemish's work, this engagement has largely been theorized with an older audience in mind. Indeed, the anxiety that parents feel, as discussed above, is linked to an unchallenged understanding of the television as an 'all-powerful medium' that poses a potential threat to children. Parents are often aware that too much television is not 'good' for their children, but *why* it is not good is often left unexplained or unconsidered.

Buckingham's work is significant insofar as it challenges the notion of children as passive victims and explains the way in which they are 'more active and sophisticated users of the medium than they are often assumed to be' (1996, 7). Following on from his book *Children Talking Television* (1993) and based on a series of 'small-group focused interviews with a total of 72 children in four age

---

[7]During the writing of this chapter, one of our sons symbolically crossed the 9.00 pm watershed when we considered him 'ready' (though how this is measured is hard to say objectively) by watching an episode of *Family Guy* (Fox/Channel 4/Sky1/BBC/ITV2 1999–). He lost this privilege due to poor behaviour the following week but continued to watch the same downloaded episode on his smartphone with headphones in the car on the morning school run, just to make the point that the 9.00 pm watershed was a parental mythology.

[8]See David Morley's (2000) *Home Territories: Media, Mobility and Identity* for a reading of the childhood home and memory.

groups,' (1996, 8) Buckingham's work in *Moving Images: Understanding Children's Emotional Responses to Television*, reveals significant areas for us to consider in terms of the memories people have of children's television. For not only does he reconsider the child-viewer as 'active' but he is also considering the emotional involvement and the 'talk' that surrounds viewing. As he states: 'Talking about television is not a neutral activity' (57). Talking about television is also about talking about ourselves and our aspirations (57) or what he refers to as 'narratives of the self' (59), which, we would add, in a neoliberal framework expects self-development and parenting from a distance rather than a command and control operation of daily life. For parents, this also means an inevitable move towards thinking about the 'effects', as Buckingham explains about his own research 'there was much more speculation about negative effects than positive ones' (64). There is an inevitable slide towards thinking about television as a 'bad' object instead of something that enables children's development and learning. Buckingham suggests that this move towards television as 'bad' may be something that participants think researchers *want* to hear, especially if, as Buckingham argues, the researchers are middle-class academics (64–5). In other words, there is an assumption that to say that television is not a 'good thing' for children is something participants think they *should* say as opposed to something they actually believe or subscribe to.[9] This now also misses the current context of viewing, in that a television text considered 'bad' can now be re-viewed on a variety of devices, some of which a parent may have confiscated, or reduced the 'screen time' on because of 'misuse', thus making the device more 'bad' than the text itself.

Interesting to this work, Buckingham discusses the way in which older children remember what they were like in terms of their television viewing, as Buckingham explains: 'a number of children described how they had been frightened or upset by television programmes they had seen when very young' (1996, 88). He notes that many of the conversations about past television memories were marked by 'irony and self-deprecating humour' (88). He goes on to notice the way in which girls, in particular, 'construct a narrative of self-development, in which their past confusions are now left well behind' (90). For instance, one girl he interviews explains in relation to *Doctor Who*, 'now you see they're selling off all the [models] and you think "why was I scared of that?!"' (88). Here the interviewee, 'Jessica (12)' demonstrates both the self-deprecation that Buckingham mentions, and also the sense of development and mastery – she looks back on her former self as naïve and silly in comparison with her present 'knowing' self. Childhood is, then, revisited through past television texts and memories of past watching practices, in order to move a certain idea of childhood forward (perhaps one that challenges the childhood-hope-futurity paradigm); while *old TV* (and the feelings

---

[9] See Ellen Seiter (1999) *Television and New Media Audiences*. Her research covers female participants who pre-screen television programmes and only select educational content for children.

that circulate/d around it) is used as a yardstick to measure self-progress. Many of the posters on the parenting website mumsnet.com, as this chapter will go on to explore, also demonstrate this sense of self-deprecation/self-development dialectic in their recollections of past television: television has allowed them to grow but their memories may be both in and out of sync with their present selves formed of those memories. Television can still move them and re-move them from the persistent need to develop while allowing them to perform self-development.

Research into the way that children remember stories reveals their ability to recall '"high-level" units of information [better] than "low-level" units' (Pugzles Lorch, Bellack and Haller Augsbach 1987, 453). Yet, by 'contrast, in studies of children's memory for televised stories, children have difficulties in discriminating plot-relevant content from less essential information' (453). The memories that we discuss from both the netnography of Mumsnet and the interviews evidences this research and underlines the fragmentary way in which people remember children's television.

The 'mamasphere': Mumsnet and past television

To explore the ways in which parents, particularly mothers, shared past television, we decided to undertake a netnography[10] of Mumsnet. We also drew from and were inspired by work on 'mothering through precarity' by Julie A. Wilson and Emily Chivers Yochim (2017). Based on interviews with twenty-nine mothers over the course of a year, *Mothering through Precarity: Women's Work and Digital Media* examines the precarity in the lives of mothers who are all trying to be '"good moms" in a highly mediated and deeply insecure milieu' (2017, 8). The focus on mothers' affective labour and feelings of insecurity chimed with the interviews from the NMeM and television industry, as discussed in the last chapter (where cultural workers care about television); and, provides a theoretical engagement with the ways in which mothers use digital media as a means of caring. Wilson and Chivers Yochim define the 'mamasphere' as a 'contradictory web of advice, friendship, information, and entertainment, fuelled by highly-organised and interactive data-mining machines, but also by the situated experiences of mothers' (27). This definition speaks perfectly to the posts and activities on Mumsnet.

Mumsnet is an online discussion site in the UK 'created by parents for parents'. Our research pursued several threads within Mumsnet. On its home page, it features 'discussions of the day', information on books to read, pregnancy, videos

---

[10]See Robert V. Kozinets (2010) *Netnography: Doing Ethnographic Research Online*. His book 'aims to provide a set of methodological guidelines, a disciplined approach to the culturally-oriented study of that technologically-mediated social interaction that occurs through the Internet and related information and communications technologies (or "ICT")' (2010, 3).

about healthy lunch ideas, events, guest posts, style and beauty advice, bloggers, exclusive offers, a link to jobs, 'talk', and 'mumsnet daily', which rounds up their most-viewed threads. The site has even hosted live webchats with key political figures. Visitors to the site can find out anything from the must have Liz Earle product to the controversy over moving *The Great British Bake Off* to a different channel (BBC Two, 2010–13; BBC One 2014–16). Although the site's tagline 'for parents by parents' speaks to all parents, the name of the website (mumsnet) and the issues it covers speaks to a gendered audience.[11] The website's iconic image, visible in the tab, is from the silhouette used in the TV series of *Charlie's Angels* (ABC, 1976–81) but the women are holding babies, toddlers and feeding bottles as opposed to guns. The site was launched in 2000 by Justine Roberts and Carolyn Longton, who met in antenatal classes (Pederson and Smithson 2013, 99). In their article 'Mothers with attitude', Sarah Pederson and Janet Smithson argue that Mumsnet can be seen as an empowering source for women and contradicts previous research on online communities that characterizes women as 'supportive' and 'polite' as opposed to men who were often 'aggressive' and 'self-promoting' (97). Indeed, they argue that Mumsnet 'is not primarily a parenting site as much as a space for women to find advice, entertainment, debate and the opportunity to compare experiences with other women' (97). Their study also reveals that the demographic of Mumsnet differs from other parenting online communities 'especially in terms of number of working mothers and higher levels of education and income' (104).

Our research found that embedded in the postings about children's television on Mumsnet is a competitive form of remembering: 'I remember this programme better than you', 'I remember more than you', 'I remember further back than you', such that self-promotion is not entirely absent from the discussion. There is a sense of competing for who can evoke the best/fondest remembered text, or who can pinpoint a particularly charged memory that will attract the most attention from other posters, and that may allow for a struggle over meaning to take shape. In many respects, this form of competitive remembering can be likened to the traumatic birth stories that women share, usually in similar forums, and it draws attention to the multidirectionality of memory as postulated by Michael Rothberg (2009). Here we might frame the examples in this chapter as performing 'competitive memory' as one version of the past is seen to be arguing with another or seeking to cancel out another. A zero-sum game that suggests that mothers on parenting sites are not always performing supportive and polite roles.

While we, as researchers, will not be making value judgements about different versions of *old TV* as more truthful, authentic, real or meaningful in the Mumsnet discussions, we do think this competitiveness in remembering needs addressing as an opportunity for comparatism. Rothberg strenuously argues: 'The greatest

---

[11]Pederson and Smithson point out that 'Despite the description of the majority of such sites as "parenting" communities, they are mainly used by women' (2013, 98).

hope for a new comparatism lies in opening up the separate containers of memory and identity that buttress competitive thinking and becoming aware of the mutual constitution and ongoing transformation of the objects of comparison' (2009, 18). In the context of remembering children's television we would argue that such competitive remembering produces paratextual memory, and allows the text to produce feelings of loss, longing, identity and experience that it originally did not convey. These women are not engaging in textual meaning-making but are inserting themselves into television history, they were 'there', and the text of 'then' is here 'now'. If remembering is a creative act, as Keightley and Pickering argue in *The Mnemonic Imagination* (2012), then paratextual memory signals 'a collective desire to reconnect with what has apparently been lost or reassess what has apparently been gained. Both reconnection and reassessment bring the past into a dynamic relationship with the present, opening up the possibility of critique in the movement made between them' (2012, 114).

Wilson and Chivers Yochim (2017) draw attention to the 'flow' of discussion posts and the way in which they adhere to the fabric of the mother's everyday lives:

> Ironically, mothers' mundane voices spoke to the 'silences and gaps' of the digital mundane. Here, media don't necessarily stand out as particularly significant – as objects worth talking about on their own – but figure as something indistinguishable from the movements of everyday life. As mothers move through their quotidian routines, dipping into social media for quick moments of adult interaction, digital culture becomes a vital thought taken-for-granted foundation for their days.
>
> (Wilson and Chivers Yochim 2017, 26)

As Wilson and Chivers Yochim's research reveals, mothers are often using digital media in a way that fits in with their daily routines. They are 'dipping in' as opposed to spending concentrated amounts of time. Digital media becomes a space of interaction, reassurance, community and, yet, also something that is non-committal and unencumbered by the demands that a face-to-face meeting with friends might necessitate. Social media provides a forum for interaction that is on their terms and with minimal demands.

In her work on contemporary media practices, Jodi Dean (2010) explains the discursive framework around blogging: 'Blogging subjectivity isn't narrativized. It's posted. It's not told as a story but presented in moments as an image, reaction, feeling or event' (2010, 47). As discussed above, the interaction is often quick, a 'dipping in' as opposed to a thoughtful and laboured response. Dean's appraisal of blogging also suggests an affective engagement that also comes through in Wilson and Chivers Yochim's research. They write that: 'Mothers are thus drawn to online environments by the "tiny affective nuggets" that circulate and accrue in the mamasphere; their encounters promise ongoing modulation and attunement to precarious family scenes' (Wilson and Chivers Yochim 2017, 28).

We are interested in these 'affective nuggets' and to what extent they offer insight into the way people care for and about television and allow it to become part of their sense of self and part of the inheritance they offer their children. What follows is the result of 'mining' Mumsnet for these 'nuggets' and an analysis of what the memories of television mean to mums. Embedded in the discourse that surrounds the netnography and in the anxiety parents express about their children's television watching is the burden on mothers to monitor and supervise their children's television inheritance as well as their contemporary television watching, with their own personal experience to draw upon as their main resource. As Wilson and Chivers Yochim argue: 'No longer able to rely on public institutions to inherited social and economic capital, mothers feel it is up to them to privatise happiness for their families on their own' (2017, 34). While not entirely the responsibility of mothers, it is clear that part of the act of caring for children in the twenty-first century is caring for their media diet through recourse to a parent's own media repertoire. Parental controls speak to the implied responsibility that parents face in making sure their children are protected from the ills of the digital world. Dangers lurk and there are moral panics and online advice about what children might see or read from certain programmes.[12]

There were three dominant themes around the threads on children's television: 'Too much television?' 'Television in nurseries or childminders? Or 'what age children should be allowed to watch TV?' And 'Do you remember this children's TV programme?' Here we recognize the anxieties about how much and what kind of television children should watch and whether the programming is age-sensitive. However, for the purposes of this chapter, and the book as a whole, we are most interested in the threads that referred to the remembering of television. Threads such as 'Come and remind me of your fav [sic] characters from children's television when WE were children' which attracted 141 posts. Here the emphasis that is on *we* suggests an invitation to indulge in one's *own* memories together, to focus on the individual and their generational milieu, rather than to be caught up in the concerns and responsibilities of parenting children's memories and viewing. In the following quotations from Mumsnet public discussions we lay out the discussion postings as they appear on screen:[13]

littlelamb Sat 01-Nov-08 10:35:07
I loved Dogtanian. It used to be shown in its entirety in the Summer holidays and I used to sit there with my brothers and watch the whole thing. I now have it on DVD for dd and realise that my mum must have been so keen fro [sic] us

---

[12]For instance, the UK children's charity, the NSPCC (National Society for the Prevention of Cruelty to Children) has a dedicated website to help parents with online safety for their children. Scholarly work from Stanley Cohen's seminal work on 'moral panics' (1972), to Martin Barker and Julian Petley's *Ill Effects* (1997) onwards questions the relationship between children and the media and the way in which the media creates a 'moral panic' around particular events or texts.

[13]For the uninitiated in online parental shorthand: 'dd' refers to darling daughter, 'ds' is darling son and 'dh' darling husband.

to watch it because it is hours and hours long. It is (and I hate to admit it now) a bit shit dated though. And I looooooooved Willy Fogg. I think I must have something for TV shows with catchy theme tunes (latest hit in this house is Wonder Pets).

In the example above, the poster, 'littlelamb', takes pleasure, reflected in the extended word 'looooooooved', in the memories of 'Willy Fogg' (*Around the World with Willy Fog*, RTVE, 1983). Littlelamb also fondly reminisces about television viewing with her/his brothers during the summer holidays and has now bought a DVD for 'dd' (darling daughter) to watch. Here there is a clear sense of inheritance that is infused with summer days, siblings and the indulgence of 'watching the whole thing'. What is also interesting is the retrospective 'judgment' littlelamb has of her/his own mother who s/he believes let the kids watch it 'because it is hours and hours long'. Thus, there is recognition about the mother's responsibility of being in charge of children's viewing and of television as a means to keep the kids occupied. Despite the fond memories of watching the programme there is also an admission that it is 'a bit shit dated' and yet, despite this reluctant judgement, s/he has still bought a DVD of it to share with his/her daughter. Instead of buying the DVD because of the quality of the programme or its moral superiority over anything else currently on television, the suggestion here is that littlelamb has bought this programme because of his/her memories of watching it as a child, memories that are bound up with being off school and spending time at home. One of the things that comes through this research is the way in which people want to share their fond memories of childhood with their own children *through* television: memories of an experience with television. Indeed, television is imagined as something that can pass on affective moments to the next generation.

Not all memories are about summer holidays and family viewings; in fact, many circulate around scary moments and fearful memories of children's television. In his work on fan memories and *Doctor Who*, Matt Hills (2014) refers to the 'memory cheats' such as the 'hiding behind the sofa' memories that abound in recollections of *Doctor Who*. He argues that: 'Whether fans actually have this memory at an individual level or not (and many will not), its construction as a shared, mythical past nonetheless represents "an act of negotiation … to define individuality and collectivity" (van Dijck 2007, 12), with fans individually diverging from collective memory even while its force as a badge of fan collectivity remains in place' (Hills 2014, 42). Alison Landsberg (2004) would have defined this as 'prosthetic memory', which considers memory as experienced by proxy, exploring how we account for the circulation of memories in mass culture that are felt and shared but not directly experienced.[14] The issue is less about 'memory cheats' (truth and

---

[14]Landsberg states that 'prosthetic memory' offers sites for experiential encounters to produce a new form of public cultural memory 'by making possible an unprecedented circulation of images and narratives about the past' that allow audiences to create 'deeply felt memory of a past event through which he or she did not live' (2004, 2).

falsity is not the issue) but rather television as a shared experience for creating community from memory, having a phatic component or its use in seeking to connect with others who may have struggled over the meanings of their shared television pasts. As this thread makes clear:

> *stinkingbishop Fri 21-Nov-14 07:24:34*
> The Enchanted Garden[15] (?) where the dinosaur statues came to life? But the freaky FREAKY thing was these sort of large mannequin things coming to life and closing down on them. Horrendous.
> The walls in the rubbish chute closing in on Star Wars still gives me the heebie jeebies.
> And don't get me started on Dr Who [*sic*]. There were some aliens with translucent skulls so you could see their pulsing veins and to this day I still can't eat blue cheese or raspberry ripple ice cream as a result!!!

> *effinandjeffin Fri 21-Nov-14 14:49:54*
> And going back to Dr Who [*sic*], my dd recently watched the one with the kid who has a gas mask for a face and says 'are you my mummy?' She won't go into the hall on her own now. I feel terrible but at the same time, being scared by Dr Who [*sic*] is almost like rite of passage.

Posts often cluster around particular emotions and affects: such as fear or happiness (more the former than the latter) and the need to connect with others in almost reunion moments as common audience members at particular point in time. The happy memories are often less to do with the programme and more to do with the social context. Posters remember warm memories of sitting together watching programmes with the family, or siblings – usually following roast dinners. And posts about scary television, such as above, search to identify where the frightening scenes come from and/or are embellished with details, which evidence the way the scenes have imprinted themselves into memory. They usually contain an affective response '(bites nails)', 'hides behind couch' or emojis with gritted teeth – to recall/express the physical response.

There is an expectation of scaffolding that operates in the posts where people are building on each other's memories, strengthening them and therefore increasing the pleasure taken in the process of re-experiencing and rediscovering memories of television. It ends up constructing a particular cultural view of family and an implicit desire for a return – to a sense of family, of belonging, of more innocent times. Here

---

[15]This is a misremembered title. The actual title is *The Enchanted Castle* (BBC, 1979). It is interesting because it clearly left an impression on a select few who have found each other online over the last few years. There is a 2007 thread of discussion on digitalspy.com concerning a poster's desperate attempt to find anyone who remembers it. See 'Surreal kids show ~ late 70's / early 80's?' that elicited this response 'OMG…….. Hurrah!…..I've found you! AT last! someone that remembers it!! Oh thank god! I thought I was going insane. I have been pestering friends and family for years trying to work out what this programme was and NOBODY remembers it! NOBODY! Not even my sister!' (Gypsylady 20 July 2007 at http://forums.digitalspy.co.uk/showthread.php?t=622004).

nostalgia is the strongest in the sense of a return, a travelling kind of memory but also a regrouping and consensus building around a concept of childhood.

Drawing on James Clifford's (1992) notion of 'travelling cultures' Astrid Erll proposes thinking about memories as travelling, particularly in an increasingly global world, where shared media facilitate and, at times, structure our mnemonic practices. Like culture, Erll argues, memories 'do not hold still' and are instead constituted 'through movement' (2011b, 11). In the case of British children's television memories, the movement is mediated through emotion. There is a movement within the memories we researched between the recollection of the television scene or theme tune or particular character (as well as other markers) to a communal/social, shared recollection and then often to YouTube or another platform to re-view the particular programme. This travelling memory is suffused with emotion and often attached to particular memories of the home, of childhood and/or of loss. As Erll writes:

> Memories do not hold still – on the contrary, they seem to be constituted first of all through movement. What we are dealing with, therefore, is not so much (and perhaps not even metaphorically) 'sites' of memory, *lieux de memoire*, but rather the 'travels' of memory, *les voyages* or *les mouvements de memoire*. Possible contexts of such movement range from everyday interaction among different social groups to transnational media reception and from trade, migration and diaspora to war and colonialism.
>
> (Erll 2011, 11)

The memories we found in the Mumsnet site are in a place (held on an online container) but they are fragmentary – television becomes a carrier of cultural memory and can produce collective memory in the present, but only in bits and bytes. They are not remembered in totality, rather in fragments, which reflects the 'dipping in' Wilson and Chivers Yochim note. This is not a full, critical memory, these are not fan memories, these are fragmentary memories – like a jigsaw puzzled together to visualize a picture. There is a lot of fact checking – from other posters or by referring to YouTube, but there is no scholarly referral to deeper television histories, which illustrates existing social frameworks and new ones that are forming on the basis of beliefs and memories and not history, evidence or positivist concepts of accurate verification. One of the issues raised within the netnography is a sense, belief or faith that past children's television is or felt more innocent, less complicated and longer. Yet, clearly this perception has a lot to do with the memories themselves – it was an innocent time for the rememberer which is not necessarily the same thing as an innocent text.

Interviewing mums

For our research we decided to interview mums who self-identified as parents who share their past television. We decided to limit our interviews to mothers and to conduct the interviews individually, to give women a chance to open up about some of the caring that frames the decisions they make about their children's viewing. This is not to say that fathers do not care about their children's viewing habits or that they do not have a say in those habits. Work from David Morley (1980, 1986, 1992) and David Morley and Charlotte Brunsdon (1978) and onwards has demonstrated the powerful influence of the father in the home in terms of viewing. However, given the parameters of this research, we turn our attention specifically to mothers both because of the way in which this engages with the netnography on Mumsnet and because of recent work, such as Wilson and Chivers Yochim, which posits the role of the mother within the precarity of social media and happiness in the domestic sphere.

The interviews were conducted in the privacy of the interviewees' homes, which often meant that mothers displayed the DVDs of past British television they watched with their child/children. We posted a call for interviews on a secure site for a children's primary school in Leeds on Facebook initially and then snowballed from these interviews. The interviews themselves were semi-structured, loosely organized by a series of questions that covered their memories of past television and television viewing habits.

The interviews were very much in the spirit of James Lull's (1990) work on television and ethnography. That is, they seek to unpick and uncover the way in which families, in this case mothers in particular, 'construct their time with television' (1990, 12) and specific to this book, how they construct their memories through television. As the introductory quotes to this chapter from Holdsworth and Helsby identify above, many people remember through television in a way that puts television in the background and their memories of family, food and furniture in the foreground. Following Lull's work, we were conscious of both the 'immediate context' and the 'referential context' of the interviews (see Lull 1990, 17–19). We spent time at the participant's home, inviting them to talk us through their collections and memorabilia as well as asking direct questions regarding the sharing they did with their children around past television. Although we recognize this as a small case study, we were also conscious to supplement our findings from Mumsnet with interviews in order to be sure that we had a key into a larger picture and not a just an 'ethnographic snapshot' out of sync (18).

Most of the respondents, predominately white, middle-class and British, were watching children's television in the late 1960s and 1970s (participants ages ranged from 40 to 49). Therefore, these respondents remember Saturday television but have no memory of there not being Saturday television, which was the case in the 1950s and most of the 1960s (Buckingham et al. 1999, 95). Nor were they aware that there did not used to be children's television scheduling in the holidays (93). The 'consolidation' that came with the 1970s meant the programmes they watched 'contributed to a degree of predictability, which enabled them to become part of domestic family routines' (85; see also Steemers 2010). The way in which television 'punctuated their lives' as many of the respondents claimed, was part of the decade they grew up in. As Julie remembers: '[There] was sort of routine [and] I remember lying on the floor with my feet on the radiator watching television' (interview with Julie 8 October 2016). Here there is both the notion of how television dictated a schedule but also a real sense of spatio-temporality. She can remember where she was and how she positioned her own body in front of the television, which many of those we interviewed did. They recalled the colour of certain chairs or fighting over where to sit in the kitchen to get the best view.

Yet, the fixed scheduling is no longer the case for children today since they can now watch television 'on demand' and through their tablets, as many do, instead of on the television screen. Thus, this chapter and research focuses on a particular *time of children's television* and reflects this – it is the same time as *our watching*, though one of us grew up watching television in the United Kingdom and the other in the United States. Moreover, one thing that we have experienced anecdotally is that our British colleagues get much more excited and animated when asked to talk about children's television than their American counterparts. Could this be because there was more regional television in the UK and more 'real life' programming as opposed to animated cartoons? Unfortunately, this question will have to wait for another project. The other experience we have shared is the act of being mothers of British children who are being raised on a regular diet of television alongside other media, all with different cultural values. We share these mothers' concerns, anxieties and excitement, and the prospect of introducing their children to new (and old) programmes.

The interviews shared a lot of similarities with the posters on Mumsnet, suggesting a convergence of female parenting website users and female TV audience members amongst this age group. There was a sense amongst the women interviewed that the real pleasure came from the memories of the time when they watched the programme, rather than the programme itself. In fact, many said that the programme was not as good as their memories of it. They often wondered why their children did not enjoy it as much as they did but soon recognized that the quality and structure was slower and less interactive than what is on children's television today. There were also several moments in which they discussed their memories and linked them to what their mothers were doing. For instance, one participant said that she was always allowed to watch television whilst her mother cleaned the house. There was a distinct sense of time and place – when she could watch and what she could watch, and television standing in for a parental eye while mum was busy.

Many of the mothers felt that television today was not as 'good' as the television they watched and that was part of the reason for showing their child/children the television they grew up with. Though one respondent, Julie, limited her buying of past television both because she did not want her children to watch 'too much' and because she felt that the programming on today's television, particularly the BBC, was much better than it was in the past (interview with Julie 8 October 2016). Others turned to past television to give their children a feeling or emotion attached to the experiences they had watching children's television. One respondent,

Debbie, kept returning to the word 'cosy' in her memories of past television and felt that she was trying to share the cosy feeling that she had watching television as a child with her daughter. She fondly recalled times sat on the couch with her brother watching television and felt there was a palpable warmth about it. She also remembered the way in which television punctuated the routines in her house or in her grandmother's house. Rules such as having no television between 6.00–7.30 pm were ingrained in her memory, and she remembered with delight having the television turned back on at 7.30 pm along with tea and supper. In discussing past British television, Debbie said that she could smell the food that her mother and her grandmother cooked while she watched television as a child (interview with Debbie 22 September 2016). The memories were evocative, sensual, ritualistic and familial.

Childhood television memories also evoked family traditions, habits and cultural traditions. Veena recalls Sundays with her family and extended family that began with television and ended with a trip to the cinema. As she explains:

Sunday mornings I remember sitting down to watch *Nai Zindagi Naya Jeevan* [BBC, 1968–82]. It was an information programme targeting Asians who were newly arrived. It was in Urdu and it was on Sunday morning and we'd all sit and watch that. You'd hear about news, you'd hear about stuff in my parents' first language. That was always a bit of coming together. Sundays were a bit ritualistic so we'd watch that and then usually we'd end up driving to Southall in London where there was a big Asian community and you'd get the food that you wanted and everything and then we'd go and see an Indian Bollywood movie and you'd get samosas and tea served in the cinema, it was lovely. It was lovely.

(interview with Veena 5 October 2016)

The 'coming together' over the television is a common theme within childhood memories, and we can see that being a second or third generation Asian in the UK did not mean British television did not function in a similar way, such that there is a sense of cultural inheritance as well as television preferences. Television in this sense bonds the family in its sense of cultural heritage as well as a unit. The fact that the day was 'ritualistic' seems to provide comfort and stability. Veena describes it as 'lovely' twice, reiterating the warmth and sense of togetherness that the memories and act of doing something as a family evokes.

A 'Brambly Hedge Moment'

Throughout her interview, as discussed, Debbie kept using the word 'cosy' to describe her television memories from childhood and the desire she had to give this to her daughter through sharing past television. It also became something she used with others. Indeed, the cosiness that she kept returning to made its way into a phrase she uses with a close friend and neighbour: the 'Brambly Hedge Moment' (interview with Debbie 22 September 2016).[16] She said they often text this to each other as a code for meeting up over tea or going out for tea and cake and talking about their family and the past. The television series she referred to evoked a sense of warmth and comfort for both of them, and they each fully understood the reference, enough to use it between them.

Amy Holdsworth argues that 'television is at once both cosy and old-fashioned yet invested with culturally specific anxieties, and it is as a paradoxical symbol of both security and potential loss that it has become a deeply nostalgic technology' (2011, 126). What comes through strongly in the interviews is the way in which television can facilitate notions of home, comfort and safety. Several mums refer to feeling 'safe' when they know that their children are watching television as opposed to being on a tablet or laptop. Some mums referred to feeling a sense of danger at knowing their child was only a click away from something inappropriate whereas the BBC's children's channel for pre-schoolers, CBeebies, reassured them that anything they watched would be acceptable. The feeling of knowing that their children were occupied with something 'safe' enabled them to get on with other domestic duties (such as cooking dinner or cleaning the house), or carrying on with work.

Many of the mums used social media to introduce their child to past television and then bought the DVDs later, if they were available, using the internet for tracing and consuming safe and known pathways into their television past. Such pre-screening of media through memory is indicative of how the sovereign consumer of televisual choice makes real decisions in an uncertain market economy, anchoring those purchases to personal and inheritable memory. They often prefaced showing the clips with stories about when they first saw it and the context in which they saw it (on Sunday mornings, or Sundays after a roast dinner, etc.) as a form of curatorial narrative voiceover. The sharing often means a chance to spend time with their children over something they both enjoy, and to engage in acts of translation from one generation to the other. One mum discussed the way in which watching a programme for the second time around meant that she saw it in a different light – there was not only re-pleasure in remembering but also in seeing the programme from a new (or more 'adult') perspective.

One of the mums spoke of her daughter's pleasure in the text as centring around the voices she heard, particularly the timbre or accent of the characters (interview with Debbie 22 September 2016) and this was also something that she remembered enjoying. Here, the evidence regarding the ways in which childhood emerges as a multisensory experience through recourse to remembering television, demonstrating how children remember, is particularly apt. The mums interviewed almost always recited a theme song, or remembered specific characters or voices,

---

[16]See the illustrated children's books by Jill Barklem (1980–2010) and the animated TV series (1996–2000) of *Brambly Hedge*.

but almost never remembered a plot line. Their memories are centred around fragments, moments of the text that they recall, rather than a full sense of the programme itself; and, this seems to be in large part a result of the way in which these fragmentary memories are attached to the fabric of their lives at the time of watching. They can recall the food they ate, the people they watched with, the time of day or whether it was after school or during the holidays. Their memories are suffused and informed by their context with very little televisual content to fall back on as evidence, suggesting that the re-creation of television memories is far more imaginative than archival, far more intimate than public.[17] The way in which they share these programmes with their children often has a lot to do with wanting to create a connection or to see whether their child has similar tastes to them. For instance, Anna explains:

> I thought [*The Flumps* (BBC One, 1977), *The Trap Door* (ITV/Channel 4, 1984) *Jamie and the Magic Torch* (ITV, 1976–9)] were brilliant as a kid and I probably wanted to see, did he think they were brilliant as well. Would that give us some closeness or what's he like, is he like me? Does he also think these are brilliant? And he loved them, especially *Trap Door* and he still watches *Trap Door* a lot.
> (interview with Anna 1 October 2016)

In a sense, Anna uses television to see to what extent she and her son share similarities and to see whether it can be something that creates a connection. Interestingly, during the interview, Anna realized that she shared television with her Dad:

> And *Batman* [ABC 1966–8; ITV 1989–92] was Saturday, I used to watch with my dad because *Batman* was from my dad's era. So my dad, that's really interesting because my dad loved *Batman* and my dad wanted me to get into *Batman*. Because I think it's from the '60s. So he really loved watching it. So we'd watch that together and he would say, 'I used to watch this.' [...] I've never really thought of that, but yes I used to watch that with my dad. So yes, three generations of real skin *Batman*, you know, I've enjoyed it.
> (interview with Anna 1 October 2016)

During the process of recalling her television memories, Anna remembered that she watched 'real skin' *Batman* (the series with real actors) with her Dad and that this is most likely the reason why she has been so keen to share it with

---

[17]In 2017 SkyMovies launched its Christmas advert with the strapline 'Christmas is all about traditions … as we show in our heart-warming story of a mother, her daughter and one very special movie' (SkyMovies 2017; ellipsis in original). Strikingly, the advert shows the stability and security of three generations of female appreciation of one movie despite changes in TV technology. Content is not important here (the film stays the same), but what is key is that upgrades in TV sets, from analogue to digital, do not shift the box's status. It stays in the corner of the room and so too the intimacy of the relationships between daughter, mother, grandmother and granddaughter remain in their direct interaction with that box.

her son. But it was not until the interview, and thinking about watching past television with her son, that she remembered this. As she says towards the end of the interview:

> It's been interesting talking about it, it's reminded me that my dad introduced me to *Batman* […] So yes, that's really interesting because I didn't realise, perhaps subconsciously I wanted Fred to enjoy that and he really does.
>
> (interview with Anna 1 October 2016)

Here Anna articulates her interest in the pattern of her own memories, recognizing that it wasn't until she started thinking about her childhood television memories that she remembered that it was her Dad and the enjoyment she had watching *Batman* with her Dad, which prompted her to share the series with her son. Many of the participants had not stopped to think about why they chose to share particular programmes or what the act of watching this kind of television created for their children – it most cases the interview prompted this reflection for the first time and engaged them to consider what they wanted out of the experience.

Interestingly, most mums were very keen to display or show their DVDs of past television (see Figure 3).

They often had them displayed in preparation for the interview, or even shared pictures of them before the interview over social media to evidence the fact that they really did collect and share the DVDs with their children. Indeed, many of

FIGURE 3 Photograph of mum's DVD collection of children's television displayed for the researcher. (Photograph Kristyn Gorton.)

the mums interviewed displayed their children's dolls or books associated with television series from their own childhood. Several of the mums referred with great fondness to *Bagpuss* (BBC One, 1974) as a key example.[18] When we asked one mum, Veena, why she bought a *Bagpuss* doll for her daughter, she replied by saying:

> To be honest I'm doing it more for me than for her, I can give her anything, I could give her some old dog or whatever, well I could, couldn't I? I mean she won't know any more but I think [...] it's probably a link to me and to my past, isn't it? It's kind of creating that connection [...] I want her to like what I like almost [...] And sometimes it works and sometimes it doesn't work. So, it's fine but it's nice to have that connection, isn't it?
>
> (interview with Veena 5 October 2016)

In one way, this accords with Jonathan Gray's argument concerning the role of the toy. In *Show Sold Separately*, Gray discusses how *Star Wars* action figures can function as, what we would term, paratextual memory: 'If *Star Wars* can act as a doorway back in time, for many fans, toys serve as a key to this door' (Gray 2010, 184). Veena is aware that the doll itself will not be understandable to her daughter, especially as she does not watch the show. Thus, in this sense the paratext (the doll) is devoid of significance for the person who has it, but full of meaning to the person who is giving it. As Veena explains, it is about creating a connection between herself and her daughter and a link between herself and her past, a form of personal inheritance. Her awareness that it sometimes does not work demonstrates the precarious ways in which television as memory is inherited, but it does not stop her from trying to create that connection, because even if she is not able to construct a connection between herself and her daughter, she is still able to take pleasure in seeing the doll as it says something to her about herself. It reminds her of something from the past that she treasures.

In contrast, George recognized that she did not share *Bagpuss* deliberately because she was afraid that her son would reject it. She initially explained the significance of *Bagpuss* as related to an early memory from her childhood of being ill and watching it whilst she was home from school:

> I remember the time when I was much younger having been ill and being off school and being at home with my mum and being warm and watching *Bagpuss* during the day, and after that thinking 'oh that was a really nice day, I can do that again!' [...] it's not a really distinct memory of a particular day, it's probably just moments that I remember, I've got a real vivid memory of the fire being on, being cold outside, being home with my mum's cardigan on and

---

[18]For an excellent analysis of the handcrafted ingenuity and impact of *Bagpuss* see Rachel Moseley's (2016) *Hand-Made Television: Stop-Frame Animation for Children in Britain 1961–1974*.

watching *Bagpuss* and really enjoying it. But it was special, it was just me and my mum at home.

(interview with George 14 October 2016)

Here, as George explains, the memories are fragmentary but suffused with emotion and warmth – of her mother's cardigan wrapped around her, the heat-filled room and of being held by her mother. The memories are very evocative and precious and yet anchored by a television programme. The interview continued on about other things, but she later returned to this memory and explained: 'That's probably why I don't think [my son] would be interested in *Bagpuss* and I wouldn't like him to slag *Bagpuss* off because, "he can't criticize *Bagpuss*!" Maybe that's why because I wouldn't want him to not like it' (interview with George 14 October 2016). Unlike Veena's attempt to create a connection, here George is very careful not to allow her son to be critical of *Bagpuss* in part because she holds the memory of being home alone with her mother in a sacred way. She does not want to create an opportunity for her son not to like it, as this might, in some way, taint the special memories she has of her childhood. In this sense, paratexts work differently – they can create connections and links to the past that can then be shared in the hopes that they construct new connections, or, as in George's example, they might also be stored away (strategically forgotten) in order to keep the memories of one's own connection intact. What is very interesting here is the awareness on the part of the mums as to why and how they want to create an inheritance and to what extent they are careful about the links they create and avoid creating.

Not all the mums described their childhood television memories with warmth and affection. For instance, Julie talked about watching television on her own and that, at times, it was a relatively lonely experience. Her father often went to the pub, her brother spent time in his room and her mother got on with her work in the kitchen, which often left Julie watching television by herself. She recalls watching programming that was a little 'old' for her but that her mum let her watch so that she could get on with other things.

[My mum] used to let me get on with [watching *Dynasty* (ABC, 1981–9)] and sort of tut at me from the other room so it was disapproved of and I was made to feel a bit stupid for watching it. But I didn't care, not enough to stop me watching it. I don't know why I liked it because it does fit in with all I'm saying I don't want Alice to see.

(interview with Julie 8 October 2016)

Here Julie realizes that although she has protected her daughter from very gendered material, she herself enjoyed it as a child and she notices a sort of hypocrisy in this decision, as well as a benchmark against which to judge her own parenting. A similar moment happened when Anna realized that she herself finds television very relaxing and looks forward to sitting on the couch at night and settling into a show, whereas she is anxious about letting her children watch too much. Implicit here is a consideration of what the children 'inherit' and what television might give them.

Similar to Seiter's 'case of a troubling interview' (1990), there was a sense that some of the mums were somewhat self-conscious about their own television consumption and that of their children in relation to being interviewed. Indeed, some mothers explained that they have more books than DVDs, or that they refuse to let their children watch television in the mornings, or after a certain time at night. They emphasized the importance and value of reading as if to reassure that this, as well as television, had an important role in their child's daily routines. As Seiter's research demonstrated there is a sense that talking about television needs to be underpinned by some sort of discussion of 'higher brow' arts, thus underscoring her point that 'the social identities of academic researchers and the social identities of our TV viewing subjects are not only different, they are differently valued' (1990, 70), even if as academics we have often worked in and with communities and the public. So, for example, one mum discussed how her daughter reads Dickens and Shakespeare as well as enjoying past television (interview with Debbie 22 September 2016). There was also a preference or snobbery for the BBC, and this appears as something that is inherited. While, we did not present ourselves as historians or experts on the specific texts they referred to, they did consider us as passing judgement. The challenge is, to rephrase Seiter (1990, 71), who draws on Bourdieu (1984), to investigate popular memories and explain how these memories are 'distributed in relation to domination. To do so will also necessitate recognizing our own dominance and our own class interests within the system of cultural distinctions.'

Television as 'time machine'

Drawing on Raymond Williams's (1974) work on television flow, William Uricchio points towards the 'role of sequence, context and association in the construction of meaning, and the tensions inherent in ordering and reordering bits of time, space and event' (2010, 28) in our memories of television. In this sense, television can be a kind of 'time machine' that transports us to another time in our own lives. The meaning we give programmes is often bound up by the 'bits of time, space and event' that surrounds them and this is what we have found articulated in the memories from Mumsnet and in the interviews. As Anna explains:

> My childhood was punctuated by TV programmes. Because now you can watch anything anytime whereas when I was a kid in the '70s and '80s, things were only on once, that was it. You watched *Worzel Gummidge* [ITV 1979–81, 1987–9] on a Sunday afternoon, you watched *Grange Hill* [BBC 1978–2008] when you came in from school, you watched *Love Boat* [ABC/BBC 1977–90] on a Sunday afternoon.
> (interview with Anna 1 October 2016)

Here Anna articulates the way in which television anchors her everyday life and constructs memories around her domestic routine. It also, as discussed earlier, has led her to feel an attachment to particular programmes, in her case *Batman,* which she associated with her father. Many of the other women interviewed and posters on Mumsnet related a similar sense that television plays a significant role in their memories of childhood and in their sense of themselves today and in their parenting style. The memories discussed in this chapter have largely been fragmentary, fleeting, sensory and evocative. They centre on images, sounds, bits of theme tunes, particular chairs or positions of viewing, associations with relatives that watched alongside, smells in the home, and food. In this sense, the memories are fragile and tenuous and yet they are strong enough to be inherited and shared. In their work on care, Mol, Moser and Pols suggest that: 'Crucially, in care practices what it is to be human has more to do with being fragile than with mastering the world' (Mol, Moser and Pols 2010, 15). In her uncomfortable interview, an experience we have had more times than not, Seiter (1990) struggles to care about the anecdotes, memories and stories of television from an interviewee who does not align with her social class and cultural capital. Our research reflects the fragility of the object of study, and of our relationship (as researchers) to it and those who remember it. Our participants do not pretend to have mastery over these memories but they do demonstrate a strong attachment to the preservation of the memories insofar as they can be passed down to their children, and they do consider them a form of property that can be a 'common-pool resource' as Allen describes it: 'What if memory itself is considered from the position of common property, not private property?' (2014, 13).

One of the expectations many mothers feel is that they must 'make memories' good ones for their children to both enjoy in the making and enjoy in the remembering, a form of creative remembrance. Television functions as a medium that provides both the creative connectivity with the present and future, and the chance to enjoy the nostalgia of their past. Simultaneously constructing new memories is often a draw for mothers who share their past television with their children. The caring that happens in this sharing of past television is one that is imbued with a sense of folding the past with and into the present. These mothers want to be remembered by their children as the creators and curators of good memories, and *old TV* is an important and cared for apparatus to demonstrate this.

In their research on care in children's television, Amy Holdsworth and Karen Lury (2016) explain that the pattern and rhythm inherent to children's programmes such as *Katie Morag* (CBeebies/CBBC, 2013–) challenge the chronological narratives of childhood and 'instead reimagines such narratives as simultaneously folding and unfolding, looping between times and spaces' (2016, 193). The looping between times and spaces that Holdsworth and Lury recognize as part of the programme's structure is also apparent in the sharing and passing down of past television between the mothers and children in our research. In talking about the programmes, watching them together, sharing a laugh or using it as a prompt to talk about other things, children's television creates an affective space to share and create new memories from *old TV*. Part of the reason for our close attention to childhood, memory, care and the materialized remembering that mums are performing in their re-consumption of children's TV is to underscore the mundane and everyday social materialities of parenting through television. This is not simply a case of drawing attention to *old TV* as consumed, commodified or played-with (in terms of merchandise), nor are we focused on changing constructions of childhood (see Derevenski 2000). In fact, our research does not privilege the particularity of the material object of television at all (our parents could not remember many of the programmes in much detail) so there is no neatly-bound *old TV* to inherit here, no singular way of seeing to make meaningful and no practice of re-viewing that is readily discoursed. The memories are autotelic (to remember *old TV* is self-rewarding) and the memories are of self-rewarding times of seemingly pointless and meaningless TV watching as a kid (see Rautio 2013), while all around was complex.

6 NOSTALGIA AND PARATEXUAL MEMORY: *COLD FEET* (ITV, 1997–2016), REMINISCENCE CLIP SHOWS AND 'VINTAGE' TELEVISION WEBSITES

The last chapter explored viewers' memories of children's television as well as considering the ways in which these are framed by a 'mothering' of the past. Indeed, care framed many of the moments within the mundane, everyday lives of the mothers who watch television with their children and/or use television as a means of teaching their children something about their past television habits and pleasures. As Roger Silverstone has argued: 'We are drawn to these otherwise mundane and trivial texts and performances by a transcendent hope, a hope and a desire that something will touch us' (1999, 55). This logic of care can also be found within television marketing, production and paratexts, which this chapter will explore along with the way the remembering of past television works within these formats. It begins by looking at the role of paratexts within television marketing and distribution and in the way viewers construct meaning about the television series through these paratexts. We do this in order to consider how these paratexts work to create a sense of history around the text and a sense of heritage.

This chapter considers the role of paratexts as circulating not only around texts but as the very vehicles for reboots, nostalgia, reminiscence and activating dormant and remembering audiences. Through a case study example on the revival of the British television comedy series *Cold Feet* (ITV, 1997–2016) we move across scales of increasing inter-textual remembering in nostalgic, vintage and legacy television shows from the United States, to the popular television 'looking back at' programmes such as Reminisce This (2018).[1]

Moreover, this chapter raises questions regarding viewers' nostalgia – what are they nostalgic for? If, as Amy Holdsworth argues, nostalgia for television is more the 'desire to remember not to re-experience; to recall not to recover' (2011, 102); then why do people make past television available (to their children, as discussed in the last chapter and through hyperlinks, as available online). 'Remember'

---

[1] *It Was Alright in the 1970s* defined as: 'Celebrities young and old look back on the television of past decades, a time before political correctness took hold and casual racism, sexism and homophobia was the order of the day' (IMDB 1990–2018)

and 'recall' both suggest surface affects, they are fleeting, superficial, ephemeral; whereas re-experience and recover, (re)store, (re)collect, curate and pass down, speak to more sustained moments and movements, deeper engagements and simulation, and sustainable memories towards which our research leans. The posters and interviewees often want to 'stay' or 'dwell' in those memories, long enough so that they can 'give' them to their children, but also long enough so that they become tangible and 'share-able'.

This chapter also considers the way in which the ephemera around programmes – their paratexts – construct expectations, sustain interest, generate significance and build story, spreading memories. How do viewers then engage with these paratexts in terms of their memories of the programmes? As discussed in the last chapter, one woman bought a *Bagpuss* stuffed toy for her daughter while the latter was still a baby, before she could meaningfully associate the stuffed toy with the series. She placed the toy on the shelf in her daughter's nursery as if to remind herself that she wanted her daughter to inherit the significance of the toy and the gift itself.[2] For in the act of buying the stuffed toy she was taking pleasure in her own memories and reminiscences but also preparing herself for sharing these with her daughter: making room for inheritance by engaging in the conspicuous consumption of television merchandise but also the mundane-ness of television's materiality. This chapter reveals similar practices, both in the way images or characters are recycled and reused to new purpose and to engage with old memories. Fans of *Cold Feet* will be excited to 'live' with their favourite characters again but might also have found themselves disappointed with the experience, primarily because the new version is not *enough like the old*. Series such as *It Was Alright in the …* are very similar to the nostalgia television websites where we are offered potted sociocultural histories of particular decades mediated by programmes that are seen to define these eras. In addition to this we are offered several vantage points from which to view these reminiscences – in the case of *It Was Alright in the …* this is created for us by people who lived during the time, who were making programming at the time or people who have never seen the television texts screened before. Thus, from whatever television place we stand and start from, at home as viewers, we are offered other places from which to make a judgement and through which to filter our own memories. The websites also mediate the memories either through personal reminiscences or categorization which leads us to make value judgements about the television and its place within history.

---

[2]It is worth noting that this act of placing on a shelf in a nursery mirrors, in a small way, the original Bagpuss toy currently on display at Canterbury Heritage Museum. The toy's repurposing to create new paratextual memories such as on a Royal Mail stamp in 2015 or being reunited with Emily Firmin for the fortieth anniversary in 2014 (the eight-year-old daughter of the creator Peter Firmin) who appeared in the series. Bagpuss appears in the museum's collections webpage alongside pilgrim badges from 1170, a mammoth tusk, Second World War artefacts, and a Rupert Bear illustration from 1920.

The looping that Holdsworth and Lury (2016) identify speaks to the way in which television conditions and constructs a sense of time and space that allows parents to give their children a sense of their past. In her work on TV time, Patricia Mellencamp writes that the 'memories TV recalls via constant reruns, remakes, and parody, the past it recreates, rarely summons or echo personal experience'; rather, she sees TV's 'democratic' past as creating an 'atrophy' of experience' (1990, 241). She goes on to argue that 'TV is rarely the material object setting off involuntary (personal) memory [...] TV triggers memories of TV in an endless chain of TV referentiality [...] With its raw appeals to and inscriptions of affect, television is a medium of remembrance more than memory' (242). Thus far, our research has demonstrated the opposite in terms of memory. Television does 'summon or echo personal experience' as evidenced in the interview with mothers who share past television with their children. In Chapter 4, we considered the way thst the materiality of television provoked affective responses from visitors as well as from people anxious to have their past television collected by museums to display and exhibit. Mellencamp's claim for television's referentiality has been seen as a key feature of contemporary television for decades (see, for example, Kaplan 1987; Joyrich 1988; and Collins [1987] 1992), but, as this chapter will go on to explore, it does not mean that television becomes a 'medium of remembrance rather than memory'.

Paratextual memory

In discussing the use of ephemera in the museum, Michael Terwey, head of curations at the National Media Museum explains that:

> the bigger assemblage of stuff and story and ephemera around a piece of technology the more likely it is that we want to acquire it because it means we understand better its significance when we come to display it, or when researchers come and look at it they have more raw material to kind of go on [...] there are incredible resources in [the ephemeral material].
>
> (interview with Michael Terwey 22 June 2016)

Although Terwey is discussing the role of ephemera in the curation of television in museums, the notion of paratexts building story and significance is the same when we come to think about it in terms of television distribution, marketing and in viewers' understanding of the series.

In his work on paratexts, Jonathan Gray draws on literary theorist Gerard Genette's (1997) work to formulate an understanding of the way in which paratexts function in television. As Gray notes, Genette understood paratexts as 'texts that prepare us for other texts' (2010, 25) and this means anything from the trailers to series, opening credits, the promotional fodder, the blogs around the series to spin-offs and revivals. Preparation may assume a chronological placing as before or prior to the text. Yet, what we have been claiming in this book, is that paratextual memory is multidirectional, multi-temporal, multi-spatial and scalable. A paratextual memory may be all we have to remember of the original text, particularly if it is lost, inaccessible or even deliberately hidden from view, so as to be only enjoyed through its paratexts. These paratexts are significant as Terwey notes for their ability to build story and construct meaning, sometimes being more enjoyable than the original text. As Gray argues: 'Each proliferation, after all, holds the potential to change the meaning of the text, even if only slightly' (2010, 2). In this sense, paratexts often work to establish or condition viewers' anxieties and hopes, and this has been the case in the lead up to the revival of series such as *Arrested Development* (Fox, 2003–06; Netflix, 2013–), *The X-Files* (Fox, 1993–2002; 2016–) and *Fuller House* (Netflix, 2016–). Audiences were primed to re-experience the joy, pleasure and fun they first experienced when these programmes initially aired. These 'returns' or 'revivals' have also been referred to in journalistic discourse as 'nostalgia TV' or legacy television by the industry. As journalist Vinnie Mancuso writes: '*Fuller House* is just the latest in the nostalgia TV trend. You miss *Arrested Development*? Blam, here's a new season. Pissed that *The X-Files* only got nine seasons and two movies? FOX is here with 6 more episodes (and possibly more)' (2016). However, as Mancuso goes on to explain: 'The problem, as *Fuller House* personifies completely, is that nostalgia does not equal need. The whole point of nostalgia isn't just straight longing, it's longing for something you know won't ever be the same again' (2016).

In *Rerun Nation* Derek Kompare (2005) starts off his chapter on 'Our Television Heritage' with a quote from journalist John Leonard of *New York Times* from 1976 who writes: 'There are very few moments from the TV past that our children will not witness, over and over again' (2005, 101). So although only some television moments are vividly remembered, as explored in the last chapter, this does not necessarily mean that these are the only things in our memory. As Kompare argues, this moment was to crystallize the importance and significance of television as a cultural art form along with a 'greater acknowledgement of the everyday culture of modernity' along with the beginning of 'television's historicity, that is, its articulation into discourses of history and memory' (2005, 102). More specifically, as Kompare goes on to elaborate, the 1970s marked the formation of television heritage (102). The shift in terms of thinking about television as something more than a valueless medium meant a change in the way people valued television and made room for 'active nostalgia, historical exploration, and cultural preservation' (104). It is this sense of 'active nostalgia' that this chapter will explore. It is also worth considering the way in which viewers are moving between platforms, much like the 'dipping in' explored in the last chapter. In her work on television and new media, Jennifer Gillan argues that:

> viewers start watching the broadcast text and then jump from it to other media platforms, a platforming strategy is a step in revising the standard broadcasting

model in which the on-air TV product exists in a hierarchical relationship to its official programming tie-ins and other affiliated secondary content.

(Gillan 2011, 18)

A good example would be *Stranger Things* (Netflix, 2016–), which is set in a fictional town in Indiana during the early 1980s. The series main cast includes four young boys and is reminiscent of *The Goonies* (1985) or *Stand by Me* (1986) both popular films in the mid-1980s and the supernatural, science fiction genre reminds us of *E.T.* (1982).[3] One of the mums interviewed in the previous chapter mentioned that she was watching *Stranger Things* with her husband and talked about the way in which it evoked *Doctor Who* for her and the moments in her childhood where she felt pleasantly afraid. In contrast to the cosiness often associated with children's television memories, the ones that circulate fear can also produce pleasure and capturing this around the text offers a paratextual pull into the programme. This is a form of nostalgia that does not seek to look backwards but actively establishes a connection with the present. Winona Ryder's presence in the series invites viewers who are familiar with her from a previous generation but then also creates new fans. As journalist Sam Adams writes in *Rolling Stones*:

> *Stranger Things* is full of nostalgic nods to the decade and its pop-cultural products, but it's also uncommonly rigorous about getting the details just right – whether it's the many pitch-perfect music cues, the hat-tipping nods and homages to Eighties movies, or simply nailing the cringeworthy fashion statements of the day (those Mom jeans!).

(Adams 2016)

Here the details are praised as being part of what draws us in and keeps us engaged in the past – both through memories of the decade and details of the time, which themselves are only reconstructed through the memories the producers and researchers have of them.

The nostalgic mode

In *The Future of Nostalgia* (2001), Svetlana Boym defines nostalgia as a 'sentiment of loss and displacement, but it is also a romance of one's own fantasy' (xiii). Her use of the word 'romance' in combination with loss and displacement is very provocative when we think about television memories. Part of the romance is with the past iterations of one's self and the fantastical side of memories, rather than a simple juxtaposition of what is dated and old with the flow of the new, as O'Sullivan defines nostalgic television (1998, 203). As the last chapter demonstrated, many

---

[3]Interestingly, Vera Dika (2003, 202) notes that there is a particular 'conflation of television and childhood […] in the films produced in the late 1980s and 1990s'.

respondents had memories about food, certain chairs or rooms, siblings who watched alongside, being ill and allowed to watch more television, and TV after school or during the holidays. While memories of TV provides the thread that stitches together social materialities of daily life, many prefaced their memories by admitting that they knew this was more of a fantastical remembering than what actually happened. They were able to distinguish between the reality of what happened and their romantic versions, but inevitably stayed longer in the latter and were happy to share the rose-tinted accounts of their past.

Although nostalgia carries a sense of longing with it, which could be constructed as depression or sadness, Boym is careful to make a distinction between melancholia and nostalgia, arguing that: 'Unlike melancholia [...] nostalgia is about the relationship between individual biography and the biography of groups or nations, between personal and collective memory' (2001, xvi). The relationship between the 'personal and collective memory' is what makes it so amenable to a discussion of television's past and it's use within television. The recycling and reviving also returns us with the sentiments housed within that collective memory. In *Cold Feet*, for instance, we have both a viewer's personal memory – when they first watched, who they watched it with, how they felt about it, combined with a collective memory – how 10 million plus watched the penultimate episode when Rachel dies, how this was covered in the press, how people may have discussed it in the workplace and other places. Both these sets of memories return in the revival, and the paratexts are key to resetting these and building on them.

In her polemic on nostalgia, Kathleen Stewart argues that: 'Nostalgia, like the economy it runs with, is everywhere. But it is a cultural practice, not a given content; its forms, meanings and effects shift with the context – it depends on where the speaker stands in the landscape of the present' (1988, 227). Here it is tempting to draw very strong lines between television and the way in which Stewart defines nostalgia. For like nostalgia, as imagined by Stewart, television is everywhere. Its ubiquity has been theorized by scholars such as Anna McCarthy (2001) and its materiality is felt by most of us – whether as a box in the corner of the room, something on our laptops or smartphones, or something above our heads to keep us distracted. In her work *Ambient Television* McCarthy argues that:

> the site-specific nature of many institutional and personal uses of TV means that it is impossible to single out one mode of spectatorship to define the relationship between screen and environment [...] Rather, the diffuse network of gazes and institutions, subjects and bodies, screens and physical structures that constitutes the televisual place sustains quite particular effects in each place.
>
> (McCarthy 2001, 3)

As McCarthy suggests, it is not just that television is everywhere but its material proliferation means that we need to understand that there is a 'diffuse network of gazes' that causes particular effects (and affects) depending on the place they are viewed. Whether we are watching television in an airport waiting for our plane to depart or someone else's to arrive, whether we are in the hospital awaiting an appointment, in the comfort of our own home, snuggled on the couch, or at a bar talking with friends. The televisual place, as McCarthy puts it, conditions the effects it has on its viewers as well as the memories they have of that viewing experience. Indeed, the last chapter highlighted how these memories are often framed by the place/places – whether the front room of the family house or hiding behind the couch.

The way we make meaning and find significance in what we watch on television can also be extended to think about television's paratexts – its forms, meanings and effects shift with the context, as Gray explains above, both in terms of our understanding of the programmes and in our own memories of these programmes and our viewing experience. In her work on television, memory and nostalgia, for instance, Holdsworth thinks back to her childhood memories of watching television and remembers the feelings that came with watching television on a sunny day; an evocative memory that many of us can relate to, particularly the feelings of both guilt and pleasure competing (2011, 25). She writes that:

> These are not memories of the detail of the programmes […] neither are they purely memories of the context, but they are an interplay between the two and the sense impressions left by the play of light, texture, colour, sound and temperature.
>
> (Holdsworth 2011, 25)

The 'interplay' that Holdsworth refers to speaks to the shifting context Stewart identifies in the movement of nostalgia. Holdsworth is also speaking from a particular position, she 'stands in the landscape of the present' and from this vantage point can remember the 'sense impressions' of her childhood television viewing. The *It Was Alright in the …* speak entirely to the notion of where we stand by including viewers in the present that stand in different places – whether as people remembering or viewing for the first time.

Case study: Cold Feet

ITV first aired *Cold Feet* from 1997 to 2003 with great acclaim. The series, created by Mike Bullen, won a British Academy Television Award, six British Comedy Awards and two National Television Awards. Set in the north England city of Manchester, the series followed the lives of a group of thirty-something friends from similar class and ethnic backgrounds. One of the main storylines centred around the romantic relationship between Rachel (Helen Baxendale) and Adam (James Nesbitt), which culminates in the birth of their son and then shortly after, her tragic death. The episode where Rachel died in a car crash had almost 11 million viewers. The series is reminiscent of the American *Thirtysomething* (ABC,

1987–91) and of *Friends* (NBC, 1994–2004) and draws on these but produces the story with a Northern flair. The Manchester landscape that the story revolves within adds a different feel to it and gives it a particular edge.

Rachel's death drew a great deal of attention from viewers and many felt upset with the end of the series and hoped it would return. However, it was not until eighteen years later (after its first debut in 1997) that the series was revived. The fact that they brought back the series comes in line with other revivals (such as *Absolutely Fabulous: The Movie*, 2016) and cynically it could be said that this is part of austerity culture in the British television industry where there is a sense that something like *Cold Feet* could guarantee an audience and has an already existing fan base. Yet, as one 'mega-fan', Sarah Hughes, writes in the the *Belfast Telegraph*:

> For every reboot that works, such as Russell T Davies's smart, sharp revival of *Doctor Who*, there's one that lingers in the memory as a bitter example of what not to do. Take *This Life* […] most fans were thrilled […] Yet the characters who'd seemed so effortlessly cool in the late Nineties were now revealed as smug, self-involved and depressing. A show that had once seemed to tap directly into the zeitgeist now appeared desperately out of touch.
>
> (Hughes 2015)

It is notable that a 'mega-fan' is put forward as someone expert enough to make a judgement on a television series in a broadsheet, they are 'paratextual completists' according to Hills (2015, 53) and their paratextual memory also leads to (re-) commodification in new fan-targeted merchandise (75). This demonstrates an evolution in how fans are seen with regards to television and its marketable memorability. The mega-fan Hughes points out that half of the reboots end up as failures partly because they are speaking to the wrong 'zeitgeist'. Hughes goes on to point out that the characters' ages will potentially make a difference in whether or not the series is successful with audiences. She argues that 'once people edge towards 50, they slowly fade from anything except procedural dramas' (Hughes 2015). This pronouncement seems relatively harsh and unfounded; however, it might be that *Cold Feet*'s warmth and cosiness, which originally appealed to viewers, may now be as trite and uninteresting as *This Life* (BBC Two, 1996–7).

Cold Feet works as a good example of 'nostalgia TV' as most viewers will have tuned in because they were nostalgic for the time when they viewed the first series. As Katherina Niemeyer and Daniela Wentz (2014) argue: 'A nostalgic series is very often the object of its audience's longing" (130). Indeed, ITV offered a free download of the first series to paratextually revive interest and perhaps to catch up viewers who did not see the first series. However, the revived series raises interesting questions about memory and time. Is there an amount of time that is too long to keep viewers attached to their favourite characters? Viewers are accustomed to waiting for the next season of their favourite programme and can reimmerse themselves in the world these series create. For example, fans of *Game of Thrones* (HBO, 2011–) will be deeply engrossed in the lives of the characters while the season is running but will have to wait until the next season to pick up on these stories. There is often some repetition in the first episode to remind viewers but most remember the stories they have been told and where they left off with these characters. Timing appears as a key issue in the journalistic reception of the series. One journalist for *The Economist* writes:

> Timing has been of key importance. There had been conversations about reviving *Cold Feet* over the years, but many felt the moment for following each character had passed. Not now. 'Enough time had gone by', says James Nesbitt, who plays Adam. 'Those familiar, yet distant, characters leapt off the page and they still had something to say.'
>
> (J.A.R.B. 2016)

The thirteen-year gap between the original series and reboot does not seem to have effected it's viewing figures which went into 7 million.[4] The series relies on viewers' being interested in the lives of the central characters as not much else happens in the series. The central plot focuses again on Adam's love life, this time whether he can successfully keep his partner in Singapore while trying to care for his teenage son in Manchester. The ending feels telegraphed and we know that he will ultimately end up with his landlord who resembles Rachel. Beyond this, we are faced with the lives of an older cast who have entered their late forties, early fifties and find life is more behind them than in front of them.

In the trailer to the new series, the audience are drawn into the cabin of a jet commuter, as gentle elevator music plays, the camera moves in on a sleeping Adam (James Nesbitt). A stewardess dressed in red leans over and taps him.

Jenny (Fay Ripley)	Hot towel, sir?
Adam	Jenny?!
Jenny	Coming back, eh?
Adam	It's been too long.
Jenny	I know someone's who's missed you.

Cut to see **Pete** [John Thomson] *in the seat next to him.*

Pete	I have mate, things haven't been the same without you.

He turns to look at **Jenny.**

Pete	Can I have some peanuts?

(ITV 2016)

At this point, Karen (Hermoine Norris) stands up from behind them and David (Robert Bathurst) enters as the pilot. The dream sequence ends abruptly and Adam is given a hot towel by a 'real' stewardess and told that they are about to land.

---

[4]Sam Wollaston writes in *The Guardian*: 'It could have been a disaster, the reboot of *Cold Feet*, 13 years on. It hasn't been – the numbers have been dead impressive. Seven million viewers, in this age of about 6m ways of watching TV, aren't easy to come by' (2016).

The sequence plays with feelings of nostalgia, longing and reunion that the producers of the revived series hope audiences will feel so that they tune in to watch. Setting it on a plane reminds us of a journey and the transition between one place (the past) and the new landscape they are heading to (the present). Adam's acknowledgement that it has 'been too long' attempts to key into feelings viewers might have, along with Pete's admission that 'things haven't been the same without you'. Each is designed to be part of the viewers' thoughts whilst simultaneously reminding viewers of the relationships between the characters: Jenny and Adam once dated, Pete and Adam are best friends, Karen and David were once married.

The revived series does not do much beyond reintroduce us to the characters and their lives thirteen years on. Adam gets married to a woman he has fallen in love with whilst working in Singapore early in the series but then suddenly realizes that he needs to be 'there' for his fifteen-year-old son, and soon the relationship is over and no longer referred to. Jenny and Pete are still together, but he has lost his job and now works two jobs, as a taxi driver and care worker, and is diagnosed with depression. Jenny's ex-lover reappears on the scene and tells their daughter Chloe, who is thirteen years old, that he is her biological father. Karen lives with her twin teenage daughters and begins an affair with Adam's wife's father, a wealthy business man. Her ex-husband, David, divorces his wife and is on trial for fraud, so has now moved back in with Karen. The various events mean that most characters have returned to the place we last saw them and to the lives they were living. In this sense, we are literally returned to the same scene, even the same sets, to watch the same storylines with the same characters. This 'sameness' seems to appeal to some viewers who see it as cosy and familiar while it may turn others off, who critique that 'sameness':

From Digital Spy Thread: 08-09-2016, 10:17
Chiltons Cane, Forum Member, Join Date: Jun 2014, Posts: 3,497
I really enjoyed it and liked seeing all the characters again. Pretty obvious Adam will end up having something with his landlady, as she is also a bit like Rachel, and i [sic] don't see the point of her being introduced otherwise. Loved seeing Pete and Jenny again.

(http://forums.digitalspy.co.uk)

'Chiltons Cane', a regular poster on Digital Spy 'loves seeing Pete and Jenny again', despite feeling the storyline is replicated. His memory of these characters appears to be the main draw in terms of his enjoyment of the programme. Cold Feet becomes a perfect case study in this sense for Hills and Garde-Hansen's (2017) explanation of 'paratextual memory'.

They define the term in part by thinking about how 'paratextual memory commemorates a favoured TV programme [and] potentially maintains an "authentic" fan self-narrative in terms of "having been there" at times of broadcast'. In the case of *Cold Feet* one of the overriding reasons viewers seem to enjoy the programme is based on their memories of the characters and their memories of watching the original series. One of the mothers interviewed in the last chapter happened to discuss watching the new series of *Cold Feet* and expresses similar reasons for her enjoyment:

JR So we watched *Cold Feet* at university and it was brilliant, and that was like an appointment viewing, we'd all sit down together all the girls I lived with and watch *Cold Feet*.

KG And you're really enjoying it now?

JR Yes.

KG What do you enjoy about it?

JR I've just always liked the characters in it and it's just good to see them you know, when you feel like you've kind of grown up with people in your, I mean they're older they're probably about ten years older than us aren't they but you still feel a bit like you've grown up with them and you can understand a bit about what they're going through with children, and it's still funny, I think, I still think they've got the good same humour in it.

(interview with Julie 8 October 2016)

Julie remembers both the context for her memories (watching with friends at university), which constructs a sense of 'having been there' at the time of the first broadcast, and is also commemorating the series through the affection she has for the characters. She feels a sense in which they have 'grown up with her' and face similar issues to the ones she faces in the present. There is a sense of affection, for the characters and for the time in which she first watched the series, which makes the programme feel significant and enjoyable. In this sense, it is precisely the 'echo of personal experience' that draws her into the text and creates an affectionate attachment.

In his blog about the reboot of *Cold Feet* in *Critical Studies in Television Online*, Tom Nicholls finds the series can offer 'a welcome break from our daily routines whilst also reflecting upon them' (2017). He recalls preparing himself for the new series fully anticipating that it would be a failure, and yet finding himself drawn in by the 'magic' of the characters and their interactions. Nicholls argues that 'comfort telly', like *Cold Feet* 'might be more complex than it first looks' particularly in terms of the way it invites viewers to question what it is that is drawing them back into the fictional worlds of the rebooted series (Nicholls 2017). His analysis chimes with the ways in which the above fans and viewers have considered what it is they liked or didn't like about the reboot. Fundamentally, as Nicholls suggests, part of what they enjoy is the reflection on what it is about the return they like. They take pleasure in the remembering and the nostalgia from their first encounter. As Julie remarks, 'it's just good to see them, you know'.

It Was Alright in the 70s (Channel 4 2014)

Using 'old' characters and storylines is one way in which past television is valued and used – it is also something that we inherit in terms of remembering the past and how we use it. Another popular form of recycling is the use of past television in archive-based programming. Old clips are used to remind us of a particular time and commentators are brought in to comment on their personal reflections both of their experience of watching the programme (or not, as is the case in some formats) and of how they see this as part of their television inheritance.[5] This reshowing of British television in order to produce shock, disgust, confusion, bafflement and superiority to past shows is also a current online trend (which we shall return to at the end of this chapter), which migrates from television to YouTube and back again, connecting with old and new audiences, national and transnational.

Here TV functions to remind us of the past but also to tell us something about the present moment (how advanced we are, what better programming we have, how different we are from our parents' generation, what we had to put up with in a time of spectrum scarcity). The curation in these programmes also reminds us of what is valued. In many cases, what is remembered is the popular, the things we enjoyed and laughed at, rather than the political. As Mark Helsby comments:

> But about 12 years ago there was a big push on archive and we made three series of what became known as the 'I Loves', I worked on *I Love 1975*, *I Love 1981* and *I Love 1997* but we made *I Love 1997* in the year 2000, so it wasn't exactly a tricky thing to ask people, 'Can you just think back 3 years, what did you think about?' whatever it was, 'Melinda Messenger becoming famous?' So they were a mixture of, basically it was all pop culture archive so nothing news. The very first programme of *I Love 1970* had a very big chunk in it about Vietnam originally, and that got dropped by the Exec quite near to transmission. But that shifted the whole focus of the series so it was TV, film, books, fashion, a little bit of sport but not too much, even daft things like sweets and food and things like that, basically anything.
>
> (interview with Mark Helsby 24 June 2014)

In Helsby's memories of producing the *I Love* series, he talks about the 'sea change' that happened in this kind of archival based programming. According to Helsby, there was a shift away from more serious and political topics to those that focused on popular culture. Holdsworth makes reference to these programmes in her analysis of nostalgia and television and questions whether 'the repurposing of the television archive through these nostalgic forms means we are simply

---

[5]Lisa Kerrigan (2015) in '"Plundering" the Archive and the Recurring Joys of Television' analyses a 1960s programme devoted to clips from the archive, evidencing a longer history of this nostalgic viewing. Inevitably, the programme ran out of archival material.

being marketed the same commercially viable memories, reproducing a narrow view of both television's own and wider social and cultural history' (2011, 101). As both Helsby and Holdsworth point towards, there is a narrowing of how the archival work is used, and this might be, in part, a reaction to how it is enjoyed and received. Audiences like to remember the 'good' things – as Helsby points out, the 'daft things like sweets and food'. In our research in the last chapter we found that many respondents remembered the food and where they sat during the programming as well as how they felt, which was mostly framed by nostalgia. For this reason, it makes sense then that what is on air matches that cosy and acceptable form of remembering. For example, in the Introduction to *I Love 1981* (BBC Two, 2001), the presenter says: 'time to immerse ourselves in nostalgia. 20 years just melts away now on BBC2'. The 'melts' refers to the way in which we just let it gloss over us and makes reference to chocolate – to simple pleasures in life.

The 1970s is a good decade to focus on given Kompare's claim that this is also when television starts to earn its street credibility. One of the popular formats for the recycling of past television and making use of the archives (as Helsby points out) is in the return to old television mediated through the people who made it, watched it and who weren't alive at the time. The programme, *It Was Alright in the …* (Channel 4, 2014) selects these groups to allow for a number of vantage points that the audience can align itself with as some will remember these programmes from watching them the first time, and many will be watching them for the first time and 'learning' about the past through them. For most viewers, these programmes are all about nostalgia. Using clips from old series and inviting people to comment on them elicits 'trips down memory lane' and encourages viewers to consider what they think of the programmes (if they haven't seen them already), what they thought of them at the time (if they did see them) and what they think of them in the context of their lives now (is life better or worse than it was?). These prompts construct a nostalgic mode of viewing. We are encouraged to think about the past and our relation to it *through* television. Indeed, television is the central focus through which our memories flow and are mediated. The commentators are there to facilitate these memories and to align us with particular viewpoints. For example, the episode titled 'Getting it all in the 70s' (*It Was Alright in the 70s* [Channel 4, 2014]), focuses on the struggle for women's equality in the 1970s. The episode begins with archival footage from the 6 March 1971 women's liberation march in London with a voiceover narration (by Matt Lucas), which tells viewers that:

> In a decade were accepted values were being challenged across the board, the first downtrodden group to demand their rights were not a minority, they were the ample body of women who made up a whacking 54% of the population [...] After years of protest and descent, by 1975 change was finally on the cards, and on the 29th of December, the Sex Discrimination Act became Law.
>
> (*It Was Alright in the 70s* 2014)

The episode cuts to the opening of a BBC Two programme entitled, *Women – Which Way Now* (1975). The camera zooms in for a close up of a cake made of female figures in various 'occupations' – there is a female figure dressed in robes, one in overalls, one in a gown, but most are exposing their breasts and one figure is completely naked except a hat and high, black boots. As Lucas goes on to say: 'Of course TV didn't want to miss the party, so the BBC commissioned a sort of cake made of ladies and a studio discussion show, surely fronted by one of the UK's outstanding female broadcasters, Joan Bakewell, Anna Ford … Oh, hello Mr Kennedy.' Lucas's ironic comment of 'hello Mr Kennedy', underscores the fact that a man has been asked to present a programme on women's liberation despite the 'outstanding' female broadcasters that might have been considered for the job. Mr Kennedy begins the programme by stating: 'For thousands of years, man has regarded woman as a thing apart: remote, mysterious, contrary, unpredictable, goddess and bitch'. The programme cuts from the clip to the reactions of two female commentators who both looked shocked and horrified. 'But is man going to lose something by women gaining equality and, are perhaps women going to lose something too.'

We have discussed the opening sequence at length because it works to establish the 'mood' of the piece through the narration, the close-up shots of reactions from present day viewers and the archive footage which has been set up to be 'vintage', 'outdated' and a relic of its time. All of this happens within the first two minutes of the programme and sets up a nostalgic look at the 1970s in terms of women's liberation. Cutting to the reactions of female commentators who were both 'big in the 70s' and 'not around in the 70s' means that the audience can take their pick at who they want to identify with, however, ideologically everyone is saying the same thing – that this sort of thinking is very out dated and it is very hard to believe it happened. And yet, there is very little reflection of what is happening now and the proximity of those injustices to the ones on their screens. So the past always remains the past as an object to study and ridicule, and primarily to laugh at. As viewers are aligned with the commentators and with the view that this sort of silliness was something that only took place in the 1970s and, fortunately, is not something reflected on our screens or in our lives today.

One of the problems with this mode of address is the false sense of inheritance it sets up. There is an implicit address here to those watching in the 'now' that we have inherited the mistakes of the past and rectified them, when statistics and feminist television analysis today would caution against such optimism. We have moved on from the 1970s of course, but to what extent is this left unanswered and unaddressed to make the show more comforting and entertaining (and less political). Even though archival material from political movements begin these episodes, the political of the struggle for women's liberation is very much left out.

As discussed in the last chapter, both of us were young children in the 1970s and only vaguely recall the television in this series. But we know as feminist television scholars the implicit critique that is offered here. Although, there is a brief reference to actual political movements, showing examples of explicit misogyny on television reminds the viewer of today how *real* the sexism was and continues to be. Indeed, couching this within a popular format and with 'daft things like sweets and food' means that people will watch this, consume the tacit message of 'you've come a long way, baby' used by Virginia Slims Cigarettes in the 1970s to market to women, and not much more.

To this end, the *It Was Alright …* series references the *now nostalgia* defined in the Introduction. As discussed, the series recirculates *old TV* as lost–found, a quest-puzzle-jigsaw, as just tucked away but *now* easily accessible, reusable and reworkable by the various 'expert' viewers in the series and by viewers at home. *Old TV* is recuperated as a 'black box' showing us what went wrong in the 1970s as a means of testifying to progress that has been (or has not been made) in the *now*. But this recuperation is uncritical and used in a way that allows it to be seen as something easily consumed and forgotten and ultimately 'alright' as the title suggests. Indeed, there is an erasure that happens despite the shocked and horrified reactions.

Reminisce This

As a means of concluding this chapter, we explore the repurposing of television's paratexts and the nostalgia for past television online through sites such as Reminisce This (2018), TV Cream (n.d.) and Nostalgia Central (2018). Reminisce This: A Very British Nostalgia Site contains 'memories and images' from 1940 to 1999 with the idea to 'get you reminiscing and maybe even chatting about all things nostalgic'. The site is indexed by decade, 'reminiscences', external links and community – where people are encouraged to share their memories and read other peoples' reminiscences. Each decade tab contains an introduction and icons section to help remind or familiarize visitors with key socio-historical moments. For instance, in the 1970s tab images and moments such as 'James Hunt', 'The Winter of Discontent' and the 'Concorde' are listed and described briefly. The 'Reminiscences' section has two names listed 'Billy' and 'Bob'. These are personal reminiscences, presumably from the site owners. These reminiscences are very lengthy and include ten 'chapters' in Bob's and twenty-three in Billy's. In 'Bob's' reminiscences there is a chapter titled 'Family Viewing (My granddad, dad and me)' which recounts the experiences Bob had watching television at his grandad's house as a child. In fact, Bob's 'Black Country memories' begin with him watching television and being startled at the presenter's framing of the 1950s as 'the middle of the last century' which for him felt like 'a sucker punch to the stomach'. He explains that it felt to him as though the presenter was making it sound like the 1950s were not far off the great Ice Age. He uses this as a prompt to reminisce about his life and the first instalment concerns their family viewing. According to Bob, his grandad had a TV set 'made by the company Bush. It was a rectangular box which stood three foot six inches high and had two controls, volume and brightness'. In contrast, his Dad 'was at the cutting edge of this now expanding media. Our set, although still black and white, had a 21-inch screen but was still only capable of receiving BBC.' He goes on to recount how his Dad could install a 'gizmo' that allowed them to also get ITV. Soon after this, his father rented a set from Radio Rentals which meant they had a colour telly. He explains that when his Dad offered to get the same for his grandad he refused the offer and said: '"When I watch the telly I don't want to see it in colour. I want it to look real!"' (Edwards 2018).

In this example, television mediates the memories and lives of those remembering. And in this case, Bob's childhood memories are solely focused on the technology and materiality of television: his father's 'cutting edge' relationship to technology versus his grandfather's resistance to change and a sense of losing the 'real' of what he has known. There is also a sense here of how television can be the very thing to evoke powerful memories or feelings, in this case, a 'sucker punch' when Bob realized he was being called 'old' by the presenter, and how these feelings can trigger a narrative about one's life.

TV Cream and Nostalgia Central are less personal and more driven by a sense of a 'golden age' of television. They are focused on the programmes and content though also include information on the socio-historical background of particular decades and spaces for people to comment and blog. For example, TV Cream highlights *The Wednesday Play* (BBC One, 1964–70), *Play for Today* (BBC One, 1970–84) and *Nationwide* (BBC One, 1969–83) amongst its main categories which emphasize the role these programmes are seen to have played within British television history. It also has a section on 'Saturday mornings' that charts 'the rise and fall' of children's programming from 1968 to the present. The notion that there has been a 'fall' in Saturday morning programming implies a kind of nostalgia for 'the way things were' as though past television was infinitely better and not as much of a 'factory' as today. This notion of television as a factory, thoughtlessly churning out content, chimes with work in the last chapter, where many posters felt that children's programming in the past was better than it is now and that was part of their motivation in showing past television to their children: to give them something that was not available today. It also echoes our television producers who speak of the supermarket shelf of television creativity.

Nostalgia Central categorizes television by decades and includes short histories of each socio-historical moment along with a list of the 'most watched television' of each decade with the viewing figures. One of the most interesting things about all this is the amount of television images that propagate the sites. There are a lot of images of 'old' televisions and of people watching old television.

In the sites discussed, nostalgia is used to categorize past television and to organize it into things that are worth watching (and therefore archiving, valuing, remembering) and things that are not. Each website has an implicit criterion it has used to organize its archive of past television, but none post this or make this an explicit part of the website. Although these sites appear to be more about remembrance as opposed to memory – some, like Reminisce This use personal experience as a way of explaining the importance of past television. The form of remembrance offered in the sites encourages a sense of participation in collective remembering. The interactive nature of the websites facilitates an active form of remembrance that encourages users to seek out other examples. In this sense, they might offer a kind of 'travelling' of memory, as discussed in Chapter 5, where users will remember a programme and then go to YouTube or similar sites to watch more of a programme or to post a link to friends or family to engage their memories.

Paratextual memory, as defined by Hills and Garde-Hansen (2017), works in different ways within this chapter but the personal is often the register for memory, and the idea is for the viewer to be moved by paratexts to reconnect with the renewed text and the memory to move the viewer to connect with other viewers' shared memories of the same textuality or period of television. Whether it is a memory of the first broadcast and then a re-engagement with the affection viewers have for the characters, or a reworking of the *now nostalgia* through past texts, or an active participation in online archives, we find that personal memory functions to drive audience development through paratextual memory. This complicates the linear notion of the paratext coming before the text, preparing the audience. As Hills and Garde-Hansen (2017) have argued in relation to the return of missing *Doctor Who* episodes (see Wallace 2013) to the United Kingdom from Nigeria:

> While it remains possible that copies of missing *Who* episodes may have been retained in countries that the programme was distributed to across its history (particularly Africa), to recover these would not simply be to reclaim 'original' texts, but rather to create new paratextual memories of contemporary restoration, (re)commodification and repatriation.
>
> (Hills and Garde-Hansen 2017, 160)

Filling in the gaps in the archive with paratextual memory (by fans, audiences, showrunners or new creative industries such as animation and online video editing), or showing old clips and programmes of British television on YouTube are becoming ways of reworking the text (and its legal constraints) to test rerunability and create new pleasures. As Ellis argues of 'fragments of texts':

> Shots, sequences sounds and lines of dialogue can be used for all kinds of purposes beyond their original textual context. Digital availabilities have intensified this process as it is much easier to retrieve archival material and to reincorporate the desired fragments into a new text.
>
> (Ellis 2014)

An emerging trend is to blend those clips with narrative commentary, framed by discourses of Britishness versus non-Britishness. In *Gogglebox*-style we can, for example, view online two, three or four young Americans watching a British show for the first time on their laptop while the back of the laptop (facing the online viewer) screens to us what they are seeing. For example, BuzzFeedVideo's 2015

FIGURE 4 Screen grab of 'Americans Watch Father Ted for the First Time' (BuzzFeedVideo 2015). The still captures the affective moment of 'shock' at the opening title sequence in which Father Jack is pushed over in his wheelchair.

upload 'Americans Watch *Father Ted* for the First Time' (currently at 1million+ views) is screen-grabbed in Figure 4 at the point in the opening title sequence in which Father Jack is pushed over in his wheelchair, this is one of many points in this video that young Americans are captured as shocked, puzzled and bemused.

The clips and critique may stretch the boundaries of 'fair use', but the videos serve a double purpose of re-pleasure for British audiences and new discomfort/ pleasure for the young Americans in their transcultural struggle over meaning with the original text, which they often see as simultaneously *out of date* yet *ahead of its time*.

Such online videos offer a compilation of the 'best bits' not only for our re-pleasure but our new pleasure (if this comedy it part of our inheritance) is to observe its cultural transferability in order to reinscribe national differences. It signals a future transnational memory television format and it works well for YouTubers who want to rewatch with the added dimension of watching others watch for the first time. For example, a young British stand-up comedian Matthew Thomas, residing in New York, currently (at the time of writing) has a YouTube channel in which his most viewed videos are 'Americans watching British TV: *Keeping up Appearances*', 'Americans watching British TV: *Bottom*', 'Americans watching British TV: *Shooting Stars*' (views in the 100,000s compared to the 100s for his own stand-up routine videos). It is the difference between past British television comedy (the shows the video maker has inherited) and Americans (of the same age) who may or may not *get it* that creates a new pleasure and a paratextual memory of television as inheritable and travelling. *Old TV* clips become a way of passing on the cultural heritage of 'collective memory' of British eccentricity, class and subcultural style to young Americans who can take new kinds of pleasure in the post-broadcast afterlife. This is only possible, though, with the curatorial voiceover and explanation of the video maker who has created what Abigail De Kosnik (2016) would call 'rogue archives' or, as we shall explore in the final chapter, regenerative television memory through fancraft.

7 REGENERATIVE TELEVISION MEMORY?: CRAFTING *DOCTOR WHO*

In Chapter 4 we discussed the role of the museum for *old TV*, where we sought to understand the challenges around storage, preservation and exhibition as articulated by senior staff in the museum, some of whom were made redundant or moved on during the period of research interviewing. The discourses of legacy and cultural inheritance they articulated may seem to be simply discourses carried by them as workers, especially when television's 'heritage' changes so fast. The precarity of material objects of *old TV* (their relevance to the museum at present) says as much about the sustainability of the medium of the museum for re-encountering media histories as it does about television's inheritability. Notably, in the middle of writing this chapter, any fixed, locatedness we could have referred to, to support an exploration of *Doctor Who* (*DW*) as regenerating interest in the city of Cardiff, for example, was met with the news that the Doctor Who Experience in the city was also to close (see Prince 2016) much to the disappointment of fans.

Nevertheless, before the National Media Museum's exhibitions (NMeM) of television came to an end, there was a significant TV anniversary to commemorate, not so much the television text itself but fifty years of *DW* fandom in the free exhibition *Doctor Who and Me* (see Figure 5).

Here the museum appeared to extol a new role that chimes with Orhan Pamuk's words, the 'aim of present and future museums must not be to represent the state, but to re-create the world of single human beings [...] The future of museums is inside our own homes' (Pamuk 2009, 56–7). It makes sense then to explore in this chapter, not television in the public space of the museum as Maeve Connolly (2014) does so well, but the museum in the private space of television viewing: the domestic sphere of the home and human relationships. In this chapter the museum turns itself and fandom inside out, handing over some curatorial power to fans and audiences, displaying objects from donors and amateur creatives, to explore not only the curiosity cabinet of fandom but the cultural and creative work of their love for television. The museum curator's role is (put simply) to know what the museum has, where it is and what it means (to the museum and to other stakeholders). But what if a museum crafts an exhibition of television based on

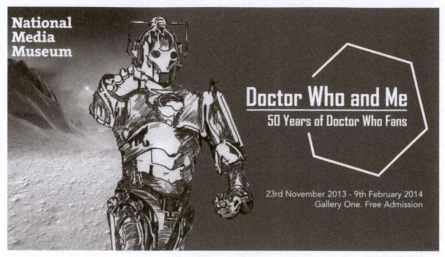

FIGURE 5 Poster for *Doctor Who and Me: 50 Years of Doctor Who*, 2013. (Reproduced with permission.)

material objects that it does not have or necessarily knows where they are, and once/if they are found (or rather they find the museum), their meaning will be determined by the public?

A museum is a public place where public recollection can take place. Connolly notes in her book *TV Museum* that we find 'the different ways in which publicness might be temporarily manifested – or contested – through practices of remembering [...] because practices of remembering television may be linked to everyday habits and routines' (Connolly 2014, 152). The challenge for any museum seeking to engage (not with artists who use television as in Connolly's study) but with members of the public who have both ordinary and extraordinary relationships with TV, is that market forces, commodification and consumer culture are integral to these everyday habits and routines. *DW*, for example, is both commercially valuable to the BBC and personally valuable to the public that has paid the licence fee. It is also valuable in another way, through craft and the real time and labour involved in demonstrating devotion.[1] What, then, is the role of the museum for regenerating *old TV* as everyday habits and routines, for exploring television's afterlife as lived and worked? One role is to create a public space in which love, affection, care and community can be understood from the perspective of the fan, the audience, the visitor rather than the broadcaster, curator or elite persons. Some may consider this nostalgia rather than history but we may also need to rethink what we mean by nostalgia when the medium of the museum re-collects (material) memories of the medium of *old TV*.

---

[1] This devotion may be of academics or aca-fans whose own participation in projects of television as heritage is through 'a range of unpaid, performative, and sacrificial labour as part of their implication in the cultures of reward and success in the workplace' (Gregg 2009, 209).

In this chapter, we add to the scholarship on *DW* through a memory studies approach by locating television's afterlife, not in the increasing mobility, transferability and scalability of transmedia platforms, complex producer-fan relationships and participatory social media cultures, but in the personal and amateur creativity curated and exhibited by the NMeM in 2013. We turn our attention to a memory institution whose primary purpose during the exhibition was to explore, understand and showcase fan devotion through both exceptional and mundane memories, memorabilia and handcrafted materials. The production of the *Doctor Who and Me* exhibition began with the personal, emotional and ordinary to invert the expert-lay knowledge relationship integral to museological practice. This was a quite explicit cultural policy of memory played out on the wave of corporate celebration of the *DW* brand and commemorative events. Yet, the NMeM's approach targeted those both inside and beyond *DW* fandom (see Wolf 2012), those who fell into the category of 'and Me', creating a space for whoever that 'me' claimed to be.

In what follows we draw on reflective interview material from the museum and other stakeholders, as well as a dossier of pre-exhibition material kindly supplied to us by the NMeM for our case study. This material reveals how they prepared – commissioning a creative design team – engaged fans and promoted the exhibition. The dossier consisted of a selection of documents, presentations, audience recordings and videos all compiled in 2013 for the purposes of research, writing copy, instructing front of house staff and work on the exhibition itself. Part of this dossier contains images, specs and costs for the extensive exhibition design work undertaken by PLB Projects Limited. What we hope to interrogate in this chapter are the different scales and sectors of *cultural memory (as) work* (amateur and professional) that converged upon *DW*. This is as much about letting the market or corporate memory determine what is an asset as it is about the public service to storytelling and the intangible heritage this creates. The museum mediates the memorability of *DW*, temporarily bringing inside, for public understanding, those memories that the museum considers valuable to attract a wider audience. This is not a welfare service, not every artefact is valuable to the museum, time cannot be spent listening to every story. The choices the museum makes curates memories into assets.

Fans in the museum

We already know from fan studies that memory and affect are fundamental to the initial devotion to the text, even if, in the case of *DW*, that devotion can turn to anti-fandom if the text deviates (see the history of the *Doctor Who* Appreciation Society, DWAS 2011/2018). In *Textual Poachers: Television Fans and Participatory Culture* (1992) Henry Jenkins presented fandom in terms of love and recounted the fable of *The Velveteen Rabbit* to describe the tension between Adorno's account of how culture is commodified and the fan who makes culture meaningful through loving memories and memories of loving:

Seen from the perspective of the toymaker, who has an interest in preserving the stuffed animal as it was made, the Velveteen Rabbit's loose joints and missing eyes represent vandalism [...] yet for the boy, they are the traces of fondly remembered experiences, evidence of his having held the toy too close and pet it too often, in short, marks of its loving use.

(Jenkins 1992, 51)

This starting point to fan studies gets a little lost in the later research of fans as consumers: 'media fans resemble ideal brand consumers, they snap up the latest thing, buy extra merchandise, participate in promotions, join official fan clubs and build collections' (Daniel Cavicchi *Tramps Like Us: Music and Meaning Among Springsteen Fans* [1998] cited in Duffett 2013, 21). On the one hand, this creates markets that extend the text's reach, thus 'commodification, which is at the heart of mass cultural representations, makes images and narratives widely available to people who live in different places and come from different backgrounds, races, and classes' (Landsberg 2004, 21). On the other hand, this commodification of texts and paratexts joins consumers (fans, non-fans and anti-fans) through shareable remembering and forgetting of the text's impact. Gunkel (2016) calls this 'remixology'[2] but it is a remix culturally constructed and mediated as 'prosthetic memories' (you may not have experienced the text but you can do so through the objects), and Landsberg would argue this would 'produce empathy' and a 'sensuous engagement with the past' (2004, 21).[3] This sensuality is captured in the official press release of 2013, in which the NMeM announces that it 'will explore people's devotion to *Doctor Who* – what the programme means to the fans, what makes a fan, and how they demonstrate their affection'. Their methodology for answering these interesting questions is to appeal for "collectibles and souvenirs" and "people who have interesting stories relating to the programme". In case the public is unclear on the parameters, the curator explains more demonstrating a clear awareness of *DW* fan objects:

Do you have a *Doctor Who* chess set? Ever knitted your own Dalek? Have you still got that Cyberman helmet in the attic? If so, these are exactly the kind of objects that might go towards creating this new exhibition. We would like to use examples of *Doctor Who* memorabilia from the past fifty years – both official merchandise and more personal homemade objects – the kind of things which show a fan's love for the Doctor. We want to know why you have this object, when you got it, and your feelings towards *Doctor Who* then and now.

(press release 8 July 2013, available from the NMeM Press Office)

---

[2]Remix is 'a kind of archival effort to preserve the memory of something that could be lost to the dustbins of history by reanimating in one's appreciation for the original and even creating new markets for the source material and the artists who created it. Remix, then, can be situated as another mode of cultural memory' (Gunkel 2016, 50).
[3]See the exploits of Fangirl Quest (n.d.) in Cardiff and other locations.

While fans are encouraged by the NMeM 'to help shape this exhibition, which will be highlighting the people who watch the show' (press release 8 July 2013), it is clear such a call or trawl for memories must be strategically aligned to the core mission of the museum.

Described by the museum as 'connoisseurs' or rather 'Connoisseur Max', fan memories and memory objects need to speak a museological language, with a 'love of the subject' that is the difference between 'enthusiasm and volunteering' states Paul Goodman (former head of collections, NMeM, interview 5 October 2014). It is worth quoting Goodman at length to highlight the multidirectional and institutional discourses of memory as story, work, feeling, cultural value and information asset, as he reflects upon the exhibition the following year:

> We have to make sure that we harvest the information that they're bringing to us for wider public consumption benefit. Not listening to them because they have a story to tell and they get excited and that's all there is to it. We haven't got time or it's not our remit and it's not our role to sit there in a room with one of them and allow them to tell you all the stories of *Doctor Who* […] So for us it's kind of what value is the information you've given to us which we can use to spit out to a wider audience then, and that again is hugely important. So again it's about harnessing that information. And fans, general members of the public. It goes back to something I said before, everybody has a story to tell. Though I think those stories can be superficial, they can be social, they can be political, they can be cultural, they can be humorous, they can be intense, they can be light touch. So you know I think stories, everybody has a story to tell and it is our duty to listen to those stories and make a reasoned, professional and intellectual judgement about the value of those stories and the value of capturing those stories for future benefit.
>
> (interview with Paul Goodman 5 October 2014)

In rest of this chapter we explore this context of mixed values being attached to TV memories, to explore how fan memorability is channelled by the museum as a new form of cultural work, both for the museum and its staff, the materialization of the objects on display, and through a mode of address that is suffused with notions of 'craft' and domestic/personal industry.

On message memories: 'I love *Doctor Who* because …'

In *Triumph of a Time-Lord: Regenerating Doctor Who in the 21st Century* (2010), Hills makes the important point that the BBC's 2005 regeneration of the text (a text whose longevity has been facilitated by the repeated renewal of 'the Doctor') creates a retooled character for serious critique. This *NüWho* can reference historical and literary figures as well as contemporary politics, thus ensuring the television text is rendered as 'an appropriate object of study' (2010, 2). Starting from Cooke's (2015, 243) claim that this is the most written about programme on British television, Hills adds to any scholarly excess in *Doctor Who: The Unfolding Event* (2015) by incorporating critical analysis of branding, marketing, merchandising and the mediatization of a television anniversary.

> Media/brand anniversaries have grown in cultural density and popularity, I would ultimately hazard, due to their over-determination: they can temporarily hold together commerce and culture, past and future, industrial template and branded uniqueness, individual and nation, live aura and mediatization, commodity and souvenir, and nostalgia and relevance.
>
> (Hills 2015, 107)

DW has not only regenerated itself and its fandom but has retooled scholarly and aca-fan (academic-fan) attention into new domains of global media business strategy and old domains of encoding/decoding theory (see Powers 2016). Hills's excellent book on the 2013 fiftieth anniversary of *DW* unpacks this well executed, sophisticated and scalable brand strategy as circulated and recirculated through discourses of invention, reinvention, generation and regeneration (see Tony Hall 'The Man in Charge' [2013], *Radio Times* 23–29 November, pp. 28–9, the BBC director general, cited in Hills 2015, 7).

The NMeM sought to extend this commemorative project by focusing on 'love' and the domestic sphere. This was effectively articulated as a devotional and emotional digital story trailer for the exhibition using still images of the objects on display and over twenty interviewees' voices ranging from older people to children, including men and women (although all seemingly British, with Northern accents most prominent). The recorded interviews the NMeM had undertaken to understand fandom were primarily important for this promotional material around answering the question: 'I love Doctor Who because …'. The trailer (NSMM 2013a) was followed by four 4–5 minute edited face-to-face interviews with male super-fans (Colin Young, Tim Neal, David Howe and David Knill) who have followed the television series for forty or more years, have been avid collectors and cross-reference each other in their interviews. While the voices of the trailer are overlaid until they became a heterogeneous chorus of declarations of love suggesting a multi-perspectival narrative, the four superfan interviews demonstrate deeper devotion as a committed community of older British men. Nevertheless, the museum teases out from these male voices stories of care, addiction, love, nostalgia, emotional literacy and desire, rather than focusing on their knowledge.

These emotional memories conveyed through voice and object (as explored in a different way in Chapter 6 on children's TV) into a validated expression of *DW* fandom (and by extension the museum) as offering something for everyone, inclusive, intergenerational and a re-liveable experience of one's own life story. As the super fan David Knill states in a way that chimes with our own interview research on memories of TV carried forward through life:

It takes you back to childhood memories where you are sat at home with a potted meat sandwich, there's *Grandstand* (BBC, 1958–2007) finished, waiting for *Doctor Who* to start […] I've always wanted a full-sized Dalek from a child, it was one of those things where you think 'Ohhh, I'd love to have one of those' and I've finally got one.

(NSMM 2013b)

For an official media anniversary, memories of *DW* need to be *on message* (the 'rite of passage' of children's terror noted by Mumsnet discussions in Chapter 6; the marking of life story with this is 'my Doctor'; and the *in sync* fandom with the broadcaster's corporate memory). The NMeM exhibition is very briefly mentioned in Hills's (2015) account of the fiftieth 'anniversary party' in 'full swing', for 'Bradford's National Media Museum represented a rare case where commemorations actually began on the anniversary date' (Hills 2015, 84; see also the review of the exhibition by Wheeler (2014) for the DWAS). The trigger to commemorate is the birthday, and that birthday is made domestic, familiar and affective. While Hills (2015) covers much of the official branding of the anniversary, we would like to add that the regeneration of the doctor (to be repeated by subsequent white, male actors) offers an ongoing inheritance of British television (as repeated renewal) on two scales. Firstly, the vertical scale of the BBC's narrative of reinvention as a pioneering broadcaster, moving back through time as an organizational memory institution, (re)writing its own history in the present for global and strategic purposes (covered so well by Hills). Secondly, the horizontal scale of the personally remembered or deeply felt (at the time) engagement with 'my Doctor' or 'my favourite Doctor' (especially the early incarnations). These moments are reactivated by the museum in the present as four white British men demonstrating how they have consistently regenerated their own fandom through memory: collecting, canonization, memorabilia and sharing their stories as a community. What is interesting, is that the museum chooses also to represent a sense of infinitely increasing circles of fandom and outlying connection to the text, as *DW* becomes domesticated through hobbies such as painting, knitting (some of which might be defined as feminine) and modelling (may be defined as masculine), handcrafted replicas and other forms of amateur creativity, which are found around the world.

Amateur creativity and conspicuous memory

Fans have been defined as 'networkers, collectors, curators, producers and more' (Duffett 2013, 21) but beyond fandom, viewers are engaged in remembering *DW* as a creative act. 'Products of memory are first and foremost creative products, the provisional outcomes of confrontations between individual lives and culture at large' (Van Dijck 2007, 7). Thus, 'mediated memory' (Van Dijck 2007) comes nearer to understanding the mechanisms by which personal, social, cultural and collective memories become mediatized. More recently this 'media and memory' research (Garde-Hansen 2011) has explored the work of memory as creating new forms of memory work. Similarly, in the paper of 'Collecting comic books: A study of the fan and curatorial consumption', Jonathan David Tankel and Keith Murphy define curatorial consumption as the behaviour that individuals put social and psychological value into the process of products, and decide to save the values (Tankel and Murphy 1998).

According to its internal documents, the NMeM anniversary exhibition sought to understand not the broadcaster nor even the text, but its impact, as the internal front of house presentation conveyed to staff:

> Main Message: This exhibition will investigate the fan culture which has built up around *Doctor Who*, its varied themes, intensity and relationships. It will explore how the series provides focus and inspiration for sparking amazing creativity and unrivalled devotion.
> (PP for FoH Doctor Who and ME.ppt, supplied
> by the NMeM 16 June 2015)

How then to articulate that devotion and intensity, that creativity and those relationships? Firstly, using media (audio and video) to engage fans and collectors in an oral-history style interviewing, to produce content for the exhibition and its promotion (as detailed above). Secondly, by curating and exhibiting the amateur creativity of fans: paintings, homemade Cybermen and Daleks (of the seven Daleks on display only one was from the museum's collection), scrapbooks, knitted items (toys, clothing) and ornaments, alongside purchased and cared-for materials and ephemera: fanzines, convention programmes, the Target books, a minted coin from New Zealand, and a replica Tardis. As the museum's director explains to staff so they understand how these items should be valued differently:

> Some of the objects on show have cost up to £2000 to create, some cost very little apart from time and hard work – the embroidered shoes for example took three days to complete, the huge David Tennant portrait took 55 hours!
> (PP for FOH Doctor Who and ME.ppt, supplied
> by the NMeM 16 June 2015)

This celebration of cultural work (the shadow economy of fan labour) expresses devotion through number: cost but mostly time. We also see that the superfan collectors (mostly males in their forties) are joined by the amateur creativity expressed through knitting (mostly female, e.g. Lotta from Germany) and painting. There is then a potential gendering of 'superfans' and superfan voices that is left uncritically presented and performed in the exhibition design and the promotional videos online. In terms of whose fan memories are being mediated we find middle-aged white men whose voices already resonate with the superfan community alongside more hidden creative labour and craft of 'amateur' fans, (gendered female) and these memories are mediated by male staff working as curators, which again is not critically reflected upon because a 'fan' is neutrally gendered in the NMeM's curatorial strategy. Having said this, there is a certain trans-gendering of the fan for it is the 'love' and 'passion' for *DW* that the exhibition seeks to display as a spectacle of labour (sometimes gendered along traditional pathways but also day-lighted as a form of confessional performance of dedication and devotion).

The NMeM's engagement with past television as emotionally and corporeally sensuous is turned into cultural value such that the spreadability of television's memory beyond the museum, audience and fan begins to incorporate other creative industries. There is apparently much less need to mourn the distance between past television and our present lives when so much *old TV* can create so much cultural, collective and personal memory. The conspicuous creativity of fans, their amateur and hobbyist productivity, their use of eBay and fan networks to create economic value from *old TV* and its ephemera, alongside the new heritage and media agencies that assist in developing, designing and touring the regeneration of *old TV*, its artefacts and ephemera. The much loved and personally valuable souvenirs (that have fewer copyright implications) allow memory institutions to retrospectively rebuild the biographical relationship between past culture and 'the public', and contribute to a new economic circulation of marketable memories. Thus, 'nostalgia' is not just 'about the relationship between individual biography and the biography of groups or nations, between personal and collective memory' (Boym 2001, xvi) but it's a shadow economy that can be re-surfaced to create new and old ideas about popular culture. 'If fans', as Matt Hills argues, 'are the target consumers for new products and franchises, they are also niche markets that represent the residue of a culture first facilitated by mass marketing' (Hills 2002, 45, cited in Duffett 2013, 21). It is this residue that becomes the very treasured stuff of the *Doctor Who and Me* exhibition.

Furthermore, 'fans productivity is not limited to the production of new texts: it also participates in the construction of the original text and thus turns the commercial narrative or performance into popular culture' (Fiske 1992, 40), and thus fans become active producers of popular memory out of and for the benefit of the television heritage economy. The way in which the 'shadow cultural economy' of fans (30) is brought into the value systems of the museum, as it seeks new methods of public engagement, demonstrates that fan memory studies has a great deal to offer cultural memory policy in action. The *Doctor Who and Me* exhibition not only operates at the personal, local and emotional scale but through the employment of paid and unpaid stakeholders who operate across scales of national (Science Museum Group), cultural (BBC and BFI) and organizational memory (from appreciation societies to heritage industries), wherein memory is viewed as a resource within the regenerative milieu of the regional city. To reframe television's history and textuality as paratextual performativity and memory work is to ensure *old TV* is made valuable to different kinds of stakeholders, not just broadcasters and fans. In what follows, we wish to emphasize the new heritage entrepreneurs and strategists that assisted the NMeM in turning memories of *DW* into cultural heritage assets that may say more about the spreadability of a 'regenerative milieu' outside *Doctor Who* and into the creative industries more generally.

Doctor Who in a regenerative milieu

We are suggesting then (as an added dimension to Hills's comprehensive account of *DW's* commemoration) one more possibility for the explosion in mediated memory culture by broadcasters and media archives: we are living in *a regenerative milieu*. One in which the creative class (through partnerships with museums and memory institutions and agents) position memory, heritage and identity as the indices of audience development for regional-national-global success. While the creative class becomes more mobile, Richard Florida clearly explores how 'place and community are more critical factors than ever before' (2005, 29). Television memory travels and it is channelled by broadcasters and YouTube, but it also has a locatedness, the cultural and political economy of remembering television is centred on particular regions and memory work clusters. One of the authors of this book researched this point in depth with the case of purchasing and exhibiting the Dennis Potter Written Archive (see Garde-Hansen and Grist 2015).

In the case of *DW*, we would argue that the NMeM spotted that personal memories of television have a currency, and they can be put to work (crafted and re-crafted) for regenerative purposes and for a much wider range of stakeholders than the broadcaster-viewer-fan paradigm suggests. The non-interested can be brought into the heritage through appreciation of the work and effort of fandom, and this is made evident through the construction of a cultural heritage by new creative industries that enable the emergence of new kinds of cultural memory work. This work envelops non-fans through the conspicuous memory noted above wherein television travels outside itself and into new domains of memory and heritage management. Fans are, then, not simply part of a changing producer-user paradigm in terms of television's regenerative capacity, they are now the collectors, curators, archivists and exhibitors who are working directly with museums, on projects that connect across resource domains within a more general regenerative milieu. This accords with the recorded conversation between Hills and Jenkins concerning the recognition of the contradictory situation of recognizing 'fans-as-intellectuals' and the rejection of the aca-fan as too intellectual whose voice carries too much authority in fandom' (Jenkins 2006, 13–14). As poachers turn into gamekeepers (in this context, as interpreters/curators of museum collections), the role of the academic who is also a fan is brought into question.

Heritage strategists such as PLB Projects Ltd who were commissioned to design and deliver the exhibition are ostensibly a hidden memory agent in the production of *DW* as cultural heritage. Like the archive entrepreneur, Philip

Morris (described by Steve Bryant of the BFI as a 'mega-fan'; interview 19 March 2014) who recovers and re-patriates lost *DW* episodes (see Hills and Garde-Hansen 2017), PLB Projects Ltd emerges from increased funding flows in the direction of regenerative culture and memory. They are a full service agency covering everything from assisting organizations to writing funding applications, feasibility studies, planning activities, developing audiences, training, mentoring, design and delivery. Their creative director is described as 'an entrepreneur and heritage specialist who regularly presents seminars to promote best practice within the sector on engagement, innovation and sustainability in museums' (PLB Projects Ltd 2016). The business has a particular focus on Heritage Lottery Funded (HLF) projects, and according to the nineteen examples of their work on the company website ensuring successful HLF funding is a feature of much of their regeneration work, with some exhibitions (notably The Tank Museum, Dorset) bearing the hallmarks of the concept design for the *DW* exhibition. As museums and heritage advisors they celebrate the connectivity of their creative storytelling across divergent projects: 'What do Charles Dickens, taxidermy, tanks, steel and sand dunes have in common?'

We are grateful to the NMeM for supplying us with the complete concept design specifications produced by PLB Projects Ltd, a business whose focus is 'Creative Sustainable Heritage' and strapline is 'Interpreting the past, designing the future'. The twenty-six-page concept design document issued on 1 November 2013 (a few weeks before the anniversary date) offers an insight into how *old TV* is reimagined and regenerated for museum visitors through the selection and curation of fan collections and craft. The through-line of the visual design is groupings of hexagons or singular hexagonal shapes either as display cases, plinths, wall art, hexagonal cut-outs of dividing screens, shelves or object displays. This emphasis upon the hexagon does beg the question as to whether the design performs a mnemonic tactic by ensuring the exhibition visually appropriates the more on-brand materials, unofficial and fan versions of *DW* that were in existence?[4] The colour palette of Dulux paints is limited to shades of purple and green. The detailed design document, also supplied to us, reveals the work involved in producing this temporary exhibition, with its 'pop-up' feel, and begs the question of whether *old TV* is sustainable on the level of preservation, exhibition and resource use. As a fit for purpose range of MDF units, acrylic panels, paint, wallpaper, substrate prints, cut vinyl, Velcro and foamex are to be constructed alongside purchased furniture,

---

[4]It is not clear from all the documentation we received and the interview material whether BBC Worldwide had any involvement in the exhibition design and how wholly separate from official practices of brand management the exhibition was. In a discussion with Matt Hills he noted that the hexagons appear as non-branded graphics that are strongly reminiscent of on-brand style guides from *DW*'s BBC Wales' return. He stated in an email exchange with us that 'Merchandise from 2005 used hexagons in its packaging, and the form has also been extensively used in official *Who* exhibitions (harking back to TARDIS "roundels" in the 9th/10 Dr's TARDIS)' (pers. comm. 24 January 2017).

the overall impression is one of creating a new domestic sphere for TV fandom. The suggestion in the design document is that chairs and shelves be supplied by IKEA, with photos of the IKEA ranges to be used, and this substantiates our argument above that the museum was moving into the home, the place where TV is watched and loved, and not simply that TV was being brought into the museum.

In the overall plan of the exhibition (see Figure 6) we can see how the space is designed to focus on the objects on display, i.e. there is a Fans' Garden with a white picket fence enclosing the replica Tardis (referring to the provenance of this object located in a fan's backyard and bringing the domestic architecture of protection into the museum). Super fan objects have significant attention around the edges of the exhibition, as paintings, posters and displays of collections, and the Dalek display is encountered by walking through a replica Tardis door. The fan object display elevates knitted items and clothes, old toys, masks, bubble bath and embroidery, for example, to museum-validated artefacts (see Figure 7). Appearing as a very neatly arranged vintage store with only one theme (*Doctor Who*) the display succeeds in turning fandom into heritage and the museum into domestic life and amateur creativity.

The 'Timeline of *Doctor Who*' takes less prominence in this exhibition, this is after all about memory not history, and the timeline only offers eleven hexagons containing photographs of each of the doctors' faces. Overall, what is striking about the design of this exhibition is its fannish, hobby-ish, crafty look and feel with a

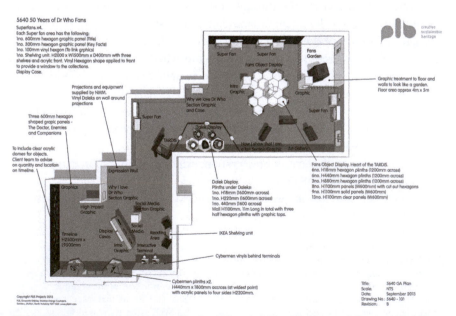

FIGURE 6 Concept design for *Doctor Who and Me: 50 Years of Doctor Who Fans*, 2013. (Reproduced with permission.)

FIGURE 7 Photograph of *Doctor Who and Me: 50 Years of Doctor Who Fans*. (Reproduced with permission.)

hint of boys' fantasy bedroom about the walls (i.e. oversized vinyl Cyberman and Dalek silhouettes are affixed).

Why might it be important for those researching television as cultural heritage to incorporate investigation of the other memory agents involved in the delivery of a public experience of television's past? Clearly, there is a deeper critical reading of the relationship between fan donors and museum staff to be undertaken, which we do not have the space in this book to more fully address. Museum curators are self-reflexively converting fan memories into vehicles for cultural and commercial value, and this has implications for fans and academics who seek to engage in impact with the public and interest groups. How fan voices, memories, stories, memorabilia and experiences are selected out of life story and community and co-opted by institutions (museums, archives, and universities) is perceived as a rather neutral act. The remembering fan, viewer or hobbyist is expected to be grateful, uncritical and yielding of their memories for exhibition and reuse, and fan craft itself is 'poached' by museum professionals to be turned into something 'valuable' with little critique of how that value is created and for whose benefit.

Moreover, heritage projects are outsourced to agencies and creative industries that work in a regenerative milieu across a range of industries and sectors and they carry their design and interpretative practices across from project to project as a form of organizational memory. This does not mean every exhibition space is designed in the same way, but it does mean that a certain 'off-the-shelf' memory work can be afforded by institutions on a budget, exemplified by PLB's DIY aesthetic and thrifty suggestions and images of IKEA furniture. This is non-elitist memory work, or flat-pack heritage at an affordable price, but also recognizable as requiring one's own labour (one's own remembering) and in accordance with the fannish hobbyism of the *DW* exhibition. In 'The "IKEA Effect": When Labor Leads to Love' (2011) Norton, Mochon and Ariely make a point that accords with our own argument in this book concerning television memory as a form of (DIY) work. Inheriting British television may be much harder than at first thought and this hard work can lead to overvaluation: 'labor enhances affection for its results. When people construct products themselves, from bookshelves to Build-a-Bears, they come to overvalue their (often poorly made) creations.' Furthermore, Norton, Mochon and Ariely show that 'labor increases valuation of completed products not just for consumers who profess an interest in "do-it-yourself" projects, but even for those who are relatively uninterested' (2011).

We have argued in this chapter that the museum and the public can work directly together to co-create popular cultural heritage in a way that exhibits Pickering and Keightley's 'interscalarity of memory' (2014), whereby personal, local, national and transnational memories are given a space for encounter and connection. However, this misses the role that hidden memory agents play in realizing the museum's policy, practice and vision and the public perception of television as heritage. These agents are trusted deliverers of public engagement projects and have a track record of regenerative culture and memory work through creative design and interpretative scripting. They are an important mediator of heritage, and while their designs are to meet the brief of the museum, we would argue that time-pressured museums with limited resources who wish to exhibit popular memory for a television anniversary are not going to deliberate too long and hard over this cultural heritage work.

In its encounter with *DW* fandom, the NMeM's own museal practice and discourse became upended as the presentation to staff (before the exhibition was launched) shows:

> With this exhibition, no matter how much time we spend researching, we're never going to match the knowledge of the fans so we're not going to try to. The exhibition will be led by the voice of the fans with as many direct quotes and references as possible.
>
> (PP for FOH Doctor Who and ME.ppt, supplied by the NMeM 16 June 2015)

Furthermore, the proliferation of paratexual memory and fan material suggests there was little need for academic consultants, broadcasters, historians, corporations, copyright holders and elite persons to construct the heritage. The documents supplied by the NMeM for analysis do state: 'There are several *Doctor Who* experts within NMeM & Science Museum Group some of whom are published authors on the subject and they are acting as content/curatorial advisors.' However, we do think it vital to ask critical questions about the role of the television historian in such new kinds of memory work, where a museum engages directly with the lay expert. *Doctor Who and Me*'s co-creation practice is fairly unique. Most museums and galleries cover the past of British television through a more formally researched chronological framing as 'a history of' (such as the permanent exhibition of 'Broadcast' at The Science Museum, London, or the touring *Story of Children's Television 1946 to Today*). Likewise, it may be framed around celebrated persons/characters such as the *BBC Faces of Comedy* (2016) or *Sherlock Holmes – The Man Who Never Lived and Will Never Die*. The NMeM exhibition clearly positioned enthusiastic and caring people at the beginning, middle and end of the process of curation (the fan, the museum worker, the visitor). 'So we've done some exhibitions,' recalls Michael Terwey of the NMeM in a 2016 interview,

> where we have been more explicitly participative or try to kind of work with audiences to create things. A lot of what we do doesn't fall into that kind of area, audiences come into the museum, they see something, they experience something, they kind of go away afterwards.
>
> (interview with Michael Terwey 22 June 2016)

Yet, he recalls in a reaffirming manner one example in which the museum worked 'with' the public: 'So the good example would be the *Doctor Who* exhibition because that was a kind of, yes, that was essentially co-curated with audiences' (interview with Michael Terwey 22 June 2016). This is the cultural inheritance of television that functions as inviting not so much a curation but a 'crafting' of memory through available resources.

Towards mo(nü)mental memories of *Doctor Who*

We can see Hills's thesis played out in miniature most clearly in yet another *Doctor Who* fiftieth anniversary, this time in 2016, to mark not the 'unfolding media event' of celebrating *Doctor Who*'s first episode (the focus of Hills's research) but the first 'renewal' of the doctor character (as actor William Hartnell is regenerated as actor Patrick Troughton on 29 October 1966, in the part-missing serial *The Tenth Planet*). *The Guardian* article 'The day *Doctor Who* changed face – and transformed TV for ever' offers the following commemorative anticipation of one single sequence of images (pictured after the headline); rendering them iconic for the many more viewers who never saw them at the time or since:

> Fifty years ago tomorrow, at 6:13pm, a unique moment in television history took place. A camera closed in on the face of an actor lying motionless on the floor. The image blurred, faded to white, then came back into focus, revealing that for the very first time, *Doctor Who* had changed his face.
>
> (Belam 2016)

Here we have the celebration of a *media moment*, that is both *old TV* and *nu TV* (the spelling of 'new' here referring to how DW fans define most incarnations of the doctor), a drilling down to the memorability *DW* finely balanced on a few moments of mostly lost footage. This should concern television historians, for 'television history' is being calibrated right down to an identifiable minute, to a short scene, that is never to be broadcast again (checked, verified, critiqued, seen in and of its time). This version of television history is important to interrogate because its industrial celebration segues nicely with the infilling of lost television memory by the new digital animations of the first Patrick Troughton episodes (we read as Nü-Classic-Who), to be released just a week after this article. Here, sequential art stands in for lost television in a way that animated chunks are being deployed across the BBC platforms of broadcasting more generally (particularly radio drama and documentary where there is no visual to support stories). This absence, deletion or failure to properly value and preserve *Doctor Who* episodes at the time (rewritten now as a necessary housekeeping and cost-reduction strategy of a prudent public service broadcaster) is both a shame and an opportunity. Surviving footage and photographs of *Doctor Who* are not simply treasured as artefactual and material traces by fans and academics, they are new (nü or nu) and valuable memory scaffolds, there to assist in the recapitalization of the text and the reanimation of dormant and new audiences. Holdsworth makes the same point in *Television*

Memory and Nostalgia (2011) concerning the delivery of a pre-existing audience in times of crisis. Thus, the BBC Store stated of *The Power of the Daleks* animation:

> Although the tapes were lost long ago, now, with the help of surviving photographs and footage, BBC Worldwide are delighted to announce that a brand new animation, accompanied by an original audio recording, will be released 50 years to the day after the story's original broadcast.
>
> (BBC Store Press Release [4 November 2016] cited on Television Heaven 2016)

Lost episodes create new opportunities to refresh and reboot. Even if they are 'lost' because, believes Mark Helsby, 'there was never that one person who'd say "no, I want to keep that, someone might want that in the future"' (interview with Mark Helsby 26 April 2016). They address the resilience during the drought in cultural resources from 1989 to 2005, and reanimate the active-creative remembering of *Classic Who* fans. Forgetting is reinstalled as a necessary part of TV heritage-making, as audiences (old and new) binge on box sets and re-engage in old merchandise. Forgotten is 'the active participatory *Doctor Who* fan culture' of the 1980s that 'had been turning its collective back on the show' (Powers 2016, 64) to become what Jonathan Gray describes as 'anti-fans' (2003). The 2013, fiftieth anniversary of *Doctor Who* (like all media events) was phatic for different generations and for different reasons (*you never forget your first doctor!*) and while it 'can never be all things to all people' it can 'surely succeed in being many things to many people' says Hills (2015, 108).

Anniversarisation of *DW* will continue as more moments, sequences and episodes are monumentalized and made memorable again. On the more recent anniversary noted above, a key aca-fan, Dene October noted on his website: 'I was seven-years-old the day William Hartnell recorded his last appearance [...] each [Doctor] will indeed regenerate but into something distinctly other than their current form. And this means a new Doctor ... for there is no disguising that this is the day *my* Doctor dies' (October 2016). A fitting metaphor for television itself ('the medium of the future' as defined in the 1950s by those establishing independent television), it is also a medium of repeated death, regeneration and reinvention. Television continues yet also creates fixed points for remembrance and commemoration as aspects of it disappear (sometimes lost forever such as *Doctor Who* episodes, sometimes rediscovered and re-patriated such as *Doctor Who* episodes). While Hayward and Fitzgerald (2013, 148) note that *Doctor Who*'s regenerative capacity as a television text exemplifies 'key aspects of the transitions that have occurred in the BBC's role' making it explainable through structural histories, Hills draws attention to those structures as new, national, global and commercial *administrations of corporate memory* by the BBC. 'It would seem that *anniversaries are present-oriented*: they celebrate the past, but only on the basis of its strategic value in and for the current moment. Anniversaries tell us about broadcasters' priorities as they stand now' (Hills 2015, 7).

What the NMeM's *Doctor Who and Me* offers, we have argued, is a different public space for television and a different television space for the public, exploring precisely the mourning-celebratory dialectic, where television is both '*just television*' as 'private affect' but also national and popular (Caughie 2010, 421). We have suggested that engagement with television (as producers, creatives and audiences) is a particular *kind of engagement* (private, affective, surprising, mundane, pleasurable and serious) that has not been lost at all. For one aca-fan the regeneration of the 1966 doctor is sensuous to the point of creating a multidirectionality of internalized, intergenerational re-readings. Remembering television is a form of time travel that helps reveal just what memory (in its creative remembering and strategic forgetting) means to our sense of self and life story:

> perhaps I have established the right for the small child in me to speak. But a word of caution. Set against this experiential agency is the admission that I'll be using my own time machine, which is not only to rely on memory with all its foibles, 'distortions' and 'misunderstandings', but also to speak hesitantly against the impressive volume of the anniversary party now in full swing. And partly, I admit, this hesitation is the adult mediator taking the young child aside and reflecting, perfectly reasonably, that Hartnell may well have saved *Doctor Who* by leaving when he did. Had he stayed, the part may indeed have remained his until the show was cancelled in – what?? – another year … another two? Not that my grief-stricken younger self wants to hear any of this.
>
> (October 2016)

In working through 'the changing configurations of subject and space' we have found television's paratextual memory and the spectacles of fan memory as key ways 'to identify the points at which the institution and its routines break open to other possibilities of meaning and engagement' (Caughie 2010, 421).

CONCLUSION: TELEVISION'S *MNEMONIC WARRIORS* – FROM MR GETTY TO ME

'Memory is *merely* one kind of evidential raw material for a historian, to be balanced against all other forms of evidence' (Ellis 2014,16; our emphasis). The 'merely' here may be seen to underplay 'memory' as only evidence. Memory research is risky. In order to capture the complexity and multidirectionality of studying the ongoingness (or loss and (re)discovery of) *old TV*, a critical memory studies approach does need to be taken seriously as a framework. Herein, remembering and forgetting television can be understood as much a process of belonging and life story as it is one of transnational and transcultural connections. 'Television', said Anna McCarthy speaking of its contemporaneity, 'looks very different, depending on whether one's level of analysis is the microlevel of the network's terminal point – the screen, a particular viewing subject or collectivity – or the standard, centralizing transmissions that appear on its face' (2001, 95). We have tried very hard not to 'choose to emphasize, or argue for, one level over the other when we invoke television' and its afterlife. To do so leads 'inevitably [to] a simplification, an artificial resolution of the dialectical tensions between the discrepant scales that comprise the phenomenal form of the medium' (95). Rather, we have chosen to evoke the 'phenomenal' of *old TV* through a critical memory studies approach that has sought to account for the 'scalar complexity' that 'can make writing about the medium's relation to places, bodies, and subjects a particularly difficult process' (95). We have sought to consider, with care and attention, the care and attention that others have given to *old TV*.

In so doing, we have opened avenues for the deeper exploration of what might be termed the activities of 'mnemonic warriors' (Bernhard and Kubik 2014)[1]

---

[1] Bernhard and Kubik (2014) use the term in the context of memory conflicts, memory regimes and the mnemonic field of politics. The 'mnemonic warrior' is a position an actor takes up when advantageous to do so, the same actor 'may find it advantageous to take a pluralist stand or to disengage from the politics of memory altogether'. Their work is useful for unpicking how in a democratic context, 'mnemonic warriors' who may 'have the advantage of setting the tone on mnemonic contests' are not able to inscribe a 'hegemonic memory regime' (2014, 18–19) but still have agency.

that might be operating within the afterlife of British television, who may or may not be dangerous to any sense of memory pluralism of fandom, audience diversity and the vernacular stories of those who care about TV, a pluralism that many TV scholars support and/or embellish. Such warriors are strengthened in certain (uncritical and nostalgic) conditions when they take stances or become compatible with a past of British TV as 'strong nation' TV creativity or 'national' texts. The danger is that they may miss or strategically forget both transnational connectivity and subnational or regional television memories. They may also miss the mundanity of everyday interaction. *As long as the television is ours it does not matter what kind of television memory we have,* would be a concerning position to give energy to, and should not go uncontested by critical memory studies.

To counter this, there is curatorial openness at work that invites scholars and the public to care about TV together, such as in the discourses of archivists in Chapter 3, the websites discussed in Chapter 6 and the fan cultures of Chapter 7. Many fans (see Young 2008) and producers are creating their own collections and archives online (histories and stories of camera equipment, studios, shooting locations and ephemera) and these demonstrate a level of expertise television scholars value and admire. While students might be our first publics to whom ideas of TV memory might matter, we have found, through our research, there are many others working hard exhibiting TV memory in ways that require support from scholarship, without lay expertise becoming instrumentalized for elite purposes. This then leads to a reflection on our scholarly subject position as a *meta-stance on memory*, observing TV memory, working with or even allowing ourselves to be instrumentalized by broadcasters, museums, archives and exhibitions to tell 'the story', 'a story' or even 'any story' of British television.

Do we remain memory scholars or television scholars if we intervene, embellish and scaffold television's memory work? If we step into the vernacular level to meet with someone who cares about the afterlife of TV, is this a strong or weak action? Where is scholarship's critical position in this action of remembering and forgetting? Is the ontology of a potentially weak subject position for this kind of scholarship – that works alongside fans, industries, archivists and popular memories – also, in fact, a strong position and, if so, on what grounds and with what effects? If we encounter memories of the storyteller of television that are deeply embedded in and imbued with stories of heritage, nation and conservatism, or myopic in their view of what *old TV* means, how should we take account of this in the analysis? In the context of the strengthening of mnemonic warriors, who may be producing a certain kind of inheritability, we would argue that to make past television matter now, then, the very survival of ideas of what TV meant to viewers and the values invested into TV's memories are at stake.

When television scholars step into archives, step across into industry or step through into new disciplines and domains of audiences and public engagement, into histories and memories of engineering, invention and technicity, and into the homes and life stories of collectors, fans and parents, they may find that provincial television memory is both not as important as it seems and yet, at the same time, is fiercely defended by participants. The dilemma is that on positing television memory as something specific, definable, locatable and scalable, it may then be more easily extracted and taken by other sectors and disciplines and only even momentarily for use. Perhaps television's afterlife is the common property of anyone and maybe it should be appropriated by fans, industries, archives and popular memory projects, which may make a meta-position on television memory stretchy, contested and without borders.

We are not seeking here to undermine research into television's memorability, rather we are asking what role have those memories and our memories played in the construction of a critical reflection of television in the present? Do memories 'scaffold' the research, reinforce collective understandings or (quite the reverse) are they being selected out of a sense of cosmo-optimism, i.e. the desire to narrate a story of British television in which a more 'cosmopolitan memory' (Levy and Sznaider 2005) of television history can be attached? Would the personal and producer-ly memories we have attached meaning to in this book be allowed to stand on their own unsupported, 'merely' raw material for a historian, yet highly valuable to industries and archives?[2] This is a key methodological challenge for television historians moving into the social sciences, the sociology of memory work or working on cultural memory projects, and of interviewing and collecting empirical data as past television re-emerges in new formats.

We are emphasizing the need for more critical reflection upon the memory work of producers of television's memory (a wide variety of actors) who are contributing to (or may be invited by universities, corporations, fans, museums and heritage organizations to contribute to) collective memories of television. We make the point that they are shaping how British television becomes a form of cultural heritage that operates in the present to frame the future. We are highlighting that the *construction of a collective memory of past television* during a key period in British broadcasting (principally from the 1950s to 90s) is a form of *organizational cultural memory* that is presented as having 'symbols', 'heroes' and 'rituals' that can be interpreted as forming the 'practices' of past British television (to refer to Hofstede et al.'s 1990 classificatory system of 'cultural dimensions' in 'Measuring Organizational Cultures').

Thus, what we are saying very simply, is that since the 1990s, the trend toward remembering British television has political and cultural economy dimensions (the former less researched than the latter). To study the underlying political economy of how television is remembered is also to understand the more implicit cultural policy of television memory appearing within multiple sectors (arts, heritage, commerce, journalism) and through multiple channels (broadcast

---

[2] These kinds of questions have become pressing, as The Cultural Base Project (Chalcraft and Delanty 2016) makes clear in its proposal for new thematic research areas for interrogating cultural memory: (1) working with difficult heritage, (2) potential of transnational memory, (3) contextualising narratives, and (4) negotiating heritage rights (Chalcraft and Delanty 2016).

channels, online archives, hobbyist websites and local screenings) alongside the economy of resources that flow in certain directions (toward STEM[3] subjects, British technical inventiveness and 'now nostalgia') and not others (toward local television identity, working-class cultural memory or ethnic minority memories of programming). How past television is being organized, managed, made accessible, commercialized and governed by a wide range of stakeholders should be increasingly scrutinized by television scholars as they benefit or not from any new administrations of television memory.

Moreover, one could argue that forgetting plays a crucial role in this administration, i.e. to construct a collective memory of a golden age of British television (and a new golden age for that matter) does rely upon or is enabled by significant gaps in the television archive (as noted by Wheatley [2007] and Jacobs [2006b]). Our cultural inheritance of television's production is then a patchy account of many dominant, male television production narratives and above the line collective memories. We have some oral history interviews with technicians that address lost practices of television production technologies that recuperate some female voices, some collected memories of television's workers great and small. The curation of memories of those who worked for Granada is now more fully the Granadaland project (Manchester Centre for Public History and Heritage n.d.)[4] and this 'produces' an *organizational memory* of Granada as inclusive of a wider variety of memories from 'presenters, producers, researchers, directors, camera operators, stagehands, production assistants, accountants and many others who worked for the company' from 1956 to 1990.[5]

However, such a project, which builds on Kelly and Jones's *Forty Years of Coronation Street: A Collection of Memories* (2000) and *Granada Television: The First Generation* edited by John Finch (2003), is becoming typical (a kind of blueprint) for how television heritage projects have evolved with industry, wherein academics, oral historians, librarians, museums and/or corporate archivists work together to select (usually visual and textual) material, to engage the public in memory work and exhibition. They collect social history and (hopefully) source concrete material artefacts for acquisition (such as memorabilia, photos, scripts, letters and artefacts). A website is produced to share the memories of those

---

[3]STEM is shorthand in the United Kingdom for Science, Technology, Engineering, Mathematics subjects, though the kickback from the Arts has been to posit STEAM as a more integrated way forward.

[4]Housed at the Manchester Centre for Regional History, Manchester Metropolitan University and funded by the Granada Foundation it is representative of a recent impact-driven turn within academia, the public sector and corporate archives to make the past meaningful, accessible, place-based and inclusive.

[5]2016 was the sixtieth anniversary of Granada Television. Of the thirty+ interviews accessible online, at the time of writing, with well-known and below-the-line producers, approximately 10 per cent are from women, which is fairly representative of the collective impression of past television production history, and most of these are recalling their work as secretaries and personal assistants, designers or researchers.

who were behind the scenes either as interview transcripts or audio excerpts, images from the archive are selected and all the partners are represented. Thus, the public-facing end of such projects is presented as corporate heritage and/ or as a social memory initiative (depending on the funding stream). The more critical questions and analysis of issues of memory (remembering and forgetting): reflecting upon and recollecting employment rights, gender, race, cultural taste, regionalism and commercial pressures, as well as the ethics of capturing and holding these memories in a sustained way, may happen in other spaces and places. Moreover, one always hopes the organizational leads of such projects remain in their organizations sustaining the website and memory work for the future.

How much a corporation, media company or public service broadcaster deeply and critically analyses its own organizational memory through reference to producer-ly memories, fan memories or archival values, or allows access to or the creation of personal and professional memories that would conflict with its legacy or brand identity is an important question for future research. Particularly in an online confessional culture wherein the creative industries are being held to account, and especially in a digital media ecology where memories emerge, are shared and are powerful enough to change histories as well as lives. Memories of British television are being produced on a wide scale (sometimes with significant resources) and in many different contexts (for museums, universities, broadcasters and national/regional identity purposes) for a variety of stakeholders (usually for educators, researchers, social historians as well as brand managers and the creative industries). They are then curated, selected and edited to produce old and new collective and collected memories of television. How much the audience (past, present and future) benefits from television memory initiatives should be an important question before, during and after projects, particularly if creating an afterlife of television requires a second tranche of public funding (the first round may have been the licence fee that paid for the creation of the source texts).

Nevertheless, these projects accord with a current trend for archival housekeeping facilitated by the internet and by commercial media organizations keen to (a) do something with or offload material that is uncatalogued and taking up space, and (b) work with universities, museums and libraries for the public good and/or for brand legacy. In *Corporate Memory: A Guide to Managing Business Archives* (2009) the chief executive of The National Archives in the UK states:

> across the globe communications and marketing teams are re-engineering corporate branding and identity to emphasise their pasts. Most successful companies have secret commercial weapons in the form of their archives, an often under-used asset that can be used to increase brand awareness, build commercial identity and help grow business.
>
> (The National Archives 2009)

There is though the bottom line for those entering the television industry, as our archive researcher outlined:

> There is Mr BFI, Mr Getty saying 'come and play in our archives, we have such riches' and knowing how great their archives are and not being able to get my hands on them because I just don't have the time and don't have the money to spend so it is having to rely on what's available and it makes me worried [...] because we just keep showing the same version [...] There's a danger that you're not showing the whole picture. I love using Getty, I love it when they have to go to Iron Mountain, their great big storage facility and they say, 'ooh I have to go to Iron Mountain, that will be so exciting!' What are you going to pull out of there? But I get the chance to do that less and less because programmes don't have the budget to pay for it.
>
> (interview with Mhairi Brennan 23 June 2014)

In theory then it can feel like we can do anything with *old TV*, remember anything, feel anything and pass down anything. The television set may be in danger of disappearing altogether as Jenner (2016a) notes, while Ellis' (2012) as noted in Chapter 1 covers all the new ways television as data could be mined for deeper insights.

In such a reformulation, *old TV* becomes data rather than story, perhaps without heritage, and one could surmise that cultural, collective and social memory becomes its metadata. Yet, this is not a fetishization of data, says Ellis, but rather 'history is needed to reassert the intrinsic nature of the data being used. History reasserts the metadata which gives sense to data by asserting its origins and its limitations. Any use of digital data in research requires that the parameters of the data are clearly understood: the conditions of production of the data have to be made clear' (Ellis 2014, 20). As we have shown, even data requires spaces, resource-intensive spaces where past television tapes are restored; digitized; re-edited; transcoded; turned into archival content for reuse; streamed to regional, national, transnational hubs/platforms; re-screened during national and regional events; socially mediated to develop audiences; exhibited through celebrations and commemorations; and made available to new creatives. *Old TV* as big data may seem less weird in a digital media ecology but it still needs to be stored and preserved, and the curatorial expertise of the widest range of experts is needed.

Thus, while Ellis reiterates the ephemerality issue we previously underscored by stating that 'much TV is suffused by things of the moment from which it sprang and for which it was made' (Ellis 2007, 163), our interviews find that those operating within the heritage and archives sectors are often selecting and working with television material repurposeable in the present, as *always, already out of sync* with the moment 'from which it sprang and for which it was made' (163). By this we mean that television is never simply of the moment and it may even draw on the past (its own past) while in the moment. Pushed toward endless innovation, freshness and creativity while pulled toward its own endless past and inheritance, television can never really win the game of being fully in the now.

Even when television is contemporary, because of its everydayness, ubiquity and imbrication into daily, lived lives, it is also quietly being carried around in memories: connecting programmes, interstitials, soundbites, tunes, slogans, flashbacks, as tangible and intangible paratextual memories of texts, equipment and technologies. It seems televisual textures, fashions, Gifs, fan memorabilia and the collections of spectacular images and sounds as noted by Wheatley (2016) and through 'fan-tracking' detailed by Gillan (2011) continually recirculate in digital formats creating new audiences and taking the core audience in new directions. As Ellis notes 'the grain of the times, the unnoticed and the everyday, which have a powerful evocative effect in retrospect' becomes the stuff of remembering television or a film, this can invert textual readings of the archival content itself. He adds:

> there are the materials that are caught by the involuntary action of camera and microphone which were not eliminated in the edit. These chance actions in the margins of the frame can become more fascinating than the action at the centre. This way lies both nostalgia (the regretful recall of a lost past) and deconstruction (the reinterpretation of texts away from the confines of their original context).
>
> (Ellis 2014, 17)

If Ellis sees these momentary 'things' (these textual elements of 'old TV') 'to be a real block to nostalgia' because there 'is so much of the intimate texture of the past in old TV programmes' (17) then this may assume that remembering does not have another purpose, and that looking backwards is not always a longing for something lost but a desire to form a relationship with *old TV* in the present, with aspirations for the future of television. We need to account for remembering the textures of television (wherein the text, the story, the series, the narrative arc may be forgotten in lieu of how TV felt) and the stickiness, weirdness (noted at the beginning of this book) and textural adhesion of those textual elements within memories, imagination and senses.

If the television programme's broadcast is a form of 'active forgetting' (Huyssen 1995) then that does not mean the forgetting is unproductive for television's memorability. Television and its texts, contexts, meanings and ephemera take on new productive meanings as they stick to new kinds of stakeholders in television's historiography. The potential to recuperate producer-ly memories from the intangible and material objects of television's past shifts the object of study from the text to the creative and administrative person in powerful ways. Emotions, memories and stories become exhibited, and life histories of working in and with the medium, anecdotes rarely shared, can make an impact on television history by diversifying the voices and opening up the study to other disciplines: policy studies, cultural geography, sociology and politics to name a few.

We have drawn upon our interviews not as empirical evidence for historical research but rather to understand how collective and collected memories of television texts, production cultures and experiences of viewing have constructed a shareable concept of British television heritage as inheritable through the means of memory work rather than history. We touch upon and open up for future research a key area of critique regarding the role of television workers' recollections in the writing of British TV history, the creativity of fans, the voices of audiences and the cultural labour of archivists and heritage professionals. Researchers ought to consider in more depth the value of the published producer memoir, the emergence of television worker reunion websites, the rogue archives of hobbyists and autodidacts and the unofficial industry working life stories of anyone connected to television's extensive creative reach.

This book has called upon the voices and stories of organizational actors who are fast becoming the memory agents of television's afterlife in the domain of television archives and heritage and they are dealing with the challenges of storage, accessibility and repurposing through the multiple ways in which a television collection becomes inheritable, useable and re-viewable. This misses the other side of their work, that they do not simply inherit a collection when they are selecting *old TV* for reuse, but with every selection they inherit the people who remember and who loved that TV and what it means to them. The attachment is strong. Viewers (formerly known as the audience) want access to their own television memories and producers who value the time they invested want to see again what was so much part of their lives, to reshare the memories of television with each other and with other generations.

To inherit an audience is to recognize its regenerative capacity and the memory capital it holds that makes demands on what and how *old TV* is re-viewed. An audience (at a re-screening and Q&A with a director, for example), or a viewer (alone in a BFI mediateque booth) or a visitor (to a television exhibition or museum installation) needs to be nurtured and challenged, developed and extended. They also need to be shown how to think inter-generationally with *old TV*. As Marcus Prince, television programmer at the BFI, notes:

MP   Well, I inherited a core audience.
JGH   Are they fans?
MP   No, I would say that they skew mainly older middle-class, people who actually remember the so-called Golden Age, so whatever I did, I knew that whatever changes I made I did not want to alienate that core audience, that they would have to be brought along with any changes. [...] So it's ways of taking that archive material and re-purposing it or putting it in a context that is going to make it a little bit more relevant to the current viewing public who are let's say under 50, as well as that core audience of 50 and over.

(interview with Marcus Prince 19 March 2014)

Consequently, while the digital turn has produced opportunities to rethink television's future it has also uniquely positioned *old TV* as repurposeable to re-engage viewers with their own pasts, address issues of culture, class and taste, and ask critical questions of futurity and medium-specific scenarios within the domains of television technology. What might emerge from this is uncertain.

'Emergence', say Hoskins and Tulloch,

> is the massively increased potential for media data to literally emerge at an unprescribed and unpredictable time after the moment of its recording, archiving, or loss. The likelihood of potentially transcendent missed or hidden or deleted images, videos, emails, and so on, emerging to transform what was known or thought to be known about a person, place, or event, constitutes a spectacular uncertainty for the future evolution of memory and of history.
>
> (Hoskins and Tulloch 2016, 7)

The emergence of *old TV* (texts + memories + industries) in a digital age is an act of day-lighting that needs to empirically engage with how we actually use the web (see Booth 2017) and how we actually remember television. We would argue that Hoskins and Tulloch's reading of 'television' as an 'earlier media ecology' that oscillated 'between amplification and containment of an array of insecurities' (2016, 244) does not account for television's afterlife and inheritability into the unpredictability of new media ecologies, crafting safe-zones, cosy-places and transnational re-inscriptions of identity and nation. Such *now nostalgia* is very spreadable and it needs deeper analysis. Digital emergence may also miss the lack of containment and the insecurity readily felt but hidden and forgotten in the earlier media ecology of television. Researching the remembering of television across scales of intimacy and family and public and nation should day-light the continuum of the struggles over meaning of one in relation to the other. This takes television history and memory in interesting interdisciplinary directions that could be productive methodologically for extending the value and meaning of *old TV*; we hesitate to assert *old TV* as *big data* (as 'Mr Getty' imagines), but we do believe that there are opportunities to rethink television memory through other disciplines, with the history of science, technology and engineering being an option alongside a deeper interrogation of ephemera, materiality, place, conspicuous craft and the environmental humanities as other possible avenues to explore. This should not overshadow the 'person' as the remembering subject, the 'me' of my memories of watching television everyday.

REFERENCES

Acland, Charles (2014) 'Dirt Research for Media Industries', *Media Industries Journal* vol. 1 no. 1, pp. 6–10. Available online: <www.mediaindustriesjournalorg/index.php/mij/article/view/18/30> (Accessed 9 December 2016).

Adams, Sam (2016) '*Stranger Things:* How Netflix's Retro Hit Resurrects the Eighties', *Rolling Stone* 21 July 2016. Available online: <www.rollingstone.com/tv/features/stranger-things-how-netflixs-hit-resurrects-the-1980s-w429804> (Accessed 3 October 2016).

ADAPT (n.d.) 'How Television Used to be Made'. Available online: <www.adapttvhistory.org.uk> (Accessed 1 November 2018).

Aldridge, Mark (2011) *The Birth of British Television: A History*, Basingstoke: Palgrave Macmillan.

Allen, Matthew (2014) *The Labour of Memory: Memorial Culture and 7/7*, Basingstoke: Palgrave Macmillan.

Allen, Matthew and Steve D. Brown (2016) 'Memorial Meshwork: The Making of the Commemorative Space of the Hyde Park 7/7 Memorial', *Organization* vol. 23 no. 1, pp. 10–28.

Amazon (1996–2018) 'A History Independent Television Wales'. Available online: <www.amazon.co.uk/History-Independent-Television-Wales/dp/0708322131> (Accessed 8 October 2017).

Anderson, Steve F. (2011) *Technologies of History: Visual Media and the Eccentricity of the Past*, Lebanon, NH: University of New England Press.

Ang, Ien (2011) 'Unsettling the National: Heritage and Diaspora', in Helmut K. Anheier and Yudhishthir Raj Isar (eds), *Heritage, Memory and Identity*, London: Sage, pp. 82–94.

Assmann, Aleida (1996) 'Texts, Traces, Trash: The Changing Media of Cultural Memory', *Representations* vol. 56, pp. 123–34.

Assmann, Aleida (2011a) 'Canon and Archive', in Jeffrey K. Olick, Vered Vinitzky-Seroussi and Daniel Levy (eds), *The Collective Memory Reader*, Oxford: Oxford University Press, pp. 334–7.

Assmann, Aleida (2011b) *Cultural Memory and Western Civilization: Arts of Memory*, Cambridge: Cambridge University Press.

Assmann, Jan (2008) 'Communicative and Cultural Memory', in Astrid Erll and Ansgar Nünning (eds), *Cultural Memory Studies: An International and Interdisciplinary Handbook*, Berlin: de Gruyter, pp. 109–118.

Assmann, Jan (2011) 'From Moses the Egyptian: The Meaning of Egypt in Western Monotheism and "Collective Memory and Cultural Identity"', in Jeffrey K. Olick, Vered Vinitzky-Seroussi and Daniel Levy (eds), *The Collective Memory Reader*, Oxford: Oxford University Press, pp. 209–15.

Attenborough, David ([2002] 2009) *Life on Air: Memoirs of a Broadcaster*, London: BBC Books.

Auslander, Philip (1999) *Liveness: Performance in a Mediatized Culture*, Abingdon: Routledge.

Baade, Christina (2012) *Victory through Harmony: The BBC and Popular Music in World War II*, Oxford: Oxford University Press.

Barker, Martin and Julian Petley (eds) (1997) *Ill Effects: The Media/Violence Debate*, Abingdon: Routledge.

Bartlett, Frederic C. (1932) *Remembering: A Study in Experimental and Social Psychology*, Cambridge: Cambridge University Press.

BBC (2004) *Building Public Value: Renewing the BBC for a Digital World*. Available online: <http://downloads.bbc.co.uk/aboutthebbc/policies/pdf/bpv.pdf> (Accessed 2 September 2015).

BBC (2013) 'Core Records Management Policy'. Available online: <http://downloads.bbc.co.uk/foi/classes/policies_procedures/bbc_records_management_policy.pdf> (Accessed 1 November 2016).

BBC Entertainment News (2016) 'Ken Loach Bemoans TV's "Fake Nostalgia" of Period Dramas', *BBC News* 18 October 2016. Available online: <www.bbc.co.uk/news/entertainment-arts-37679158> (Accessed 20 October 2016).

BBC History (2014) 'John Logie Baird (1888–1946)'. Available online: <www.bbc.co.uk/history/historic_figures/baird_logie.shtml> (Accessed 14 June 2016).

Belam, Martin (2016) 'The Day *Doctor Who* Changed Face – and Transformed TV For Ever', *The Guardian* 28 October 2016. Available online: <www.theguardian.com/tv-and-radio/2016/oct/28/doctor-who-changed-face-and-transformed-tv-for-ever> (Accessed 16 October 2017).

Benjamin, Walter (1940) 'On the Concept of History'. Available online: <www.marxists.org/reference/archive/benjamin/1940/history.htm> (Accessed 4 November 2017).

Bennett, Tony, Colin Mercer and Janet Woolacott (eds) (1986) *Popular Culture and Social Relations*, Milton Keynes: Open University Press.

Berger, Jake (2011) 'Digital Archive Opportunities and BBC Digital Public Space – Jake Berger' [video], YouTube 15 October 2011. Available online: <www.youtube.com/watch?v=4d6KhsB5A_0> (Accessed 30 May 2013).

Berlant, Laurent (2008) *The Female Complaint: The Unfinished Business of Sentimentality in American Culture*, Durham, NC: Duke University Press.

Bernhard, Michael and Jan Kubik (eds) (2014) *Twenty Years after Communism: The Politics of Memory and Commemoration*, Oxford: Oxford University Press.

Bignell, Jonathan (2004) *An Introduction to Television Studies*, London: Routledge

Bignell, Jonathan and Stephen Lacey (eds) (2005) *British Television Drama: Past, Present and Future*, 1st edition, Manchester: Manchester University Press.

Bjarkman, Kim (2004) 'To Have and to Hold: The Video Collector's Relationship with an Ethereal Medium', *Television and New Media* vol. 5 no. 3, pp. 217–46.

Blandford, Steve and Ruth McElroy (2013) 'Memory, Television and the Making of the BBC's *The Story of Wales*', *VIEW: Journal of European Television History and Culture* vol. 2 no. 3, pp. 118–25. Available online: <http://viewjournal.eu/european-television-memories/memory-television-and-the-making-of-the-bbcs-the-story-of-wales/> (Accessed 2 November 2018).

Bolin, Göran (2016) *Media Generations: Experience, Identity and Mediatised Social Change*, Abingdon: Routledge.

Bonner, Paul and Lesley Aston (1998) *Independent Television in Britain, Volume 5: ITV and IBA, 1981–1992: The Old Relationship Changes*, London: Macmillan.

Bonner, Paul with Lesley Aston (2003) *Independent Television in Britain, Volume 6: New Developments in Independent Television, 1981–1992, Channel 4, TV-AM, Cable and Satellite*, Basingstoke: Palgrave Macmillan.

Booth, Paul (2017) *Digital Fandom 2.0*, New York: Peter Lang.

Born, Georgina (2000) 'Inside Television: Television Studies and the Sociology of Culture', *Screen* vol. 41 no. 4, pp. 404–24.

Born, Georgina (2005) *Uncertain Vision: Birt, Dyke and the Reinvention of the BBC*, London: Secker & Warburg.

Bourdieu, Pierre (1984) *Distinction: A Social Critique of the Judgement of Taste*, translated by Richard Nice, Cambridge, MA: Harvard University Press.

Bourdon, Jérôme (2003) 'Some Sense of Time: Remembering Television', *History and Memory* vol. 15 no. 2, pp. 5–36.

Boyle, Frankie (2016) 'TV Comedy Has Gone Back to the 70s', *The Guardian* 26 August 2016. Available online: <www.theguardian.com/media/2016/aug/26/tv-comedy-back-to-the-70s-frankie-boyle> (Accessed 1 July 2016).

Boym, Svetlana (2001) *The Future of Nostalgia*, New York: Basic Books.

Boym, Svetlana (2007) 'Nostalgia and Its Discontents', *The Hedgehog Review* vol. 9 no. 2, Summer. Available online: <www.iasc-culture.org/eNews/2007_10/9.2CBoym.pdf> (Accessed 1 September 2016).

Brabazon, Tara M. (2005) *From Revolution to Revelation: Generation X, Popular Memory, Cultural Studies*, Aldershot: Ashgate Publishing.

Brennan, M. (2008) 'Happy to Help? Gaining Access to Interview Media Practitioners', *Australian Journal of Communication* vol. 35 no. 1, pp. 15–26.

Briggs, Asa (1961–70) *The History of Broadcasting in the United Kingdom, Volumes 1–3*, Oxford: Oxford University Press.

Briggs, Asa (1979) *The History of Broadcasting in the United Kingdom, Volume 4: Sound and Vision 1945–1955*, Oxford: Oxford University Press.

Briggs, Asa (1985) *The BBC: The First Fifty Years*, Oxford: Oxford University Press.

Briggs, Asa (1995) *The History of Broadcasting in the United Kingdom, Volume 5: Competition 1955–1974*, Oxford: Oxford University Press.

Brinkmann, Svend and Steinar Kvale (2014) *InterViews: Learning the Craft of Qualitative Interviewing*, 3rd edition, London: Sage.

Brockway, Merrill (2010) *Surprise Was My Teacher: Memories and Confessions of a Television Producer/Director Who Came of Age during Television's Adolescence*, Santa Fe, NM: Sunstone Press.

Brown, Steven D. and Andrew Hoskins (2010) 'Terrorism in the New Memory Ecology: Mediating and Remembering the 2005 London Bombings', *Behavioural Sciences of Terrorism and Political Aggression* vol. 2 no. 2, pp. 87–107.

Brunsdon, Charlotte (2008) 'Is Television Studies History?' *Cinema Journal* vol. 47 no. 3, pp. 127–37.

Brunsdon, Charlotte (2010) 'Bingeing on Box-Sets: The National and the Digital in Television Crime Drama', in Jostein Gripsrud (eds), *Re-Locating Television: Television in a Digital Context*, Abingdon: Routledge, pp. 63–75.

Bryant, Steve George (2015) 'Archive Footage in New Programmes Presentational Issues and Perspectives', *VIEW Journal of European Television History and Culture* vol. 4 no. 8, pp. 61–6. Available online: <http://viewjournal.eu/archive-based-productions/archive-footage-in-new-programmes/> (Accessed 2 November 2018).

Buckingham, David (1993) *Children Talking Television*, London: Psychology Press.

Buckingham, David (1996) *Moving Images: Understanding Children's Emotional Responses to Television*, Manchester: Manchester University Press.

Buckingham, David (1999) *Children's Television in Britain: History, Discourse and Policy*, London: BFI.

Buckingham, David, Hannah Davies, Ken Jones and Peter Kelley (1999) *Children's Television in Britain: History, Discourse and Policy*, London: BFI.

Bull, Michael (2009) 'The Auditory Nostalgia of iPod Culture', in Karin Bijsterveld and José van Dijck (eds), *Sound Souvenirs: Audio Technologies, Memory and Cultural Practices*, Amsterdam: Amsterdam University Press, pp. 83–93.

Buonanno, Milly (2008) *The Age of Television*, translated by Jennifer Radice, Bristol: Intellect Books.

Buscombe, Ed (1974) 'Television Studies in Schools and Colleges', *Screen Education* no. 12 (Autumn), pp. 5–36.

BuzzFeedVideo (2015) 'Americans Watch Father Ted for the First Time' [video], YouTube 17 August 2015. Available online: <https://www.youtube.com/watch?v=UJ1Akr-UBis> (Accessed 18 December 2016).

Caldwell, John Thornton (1995) *Televisuality: Style, Crisis, and Authority in American Television*, New Brunswick, NJ: Rutgers University Press.

Caldwell, John Thornton (2008) *Production Culture: Industrial Reflexivity and Critical Practice in Film and Television*, Durham, NC: Duke University Press.

Caldwell, John Thornton (2009) 'Cultures of Production', in Jennifer Holt and Alisa Perren (eds), *Media Industries: History, Theory and Method*, Oxford: Wiley Blackwell, pp. 199–212.

Callender, Colin (2014) 'Why We Should Cherish BBC Drama', *The Guardian* 12 September 2014. Available online: <www.theguardian.com/media/2014/sep/12/why-we-should-cherish-bbc-drama> (Accessed 11 July 2016).

Castrique, Sue (1987) 'WTVA: Wider Television Access', *Media International Australia* vol. 45 no. 1, p. i.

Caughie, John (2000) *Television Drama: Realism, Modernism and British Culture*, Oxford: Oxford University Press.

Caughie, John (2010) 'Mourning Television: The Other Screen', *Screen* vol. 51 no. 4, pp. 410–42.

Cavicchi, Daniel (1998) *Tramps Like Us: Music and Meaning among Springsteen Fans*, Oxford: Oxford University Press.

Chalcraft, Jasper and Gerard Delanty (2016) 'Synthetic Report on Cultural Memory', Cultural Base Project. Available online: <http://culturalbase.eu/cultural-memory-2/> (Accessed 13 December 2016).

Channel 4 (2013) 'Channel Four Television Corporation Records Management Policy Statement'. Available online: <www.channel4.com/media/documents/corporate/foi-docs/RMPolicy2013.pdf> (Accessed 1 November 2016).

Chapman, James (2002) *Saints and Avengers: British Adventure Series of the 1960s*, London: I.B.Tauris.

Clifford, James (1992) 'Travelling Cultures', in Lawrence Grossberg and Cary Nelson (eds), *Cultural Studies*, New York: Routledge, pp. 96–116.

Cohen, Stanley (1972) *Folk Devils and Moral Panics*, London: MacGibbon and Kee.

Collie, Hazel (2013) '"It's Just So Hard to Bring it to Mind" The Significance of "Wallpaper" in the Gendering of Television Memory Work', *VIEW: Journal of European Television History and Culture* vol. 2 no. 3, pp. 13–21. Available online: <http://viewjournal.eu/european-television-memories/its-just-so-hard-to-bring-it-to-mind/> (Accessed 2 November 2018).

Collingwood, Robin George ([1946] 1999) *The Idea of History*, Oxford: Clarendon.

Collins, Jim ([1987] 1992) 'Postmodernism and Television', in Robert C. Allen (ed.), *Channels of Discourse, Reassembled: Television and Contemporary Criticism*, 2nd edition, Chapel Hill: University of North Carolina Press, pp. 327–53.

Connerton, Paul (2008) 'Seven Types of Forgetting', *Memory Studies* vol. 1 no. 1, pp. 59–71.

Connerton, Paul (2011) 'From *How Societies Remember*', in Jeffrey K. Olick, Vered Vinitzky-Seroussi and Daniel Levy (eds), *The Collective Memory Reader*, Oxford: Oxford University Press, pp. 338–42.

Connolly, Maeve (2014) *TV Museum Contemporary Art and the Age of Television*, Bristol: Intellect.

Cooke, Les (2003) *British Television Drama: A History*, 1st edition, London: BFI.

Cooke, Les (2015) *British Television Drama: A History*, 2nd edition, London: BFI.

Corner, John (1991) *Popular Television in Britain: Studies in Cultural History*, London: BFI.

Cottle, Simon (2004) 'Producing Nature(s): On the Changing Production Ecology of Natural History TV', *Media Culture and Society* vol. 26 no. 1, pp. 81–101.

Creeber, Glen, Toby Miller and John Tulloch (2008) *The Television Genre Book*, London: BFI.

Crosby, Nat (2002) *A Cameraman Abroad: From Panorama to Paranoia*, Dereham: Larks Press.

Curran, James and Jean Seaton (2010) *Power without Responsibility: Press, Broadcasting and the Internet in Britain*, 7th edition, Abingdon: Routledge.

Darian-Smith, Kate and Sue Turnbull (eds) (2012) *Remembering Television: Histories, Technologies, Memories*, Newcastle-upon-Tyne: Cambridge Scholars Publishing.

Davies, Máire Messenger (2001) *"Dear BBC": Children, Television Storytelling and the Public Sphere*, Cambridge: Cambridge University Press.

Davies, Máire Messenger (2010) *Children, Media and Culture*, Maidenhead: Open University Press.

Davis, Glyn and Gary Needham (2009) *Queer TV: Theories, Histories, Politics*, Abingdon: Routledge.

Dayan, Daniel and Elihu Katz (1992) *Media Events: The Live Broadcasting of History*, Cambridge, MA: Harvard University Press.

Dean, Jodi (2010) *Blog Theory: Feedback and Capture in the Circuits of Drive*, London: Polity.

De Cesari, Chiara and Ann Rigney (eds) (2014) *Transnational Memory: Circulation, Articulation, Scales*, Berlin: De Gruyter.

De Kosnik, Abigail (2016) *Rogue Archives: Digital Cultural Memory and Media Fandom*, Cambridge, MA: MIT Press.

Derevenski, Joanna Sofaer (ed.) (2000) *Children and Material Culture*, London: Routledge.

Dika, Vera (2003) *Recycled Culture in Contemporary Art and Film: The Uses of Nostalgia*, Cambridge: Cambridge University Press.

Dillon, Robert (2010) *History on British Television: Constructing Nation and Collective Memory*, Manchester: Manchester University Press.

Dowell, Ben (2016) 'BBC4 to Recreate the First Ever Night of British Television 80 Years to the Day', *Radio Times* 26 August 2016. Available online: <www.radiotimes.com/news/2016-08-26/bbc4-to-recreate-the-first-ever-night-of-british-television-80-years-to-the-day> (Accessed 1 November 2016).

Drotner, Kirsten and Sonia Livingstone (eds) (2008) *The International Handbook of Children, Media and Culture*, Los Angeles: Sage.

Duffett, Mark (2013) *Understanding Fandom*, London: Bloomsbury Academic.

DWAS (*Doctor Who* Appreciation Society) (2011/2018) 'Home'. Available online: <www.dwasonline.co.uk/> (Accessed 2 November 2018).

Edgerton, Gary E. and Peter C. Rollins (2001) *Television Histories: Shaping the Collective Memory in the Media Age*, Lexington: University of Kentucky Press.

Edwards, Bob (2018) 'Black Country Memories'. Available online: <www.reminiscethis.co.uk/reminiscing/black-country?start=2> (Accessed 2 November 2018).

Ellis, John (2005) 'Importance, Significance, Cost and Value: Is an ITV Canon Possible?', in Catherine Johnson and Rob Turnock (eds), *ITV Cultures: Independent Television over Fifty Years*, Maidenhead: Open University Press, pp. 36–56.

Ellis, John (2007) *TV FAQ: Uncommon Answers to Common Questions about TV*, London: I.B.Tauris.

Ellis, John (2012) 'Why Digitise Historical Television?', *VIEW: Journal of European History and Culture* vol. 1 no. 1, pp. 27–33. Available online: <http://ojs.viewjournal.eu/index. php/view/article/viewFile/jethc005/5> (Accessed 2 November 2018).

Ellis, John (2014) 'TV and Cinema: What Forms of History Do We Need?', in Laura Mee and Johnny Walker (eds), *Cinema, Television and History: New Approaches*, Newcastle-upon-Tyne: Cambridge Scholars Publishing, pp. 12–25.

Elstein, David (2015) '"Pinkoes and Traitors": A Tunnel Vision of Broadcasting History', Open Democracy. Available online: <www.opendemocracy.net/ourbeeb/david-elstein/'pinkoes-and-traitors'-tunnel-vision-of-broadcasting-history>.

Erll, Astrid (2011a) *Memory in Culture*, translated by Sara B. Young, Houndmills: Palgrave Macmillan.

Erll, Astrid (2011b) 'Travelling Memory', special issue of *Parallax* vol. 17 no. 4, pp. 4–18.

Ernst, Wolfgang (2011) 'Media Archaeography: Method and Machine versus History and Narrative of Media', in Erkki Huhtamo and Jussi Parikka (eds), *Media Archaeology: Approaches, Applications, and Implications*, Berkeley: University of California Press, pp. 239–55.

Fangirl Quest (n.d.) 'Home'. Available online: <www.fangirlquest.com> (Accessed 2 November 2018).

Fiddy, Dick (2001) *Missing Believe Wiped: Searching for the Lost Treasures of British Television*, London: BFI.

Finch, John (ed.) (2003) *Granada Television: The First Generation*, Manchester: Manchester University Press.

Fiske, John (1992) 'The Cultural Economy of Fandom', in Lisa A. Lewis (ed.), *The Adoring Audience: Fan Culture and Popular Media*, London: Routledge, pp. 30–49.

Fitzwalter, Raymond (2008) *The Dream that Died: The Rise and Fall of ITV*, Leicester: Matador.

Flewin, John (ed.) (2016) 'ITN Source to Cease Operations as Getty Takes over News Collection Licensing', FootageInfo.com 10 November 2016. Available online: <Footageinfo.com> (Accessed 2 November 2018).

Florida, Richard (2005) *Cities and the Creative Class*, New York: Routledge.

Forman, Denis (1997) *Persona Granada: Some Memories of Sidney Bernstein and the Early Days of Independent Television*, London: André Deutsch.

Franklin, Ieuen (2014) 'Documenting the Social and Historical Margins in the Films of Philip Donnellan', *LIAS* vol. 17 no. 1. Available online: <https://journals.openedition. org/lisa/5606> (Accessed 1 December 2017).

Fry, Stephen (2015) *More Fool Me*, London: Penguin.

Garde-Hansen, Joanne (2011) *Media and Memory*, Edinburgh: Edinburgh University Press.

Garde-Hansen, Joanne (2015) 'Digital Memories and Media of the Future', in Martin Conboy and John Steel (eds), *Routledge Companion to British Media History*, Abingdon: Routledge, pp. 582–93.

Garde-Hansen, Joanne and Kristyn Gorton (2013) *Emotion Online: Theorising Affect on the Internet*, Houndmills: Palgrave Macmillan.

Garde-Hansen, Joanne and Hannah Grist (2014) *Remembering Dennis Potter through Fans, Extras and Archives*, Houndmills: Palgrave Macmillan.

Garnett, Tony (2014) 'Context', in Jonathan Bignell and Stephen Lacey (eds), *British Television Drama: Past, Present and Future*, 2nd edition, Basingstoke: Palgrave Macmillan, pp. 16–32.

Garnett, Tony (2016) *The Day the Music Died: A Memoir*, London: Constable.

Genette, Gerard (1997) *Paratexts: Thresholds of Interpretation*, Cambridge: Cambridge University Press.

Geraghty, Christine (2015) 'Old TV', keynote lecture at the launch of the Centre for TV History, Heritage and Memory, University of Warwick, 28 October 2015.

Giddens, Anthony (1976) *New Rules of Sociological Method: A Positive Critique of Interpretative Sociologies*, London: Hutchinson.

Gill, A.A. (2016) 'Brexit: AA Gill argues for In', *The Sunday Times* 12 June 2016. Available online: <www.thetimes.co.uk/article/aa-gill-argues-the-case-against-brexit-kmnp83zrt> (Accessed October 30, 2018).

Gill, Rosalind and Andy Pratt ([2008] 2009) 'Precarity and Cultural Work in the Social Factory? Immaterial Labour, Precariousness and Cultural Work', reproduced in *On Curating* vol. 16 no. 13, pp. 26–40. Available online: <www.on-curating.org/files/oc/dateiverwaltung/old%20Issues/ONCURATING_Issue16.pdf> (Accessed 13 December 2016).

Gillan, Jennifer (2011) *Television and New Media: Must-Click TV*, New York: Routledge.

Gorton, Kristyn (2009) *Media Audiences: Television, Meaning and Emotion*, Edinburgh: Edinburgh University Press.

Grainge, Paul (ed.) (2003) *Memory and Popular Film*, Manchester: Manchester University Press.

Gras, Vernon W. and John R. Cook (eds) (2000) *The Passion of Dennis Potter: International Collected Essays*, New York: St Martin's Press.

Gray, Ann and Erin Bell (2013) *History on Television*, Abingdon: Routledge.

Gray, Jonathan (2003) 'New Audience, New Textualities: Anti-fans and Non-Fans', *International Journal of Cultural Studies* vol. 6 no. 1, pp. 64–81.

Gray, Jonathan (2010) *Show Sold Separately: Promos, Spoilers, and Other Media Paratexts*, New York: New York University Press.

Gray, Jonathan and Amanda Lotz (2012) *Television Studies*, Cambridge: Polity Press.

Gregg, Melissa (2009) 'Learning to (Love) Labour: Production Cultures and the Affective Turn', *Communication and Critical/Cultural Studies* vol. 6 no. 2, pp. 209–14.

Griffin, Ken (2014) 'The Impact of Archival Silences on Historical Narratives Surrounding Ulster Television (UTV)', PhD thesis, Ulster University. Available online: <http://ethos.bl.uk/OrderDetails.do?uin=uk.bl.ethos.669691> (Accessed 16 December 2017).

Griffin, Ken (2015) 'The Lessons of Counterpoint Wolfgang Ernst's Media Archaeology And Television Archive Research', *VIEW: Journal of European Television History and Culture* vol. 4 no. 7, pp. 11–20.

Groom, Elinor (2014) 'The South, Southern and *Southerner*: Regional Identity and Locations in Southern Television's *Freewheelers*', *Historical Journal of Film, Radio and Television* vol. 34 no. 3, pp. 434–51.

Gunkel, David J. (2016) *Of Remixology*, Cambridge, MA: MIT Press.

Hagerdoorn, Berber (2013) 'Television as a Hybrid Repertoire of Memory: New Dynamic Practices of Memory in the Multi-platform Era', *VIEW: Journal of Television History and Culture* vol. 2 no. 3, pp. 52–64.

Halberstam, Judith (2005) *In a Queer Time and Place: Transgender Bodies, Subcultural Lives*, New York: New York University Press.

Halbwachs, Maurice (2011) 'The Collective Memory', in Jeffrey K. Olick, Vered Vinitzky-Seroussi and Daniel Levy (eds), *The Collective Memory Reader*, Oxford: Oxford University Press, pp. 139–49.

Hall, Tony (2013) 'Tha Man in Chatge', *Radio Times* 23–29 November, pp. 28–9.

Hartley, John (2008) *Television Truths: Forms of Knowledge in Popular Culture*, Oxford: Blackwell.

Harvey, Colin B. (2015) *Fantastic Transmedia: Narrative, Play and Memory across Science Fiction and Fantasy Storyworlds*, Houndmills: Palgrave Macmillan.

Haug, Frigga (2000) 'Memory Work: The Key to Women's Anxiety', in Susannah Radstone (ed.), *Memory and Methodology*, Berg: Oxford, pp. 155–78.

Haywood, Jo (2010) 'Meet Iain Logie Baird of the National Media Museum', *Yorkshire Life* 17 March 2010. Available online: <www.yorkshirelife.co.uk/people/meet_iain_logie_baird_of_the_national_media_museum_1_1637009> (Accessed 16 December 2016).

Hayward, Philip and Jon Fitzgerald (2013) 'Rematerialization: Musical Engagements with the British TV Series *Doctor Who*', in K.J. Donnelly and Philip Hayward (eds), *Music in Science Fiction Television: Tuned to the Future*, Abingdon: Routledge, pp. 135–50.

Herzog, Christian and Ali Christopher (2015) 'Elite Interviewing in Media and Communications Policy Research', *International Journal of Media and Cultural Politics* vol. 1 no. 1, pp. 37–54.

Hills, Matt (2002) *Fan Cultures*, London: Routledge.

Hills, Matt (2010) *Triumph of a Time-Lord: Regenerating Doctor Who in the 21st Century*, New York: I.B.Tauris.

Hills, Matt (2014) '*Doctor Who*'s Textual Commemorators', *Journal of Fandom Studies* vol. 2 no. 1, pp. 31–51.

Hills, Matt (2015) *Doctor Who: The Unfolding Event*, Basingstoke: Palgrave Macmillan.

Hills, Matt and Joanne Garde-Hansen (2017) 'Fandom's Paratextual Memory: Remembering, Reconstructing and Repatriating "Lost" *Doctor Who*', special issue of *Critical Studies in Media Communication* vol. 34 no. 2, pp. 158–67.

Hilmes, Michele (ed.) (2003) *The Television History Book*, London: BFI.

Hofstede Geert, Bram Neuijen, Denise Daval Ohayv and Geert Sanders (1990) 'Measuring Organizational Cultures: A Qualitative and Quantitative Study Across Twenty Cases', *Administrative Science Quarterly* vol. 35 no. 2, pp. 286–316.

Holdsworth, Amy (2011) *Television, Memory and Nostalgia*, Basingstoke: Palgrave Macmillan.

Holdsworth, Amy and Karen Lury (2016) 'Growing up and Growing old with Television: Peripheral Viewers and the Centrality of Care', *Screen* vol. 57 no. 2, pp. 184–96.

Holland, Patricia (2000) *The Television Handbook*, 2nd edition, Abingdon: Routledge.

Holmes, Su (2008) *The Quiz Show*, Edinburgh: Edinburgh University Press.

Holmes, Su and Deborah Jermyn (eds) (2004) *Understanding Reality Television*, Abingdon: Routledge.

Holt, Jennifer, Greg Steirer and Karen Petruska (2016) 'Introduction: The Expanded Landscape of Connected Viewing', *Convergence* vol. 22 no. 4, pp. 341–7.

Hooberman, Lucy (2014) 'Recalling Some of BBC Online's History', BBC blog, 11 April 2014. Available online: <www.bbc.co.uk/blogs/aboutthebbc/entries/e0ec7290-6b0f-3395-b209-de2999322126> (Accessed 28 November 2016).

Horrie, Chris and Steve Clarke (2000) *Citizen Greg: The Extraordinary Story of Greg Dyke and How He Captured the BBC*, London: Simon and Schuster.

Hoskins, Andrew (2004) 'Television and the Collapse of Memory', *Time and Society* vol. 13 no. 1, pp. 109–27.

Hoskins, Andrew (2005) 'Flashframes of History: American Televisual Memories', in John Beck and David Holloway (eds), *American Visual Cultures*, London: Continuum, pp. 299–305.

Hoskins, Andrew (2007) 'Ghost in the Machine: Television and War Memory', in Sarah Maltby and Richard Keeble (eds), *Communicating War: Memory, Media and Military*, Suffolk: Arima Publishing, pp. 18–28.

Hoskins, Andrew (2009) 'Flashbulb Memories, Psychology And Media Studies: Fertile Ground for Interdisciplinarity?', *Memory Studies* vol. 2 no. 2, pp. 147–50.

Hoskins, Andrew and John Tulloch (2016) *Risk and Hyperconnectivity: Media and Memories of Neoliberalism*, Oxford: Oxford University Press.

Hughes, Sarah (2015) 'Cold Feet is Coming Back to ITV, But One-Time Mega-Fan Doesn't Want to See a Reboot', *Belfast Telegraph* 2 December 2015. Available online: <www.belfasttelegraph.co.uk/life/features/cold-feet-is-coming-back-to-itv-but-onetime-megafan-doesnt-want-to-see-a-reboot-34251180.html> (Accessed 3 October 2016).

Huyssen, Andreas (1995) *Twilight Memories: Marking Time in a Culture of Amnesia*, New York: Routledge.

Ibbotson, Anne (2012) *Coming Full Circle: A Memoir*, London: Ashgrove.

IMDB (1990–2018) 'It Was Alright in the…'. Available online: <www.imdb.com/title/tt4202570/> (Accessed 2 November 2018).

Index Stock Shots (n.d.) 'Home'. Available online: <www.indexfootage.com> (Accessed 2 November 2018).

Inglis, Ian (ed.) (2010) *Popular Music and Television in Britain*, Farnham: Ashgate.

Isaacs, Jeremy (2006) *Look Me in the Eye: A Life in Television*, London: Little Brown.

ITV (2016) 'Cold Feet | Series 6 | Official Trailer | ITV' [video], YouTube 28 July 2016. Available online: <www.youtube.com/watch?v=vmsnlukx_oa> (Accessed 2 November 2018).

Jackson, Jasper (2016) 'Ken Loach: BBC News Manipulative and Deeply Political', *The Guardian* 18 October 2016. Available online: <www.theguardian.com/media/2016/oct/18/ken-loach-bbc-news-manipulative-and-deeply-political> (Accessed 30 December 2016).

Jackson, Vanessa (2014) 'Using Social Media to Build Screen Histories: A Case Study of the *Pebble Mill Project*', in Laura Mee and Johnny Walker (eds), *Cinema, Television & History: New Approaches*, Newcastle-Upon-Tyne: Cambridge Scholars Publishing, pp. 239–59.

Jackson-Edwards, Phoebe (2016) '"What the f*** did I Just Watch?" Bizarre Clip from Old British Children's TV Show Confuses Twitter after Going Viral (Completely Baffling US Viewers)', *The Daily Mail* 12 May 2016. Available online: <www.dailymail.co.uk/femail/article-3586427/What-f-did-just-watch-Bizarre-clip-old-British-children-s-TV-confuses-Twitter-going-viral-viewers-left-completely-baffled.html#ixzz4TJ6SQ3cc> (Accessed 12 December 2016).

Jacobs, Jason (2000) *The Intimate Screen: Early British Television Drama*, Oxford: Oxford University Press.

Jacobs, Jason (2006a) 'Television and History: Investigating the Past', in Glen Creeber (ed.) *TeleVisions: An Introduction to Studying Television*, London: BFI, pp. 107–15.

Jacobs, Jason (2006b) 'The Television Archive: Past, Present And Future', *Critical Studies in Television* vol. 1 no. 1, pp. 13–20.

Jacobs, Jason (2011) 'The Medium in Crisis: Caughie, Brunsdon and The Problem of US Television', *Screen* vol. 52 no. 4, pp. 503–11.

J.A.R.B. (2016) 'A Lukewarm Reboot of "Cold Feet"', *The Economist* Prospero blog, 16 September 2016. Available online: <www.economist.com/blogs/prospero/2016/09/tepid-television> (Accessed 27 September 2016).

Jenkins, Henry (1992) *Textual Poachers: Television Fans & Participatory Culture*, New York: Routledge.

Jenkins, Henry (2006) *Fans, Bloggers, and Gamers: Exploring Participatory Culture*, New York: New York University Press.

Jenner, Mareike (2016a) 'The Disappearing Television: What is Television without a Television Set?', Material Cultures of Television conference, University of Hull, 21 March 2016.

Jenner, Mareike (2016b) 'Is this TVIV? On Netflix, TVIII and Binge-Watching', *New Media and Society* vol. 18 no. 2, pp. 257–73.

Johnson, Catherine and Rob Turnock (2005) *ITV Cultures: Independent Television Over Fifty Years*, Maidenhead: Open University Press.

Jones, Ian (2004) *Morning Glory: A History of British Breakfast Television*, Devon: Kelly Publications.

Joyrich, Lynne (1988) 'All that Television Allows: TV Melodrama, Postmodernism and Consumer Culture', *Camera Obscura* vol. 6 no. 1, pp. 128–53.

Kansteiner, Wulf (2002) 'Finding Meaning in Memory: A Methodological Critique in Collective Memory Studies', *History and Theory* vol. 41 no. 2, pp. 179–97.

Kaplan, E. Ann (ed.) (1987) *Rocking around the Clock: Music Television, Post Modernism and Consumer Culture*, Abingdon: Routledge.

Keightley, Emily and Michael Pickering (2012) *The Mnemonic Imagination*, Basingstoke: Palgrave Macmillan.

Kelly, Stephen F. and Judith Jones (2000) *Forty Years of Coronation Street: A Collection of Memories*, London: Boxtree.

Kerrigan, Lisa (2015) '"Plundering" the Archive and the Recurring Joys of Television', *VIEW Journal of European Television History and Culture* vol. 4 no. 8, pp. 4–9. Available online: <http://viewjournal.eu/archive-based-productions/plundering-the-archive-and-the-recurring-joys-of-television/> (Accessed 2 November 2018).

Khomami, Nadia (2018) 'Outdated thinking is still holding Female TV Writers Back', *The Guardian* 28 February 2018.

Kiss, Jemima (2016) 'BBC Digital Expert Tony Ageh Poached by New York Public Library', *The Guardian* 6 April 2016. Available online: <www.theguardian.com/media/2016/apr/06/bbc-tony-ageh-new-york-public-library> (Accessed 7 April 2016).

Koivunen, Anu (2016) 'Affective Historiography: Archival Aesthetics and the Temporalities of Televisual Nation-Building', *International Journal of Communication* vol. 10, pp. 5270–83.

Kompare, Derek (2005) *Rerun Nation: How Repeats Invented American Television*, New York: Routledge.

Kozinets, Robert V. (2010) *Netnography: Doing Ethnographic Research Online*, London: Sage.

Kraftl, Peter (2008) 'Young People, Hope and Childhood-Hope', *Space and Culture* vol. 11 no. 2, pp. 81–92.

Kuhn, Annette (2002) *An Everyday Magic: Cinema and Cultural Memory*, London: I.B.Tauris.

Lacey, Stephen (2006) 'Some Thoughts on Television History and Historiography: A British Perspective', *Critical Studies in Television* vol. 1 no. 1, pp. 3–12.

Lagerkvist, Amanda (2013) *Media and Memory in New Shanghai: Western Performances of Futures Past*, Basingstoke: Palgrave Macmillan.

Landsberg, Alison (2004) *Prosthetic Memory: The Transformation of American Remembrance in the Age of Mass Culture*, Columbia, NY: Columbia University Press.

Latour, Bruno (2004) 'Why Has Critique Run Out of Steam? From Matters of Fact to Matters of Concern', *Critical Inquiry* vol. 30 no. 2, pp. 225–48.

Latour, Bruno (2005) *Reassembling the Social: An Introduction to Actor-Network-Theory*, Oxford: Oxford University Press.

Law, John (2004) *After Method: Mess in Social Science Research*, New York: Routledge.

Lemish, Dafna (2006) *Children and Television: A Global Perspective*, Chichester: John Wiley and Sons Ltd.

Levy, Daniel and Natan Sznaider (2005) *The Holocaust and Memory in the Global Age*, translated by Assenka Oksiloff, Philadelphia, PA: Temple University Press.

Lindroos, Kia (1998) *Now-Time/Image-Space: Temporalization of Politics in Walter Benjamin's Philosophy of History and Art*, Jyvaskyla: University of Jyvaskyla.

Lipsitz, George (1990) *Time Passages: Collective Memory and American Popular Culture*, Minneapolis: University of Minnesota Press.

Lizardi, Ryan (2015) *Mediated Nostalgia: Individual Memory and Contemporary Mass Media*, Lanham, MD: Lexington Books.

Long, Paul (2011a) 'Philip Donnellan's 'The Colony' – Paul Long' Pebble Mill blog, 11 October 2011. Available online: <www.pebblemill.org/blog/the-colony-paul-long/> (Accessed 2 November 2018).

Long, Paul (2011b) 'Representing Race, and Place: Black Midlanders on Television in the 1960s and 1970s', *Midland History* vol. 36 no. 2, pp. 261–76.

Lotz, Amanda (2015) 'Why 2015 Was the Year That Changed TV Forever', *New Republic* 31 December 2015. Available online: <https://newrepublic.com/article/126732/2015-year-changed-tv-forever> (Accessed 7 December 2016).

Lotz, Amanda (2007) *The Television Will Be Revolutionized*, New York: New York University Press.

Lull, James (1990) *Inside Family Viewing: Ethnographic Research on Television's Audiences*, Abingdon: Routledge.

Lury, Celia and Nina Wakeford (eds) (2011) *Inventive Methods: The Happening of the Social*, Abingdon: Routledge.

Lury, Karen (1995) *British Youth Television: Cynicism and Enchantment*, Oxford: Oxford University Press.

McAleer, Jill and Barrie Gunter (1990) *Children and Television: The One-eyed Monster?* London: Routledge.

McCarthy, Anna (2001) *Ambient Television*, Durham, NC: Duke University Press.

McCarthy, Anna (2016) 'Things to Do with TV Sets', keynote address at Material Cultures of Television conference, University of Hull, 21 March 2016.

McLuhan, Marshall (1964) *Understanding Media*, London: Routledge.

McMahon, Ed (2007) *When Television was Young: The Inside Story with Memories by Legends of the Small Screen*, Nashville, TN: Thomas Nelson.

MacMumraugh-Kavanagh, M.K. (n.d.) 'Kicking Over the Traces – Interview with Tony Garnett', *Tony Garnett*. Available online: <www.tonygarnett.com/site/?p=169> (Accessed 1 November 2018).

Manchester Centre for Public History and Heritage (n.d.) 'Granadaland: Histories and Memories of Granada TV in the Northwest of England 1954-1990'. Available online: <https://mcphh.org/granadatv/> (Accessed 1 January 2018).

Mancuso, Vinnie (2016) 'Death to Nostalgia TV', *Observer* 26 February 2016. Available online: <www.observer.com/2016/02/death-to-nostalgia-tv> (Accessed 12 November 2016).

Masterman, Len (1983) *Media Education in the United Kingdom: An Annotated Bibliography*. In association with UNESCO (United Nations Educational, Scientific and Cultural Organization). Available online: <http://unesdoc.unesco.org/images/0009/000901/090171eb.pdf> (Accessed 23 July 2015).

Matrix, Sidney Eve (2014) 'The Netflix Effect: Teens, Binge Watching and on-Demand Digital Media Trends', *Jeuneese: Young People, Texts, Cultures* vol. 6 no. 1, pp. 119–38.

Maxwell, Richard and Toby Miller (2012) *Greening the Media*, Oxford: Oxford University Press.

Mayer, Vicki (2011) *Below the Line: Producers and Production Studies in the New Television Economy*, Durham, NC: Duke University Press.

Mayer, Vicki, Miranda J. Banks and John Thornton Caldwell (2009) *Production Studies: Cultural Studies of Media Industries*, New York: Routledge.

Medhurst, Jamie (2010) *A History of Independent Television in Wales*, Cardiff: University of Wales Press.

Mellencamp, Patricia (1990) 'TV Time and Catastrophe, or *Beyond the Pleasure Principle of Television*', in Patricia Mellencamp (ed.), *Logics of Television: Essays in Cultural Criticism*, London: BFI, pp. 240–66.

Merrin, William (2014) *Media Studies 2.0*, Abingdon: Routledge.

Michael, Mike (2012) 'Anecdote', in Celia Lury and Nina Wakeford (eds), *Inventive Methods: The Happening of the Social*, Abingdon: Routledge, pp. 25–35.

Miller, Toby (2008) 'Who Are These People?', *Cinema Journal* vol. 47 no. 4, pp. 121–6.

Mills, Tom (2016) *The BBC: The Myth of a Public Service*, London: Verso.

Mol, Annemarie, Ingunn Moser and Jeannette Pols (2010) 'Care: Putting Practice into Theory', in A. Mol, I. Moser and J. Pols (eds), *Care in Practice: On Tinkering in Clinics, Homes and Farms*, Bielefeld: Transcript, pp. 7–21.

Molesworth, Richard (2013) *Wiped! Doctor Who's Missing Episodes*, revised edition, Prestatyn: Telos Publishing.

Monaco, Jeanette (2010) 'Memory Work, Autoethnography and the Construction of a Fan-ethnography', *Particpations: Journal of Audience and Reception Studies* vol. 7 no. 1, pp. 102–42.

Moran, Joe (2013) *Armchair Nation: An Intimate History of Britain*, London: Profile Books.

Morley, David (1980) *The Nationwide Audience*, London: BFI.

Morley, David (1986) *Family Television: Cultural Power and Domestic Leisure*, London: Comedia.

Morley, David (1992) *Television, Audiences and Cultural Studies*, Abingdon: Routledge.

Morley, David (2000) *Home Territories: Media, Mobility and Identity*, London: Routledge.

Morley, David and Charlotte Brunsdon (1978) *Everyday Television: Nationwide*, London: BFI.

Moseley, Rachel (2016) *Hand-Made Television: Stop-Frame Animation for Children in Britain 1961–1974*, Basingstoke: Palgrave Macmillan.

Moseley, Rachel, Helen Wheatley and Helen Wood (eds) (2017) *Television for Women: New Directions*, Abingdon: Routledge.

Murphy, Amanda, Rowan Aust, Vanessa Jackson and John Ellis (2015) '16mm Film Editing: Using Filmed Simulation as a Hands-On Approach to TV History', *VIEW: Journal of European Television History and Culture* vol. 4 no. 7, pp. 7–10. Available online: <http://viewjournal.eu/archaeologies-of-tele-visions-and-realities/16mm-film-editing/> (Accessed 2 November 2018).

National Archives (2009) *Corporate Memory: A Guide to Managing Business Archives*. Available onlne: <www.nationalarchives.gov.uk/documents/information-management/corporate-memory.pdf> (Accessed 15 July 2016).

Neame, Christopher (2004) *A Take on British TV Drama: Stories from the Golden Years*, Oxford: Scarecrow.

Needham, Gary (2009) 'Scheduling Normativity: Television, the Family, and Queer Temporality', in Glyn Davis and Gary Needham (eds), *Queer TV: Theories, Histories, Politics*, Abingdon: Routledge, pp. 143–58.

Nicholls, Tom (2017) 'Comfort Telly 2: *Cold Feet*, The Case of the Comforting Resurrection', *CST online* blog, 8 September 2017. Available online: <http://cstonline.net/comfort-telly-2-cold-feet-the-case-of-the-comforting-resurrection-by-tom-nicholls/> (Accessed 1 November 2017).

Niemeyer, Katharina and Daniela Wentz (2014) 'Nostalgia is Not What it Used to Be: Serial Nostalgia and Nostalgic Television Series', in Katharina Niemeyer (ed.), *Media* and Nostalgia: Yearning for the Past, Present and Future, Basingstoke: Palgrave Macmillan, pp. 129–38.

NLW (National Library of Wales) (2017) 'National Library of Wales Broadcast Archive', *LLGC* blog, 22 September 2017. Available online: <www.llgc.org.uk/blog/?p=15858> (Accessed 1 November 2017).

Nora, Pierre (2002) 'Reasons for the Current Upsurge On Memory', *Eurozine* 19 April 2002. Available online: <www.eurozine.com/articles/2002-04-19-nora-en.html> (Accessed 20 May 2013).

Norden, Dennis (1985) *Coming to You Live! Behind the Scenes of Forties and Fifties Television*, London: Methuen.

Norton, Michael I., Daniel Mochon and Dan Ariely (2011) 'The "IKEA Effect": When Labor Leads to Love', *Harvard Business School Working Paper*. Available online: <www.hbs.edu/faculty/Publication%20Files/11-091.pdf> (Accessed 20 November 2016).

Nostalgia Central (2018) 'Nostalgia Central: The Way Things Used to Be'. Available online: <https://nostalgiacentral.com> (Accessed 2 November 2018).

NSMM (National Science and Media Museum) (2013a) 'Doctor Who and Me: 50 Years of Doctor Who Fans' [video], YouTube 13 November 2013. Available online: <www.youtube.com/watch?v=1crHCJcxpMc> (Accessed 2 November 2018).

NSMM (National Science and Media Museum) (2013b) 'Doctor Who Superfans: David Knill' [video], YouTube 22 November 2013. Available online: <www.youtube.com/watch?v=BF8kUznLUlc> (Accessed 2 November 2018).

October, Dene (2016) 'The Day my Doctor Died: A Child's Experience of the First Regeneration', *FBI-Spy*. Available online: <www.fbi-spy.com/doctor-who-day-died> (Accessed 1 November 2016).

Olick, Jeffrey K. (1999) 'Collective Memory: The Two Cultures', *Sociological Theory* vol. 17 no. 3, pp. 333–48.

Olick, Jeffrey K., Vered Vinitzky-Seroussi and Daniel Levy (eds) (2011) *The Collective Memory Reader*, Oxford: Oxford University Press.

Orlebar, Jeremy (2013) *The Television Handbook*, 4th edition, Abingdon: Routledge.

O'Sullivan, Tim (1998) 'Nostalgia, Revelation and Intimacy: Tendencies in the Flow of Modern Popular Television', in Christine Geraghty and David Lusted (eds), *The Television Studies Book*, London: Arnold, pp. 198–209.

Pamuk, Orham (2009) *The Museum of Innocence*, London: Faber & Faber Ltd.

Panos, Leah (2014) 'Introduction: Special Issue – Spaces of Television Production, Site and Style', special issue of *Historical Journal of Film, Radio and Television* vol. 34 no. 3, pp. 329–30.

Parikka, Jussi (2011) 'Operative Media Archaeology: Wolfgang Ernst's Materialist Media Diagrammatics', *Theory, Culture and Society* vol. 28 no. 5, pp. 52–74.

Parikka, Jussi (2012) *What is Media Archaeology?* Cambridge: Polity Press.

Pearson, Roberta (2016) 'Googling Sherlock Holmes: Popular Memory, Platforms, Protocols and Paratexts', in Sara Pesce and Paolo Nota (eds), *The Politics of Ephemeral Digital Media: Permanence and Obsolescence in Paratexts*, Abingdon: Routledge, pp. 77–94.

Pederson, Sarah and Janet Smithson (2013) 'Mothers with Attitude – How the Mumsnet Parenting Forum Offers Space for New Forms of Femininity to Emerge Online', *Women's Studies International Forum* vol. 38, 97–106.

Pickering, Michael and Emily Keightley (2014) 'Interscalarity and Memory Studies Methodology', Making Sense of Memory & History, ICA pre-conference sponsored by the Communication History Interest Group of ICA Seattle, Museum of History & Industry (MOHAI), 22 May 2014.

Piper, Helen (2011) 'Vintage Entertainment: Nostalgia, the Archive and the Disappearing Pleasures of Collective Television Viewing', *Journal of British Cinema and Television* vol. 8 no. 3, pp. 411–29.

Piper, Helen (2015) 'The Way We Watched: Vintage Television Programmes, Memories, and Memorabilia', *NECSUS: Journal of European Media Studies*, 24 November 2015, Autumn 2015 'Vintage'. Available online: <www.necsus-ejms.org/the-way-we-watched-vintage-television-programmes-memories-and-memorabilia/> (Accessed 10 October 2016).

PLB Projects Ltd (2016) 'Our Team'. Available online: <www.plbltd.com> (Accessed 1 October 2017).

Plunkett, John (2015) 'The BBC Has Deep Specialism, 50 or 60 Years of Heritage. Netflix Can't Buy That', *The Guardian* 18 January 2015. Available online: <www.theguardian.com/media/2015/jan/18/bbc-in-house-production-netflix-independents> (Accessed 12 November 2016)

Poole, Peter (2012) 'Memories of Philip Donnellan – Peter Poole', Pebble Mill blog, 26 March 2012. Available online: <www.pebblemill.org/blog/memories-of-philip-donnellan-peter-poole/> (Accessed 2 November 2018).

Popular Memory Group (2011) 'From "Popular Memory: Theory, Politics, Method"', in Jeffrey K. Olick, Vered Vinitzky-Seroussi and Daniel Levy (eds), *The Collective Memory Reader*, Oxford: Oxford University Press, pp. 254–9.

Potter, Simon (2012) *Broadcasting Empire: The BBC and the British World, 1922–1970*, Oxford: Oxford University Press.

Potter, Dennis (2015) *The Art of Invective: Selected Non-Fiction 1953–1994*, edited by Ian Greaves, David Rolinson and John Williams, London: Oberon Books.

Powers, Tom (2016) *Gender and the Quest in British Science Fiction Television: An Analysis of Doctor Who, Blake's 7, Red Dwarf and Torchwood*, Jefferson, NC: MacFarland.

Prince, David (2016) 'Cardiff's Doctor Who Experience will Close Next Year', *Wales Online* 7 November 2016. Available online: <www.walesonline.co.uk/whats-on/whats-on-news/cardiffs-doctor-who-experience-close-12138399> (Accessed 2 December 2016).

Pugzles Lorch, Elizabeth, Daniel R. Bellack and Lynn Haller Augsbach (1987) 'Young Children's Memory for Televised Stories: Effects of Importance', *Child Development* vol. 58 no. 2, pp. 453–63.

Quinton-Tulloch, Jo (2016) 'My Message to Bradford', National Media Museum blog, 4 February 2016. Available online: <http://blog.nationalmediamuseum.org.uk/my-message-to-bradford/> (Accessed 11 November 2016).

Radstone, Susannah (ed.) (2000) *Memory and Methodology*, Oxford: Berg.

Rautio, Pauliina (2013) 'Children Who Carry Stones in Their Pockets: On Autotelic Material Practices in Everyday Life', *Children's Geographies* vol. 11 no. 4, pp. 394–408.

Reading, Anna (2016) *Gender and Memory in the Globital Age*, Basingstoke: Palgrave Macmillan.

Reminisce This (2018) 'What's it all about'. Available online: <www.reminiscethis.co.uk> (Accessed 2 November 2018).

Root, Jane (1986) *Open the Box: About Television*, London: Comedia.

Rothberg, Michael (2009) *Multidirectional Memory: Remembering the Holocaust in the Age of Decolonization*, Stanford, CA: Stanford University Press.

Samuel, Raphael (1994) *Theatres of Memory*, London: Verso.

Sandon, Emma (2007) 'Nostalgia as Resistance: The Case of the Alexandra Palace Television Society and the BBC', in Helen Wheatley (ed.), *Re-viewing Television History: Critical Issues in Television Historiography*, I.B.Tauris, pp. 99–112.

Sarikakis, Katharine (2004) 'Media and Communications Policy: A Definition'. Available online: <http://mediacompolicy.univie.ac.at/wp-content/uploads/2013/03/Media-and-communications-policy.pdf> (Accessed 1 October 2016).

Schoell-Glass, Charlotte (2008) *Aby Warburg and Anti-Semitism: Political Perspectives on Images and Culture*, translated by Samuel Pakucs-Willcox, Detroit, MI: Wayne State University Press.

Sconce, Jeffrey (2000) *Haunted Media: Electronic Presence from Telegraphy to Television*, Durham, NC: Duke University Press.

Scott, Suzanne (2013) 'Who's Steering the Mothership? The Role of the Fanboy Auteur in Transmedia Storytelling', in Aaron Delwich and Jennifer Jacobs Henderson (eds), *The Participatory Cultures Handbook*, New York: Routledge, pp. 43–52.

Seaton, Jean (2015) *Pinkoes and Traitors: The BBC and the Nation 1974–1987*, London: Profile Books.

Seiter, Ellen (1990) 'Making Distinctions in TV Audience Research: Case Study of a Troubling Interview', *Cultural Studies* vol. 4 no. 1, pp. 61–84.

Seiter, Ellen (1999) *Television and New Media Audiences*, Oxford: Oxford University Press.

Semon, Richard (1921) *The Mneme*, London: George Allen & Unwin.

Semon, Richard (1923) *The Mneme*, London: George Allen & Unwin.

Sennett, Richard (2011) 'Disturbing Memories', in Jeffrey K. Olick, Vered Vinitzky-Seroussi and Daniel Levy (eds), *The Collective Memory Reader*, Oxford: Oxford University Press, pp. 283–6.

Sharp, Elsa (2009) *How to Get a Job in Television: Build you Career from Runner to Series Producer*, London: A & C Black.

Shubik, Irene (2014) 'Television Drama Series: A Producer's View', in Jonathan Bignell and Stephen Lacey (eds), *British Television Drama: Past, Present and Future*, Basingstoke: Palgrave Macmillan, pp. 45–51.

Silverstone, Roger (1999) *Why Study the Media?* London: Sage.

Singer Dorothy G. and Jerome L. Singer (2012) *Handbook of Children and the Media*, 2nd edition, Los Angeles: Sage.

Singh, Anita (2015) 'Super Ted, Pingu and Humpty from Playschool Could Rival Peter Pan', *Daily Telegraph* 16 May 2015.

Skutch, Ira (1998) *The Days of Live*, Lanham, MD: Scarecrow Press.

SkyMovies (2017) 'Christmas Advert'. Available online: <www.sky.com/tv/channel/skycinema/video/christmas-advert> (Accessed 28 December 2017).

Smith, Janet (2016a) 'Volume 1 – Summaries and Conclusions of the Savile and Hall investigation reports'. Available online: <www.bbc.co.uk/bbctrust/dame_janet_smith> (Accessed 1 November 2017).

Smith, Janet (2016b) 'Volume 2 - The Jimmy Savile investigation report'. Available online: <www.bbc.co.uk/bbctrust/dame_janet_smith> (Accessed 1 November 2017).

Smith, Janet (2016c) 'Volume 3 - The Stuart Hall investigation report'. Available online: <www.bbc.co.uk/bbctrust/dame_janet_smith> (Accessed 1 November 2017).

SONY (2016) 'UK Technology Centre'. Available online: <https://pro.sony/en_GB/solutions/archive-management> (Accessed 1 November 2018).

Spigel, Lynn (1995) 'From the Dark Ages to the Golden Age: Women's Memories and Television Ruins', *Screen* vol. 36 no. 1, pp. 16–33.

Spigel, Lynn (2004) 'Introduction', in Lynn Spigel and Jan Olsson (eds), *Television after TV: Essays on a Medium on Transition*, Durham, NC: Duke University Press, pp. 1–39.

Spigel, Lynn (2005a) 'Our TV Heritage: Television, the Archive and the Reasons for Preservation', in Janet Wasko (ed.), *The Television Companion*, Oxford: Blackwell, pp. 67–99.

Spigel, Lynn (2005b) 'TV's Next Season', *Cinema Journal* vol. 45 no. 1, 83–90.

Spilsbury, Tom (2013) 'The Hero of the World!', *Doctor Who Magazine* no. 466, pp. 14–17.

Steemers, Jeanette (2010) *Creating Preschool Television: A Story of Commerce, Creativity and Curriculum*, Basingstoke: Palgrave Macmillan.

Stewart, Kathleen (1988) 'Nostalgia – A Polemic', *Cultural Anthropology* vol. 3, no 3, pp. 227–41.

Sweney, Mark (2016) 'Janice Hadlow to leave the BBC', *The Guardian* 22 January 2016. Available online: <www.theguardian.com/media/2016/jan/22/bbc-executive-janice-hadlow-to-leave-the-corporation> (Accessed 1 November 2018).

Sydney-Smith, Susan (2002) *Beyond Dixon of Dock Green: Early British Police Series*, London: I.B.Tauris & Co Ltd.

Tankel, Jonathan David and Keith Murphy (1998) 'Collecting Comic Books: A Study of the Fan Curatorial Consumption' in C. Harris and A. Alexander (eds), *Theorizing Fandom: Fans, Subculture and Identity*, Cresskill, NJ: Hampton Press, pp. 55–70.

Taylor, Charles (1994) *Multiculturalism and The Politics of Recognition*, edited by Amy Gutmann, Princeton, NJ: Princeton University Press.

Taylor, Diana (2011) 'Save As … Knowledge and Transmission in the Age of Digital Technologies', *Foreseeable Futures* 10. Available online: <http://imaginingamerica.org/wp-content/uploads/2011/05/Foreseeable-Futures-10-Taylor.pdf> (Accessed 3 October 2016).

Television Heaven (2016) 'Television Heaven Recommends - On The Box'. Available online: <www.televisionheaven.co.uk/dvd_releases.html> (Accessed 1 January 2017).

Trodd, Kenith (2014) '"I'M OUT OF HERE IN THE MORNING": Is There a Future for The Past?', presentation at the Inheriting British Television Symposium, National Media Museum, Bradford, 11 February 2014.

Turnbull, Sue (2012) 'A Gap in the Records: Television Audiences and the History of "Us"', in Kate Darian-Smith and Sue Turnbull (eds), *Remembering Television: Histories, Technologies, Memories*, Newcastle-upon-Tyne: Cambridge Scholars Publishing, pp. 17–29.

Turnock, Rob (2007) *Television and Consumer Culture: Britain and the Transformation of Modernity*, London: I.B.Tauris.

TV Cream (n.d.) 'TV Cream'. Available online: <www.tvcream.co.uk> (Accessed 2 November 2018).

TV Studio History (n.d.) 'An Incomplete History of London's Television Studios'. Available online: <www.tvstudiohistory.co.uk> (Accessed 1 November 2018).

Uricchio, William (2010) 'TV as Time Machine: Television's Changing Heterochronic Regimes and the Production of History', in Jostein Gripsrud (ed.), *Relocating Television: Television in the Digital Context*, London: Routledge, pp. 27–40.

Van Dijck, José (2007) *Mediated Memories in the Digital Age*, Stanford, CA: Stanford University Press.

Van Dijck, José (2011) 'Flickr and the Culture of Connectivity: Sharing Views, Experiences, Memories', *Memory Studies* vol. 4 no. 4, pp. 401–15.

Wallace, Richard (2013) 'Joint Ventures and Loose Cannons: Reconstructing *Doctor Who*'s Missing Past', in Paul Booth (ed.), *Fan Phenomena: Doctor Who*, Bristol: Intellect, pp. 28–37.

Warburg, Aby (1929) *Mnemosyne Atlas*. Available at Cornell University Library's *Mnemosyne: Meandering through Aby Warburg's Atlas*. Available online: <https://warburg.library.cornell.edu/> (Accessed 11 December 2017).

Wheatley, Helen (2016) *Spectacular Television: Exploring Televisual Practice*, London: I.B.Tauris.

Wheatley, Helen (ed.) (2007) *Re-viewing Television History: Critical Issues in Television Historiography*, London: I.B.Tauris.

Wheatley, Helen and Rachel Moseley (2008) 'Is Archiving a Feminist Issue? Historical Research and the Past, Present, and Future of Television Studies', *Cinema Journal* vol. 47 no. 3, pp. 152–8.

Wheeler, Ian (2014) 'Event Review: Doctor Who and Me', *Celestial Toyroom* no. 429.

Williams, John (2014) 'Intensity of Working with Philip Donnellan', Pebble Mills blog, 4 April 2014. Available online: <www.pebblemill.org/blog/intensity-of-working-with-philip-donnellan/> (Accessed 2 November 2018).

Williams, Raymond (1974) *Television: Technology and Cultural Form*, New York: Schocken Books.

Wilson, Julie A. and Emily Chivers Yochim (2017) *Mothering through Precarity: Women's Work and Digital Media*, Durham, NC: Duke University Press.

Wolf, Mark J.P. (2012) *Building Imaginary Worlds: The Theory and History of Subcreation*, New York: Routledge.

Wollaston, Sam (2016) '*Cold Feet* Finale – I Dreaded This Reunion But It Was Good to Catch up with Old Friends', *The Guardian* 24 October 2016. Available online: <www.theguardian.com/tv-and-radio/2016/oct/24/cold-feet-finale-review-i-dreaded-this-reunion-but-it-was-good-to-catch-up-with-old-friends> (Accessed 7 December 2016).

Woods, Faye (2016) *British Youth Television: Transnational Teens, Industry, Genre*, Houndmills: Palgrave.

Worcman, Karen and Joanne Garde-Hansen (2016) *Social Memory Technology: Theory, Practice, Action*, New York: Routledge.

Young, Clive (2008) *Homemade Hollywood: Fans behind the Camera*, New York: Continuum.

Film and Television References

Absolutely Fabulous: The Movie (dir. Mandie Fletcher, BBC Films, 2016)

Arrested Development (Fox 2003–06; Netflix 2013–)

Around the World with Willy Fog (RTVE, 1983)

Bagpuss (BBC One, 12 February–7 May 1974)

Batman (ABC, Greenway Productions,1966–8; ITV 1989–92)

Bananaman (BBC 1983–6)

A Beast with Two Backs (BBC One, 1968).

Big Brother (Channel 4, 2000–10; E4, 2001–10; Channel 5, 2011–)

Bill Brand (Thames/ITV, 1976)

Brambly Hedge (BBC, 1996–2000)

Brideshead Revisited (ITV, 1981)

Buck Rogers in the 25th Century (NBC, Glen A. Larson Productions, 1979–81)

Button Moon (ITV, 1980–8)

Call the Midwife (BBC, 2012–)

Cathy Come Home (dir. Ken Loach, 1967)

Charlie's Angels (ABC, Aaron Spelling, 1976–81)

Cold Feet (ITV, 1997–2016)

Compact (BBC, 1962–5)

Coronation Street (ITV, Granada Television,1960–)

Countdown (Channel 4, Granada/ITV Studios, 1982–)

Counterpoint (UTV, 1978–96)

Dad's Army (BBC One, 1968–77)

Danger Mouse (ITV, Cosgrove Hall Films, Thames Television, 1981–92)

Doctor Finlay's Casebook (BBC, 1962–71)

Doctor Who (BBC One, 1963–)

Dogtanian and the Three Muskehounds (BRB Internacional [Spain], Nippon Animation [Japan] and MBS [Japan], 1981–2)

Downton Abbey (ITV, 2010–15)

Dungeons & Dragons (CBS, Marvel Productions, 1983–5)

Dynasty (ABC, Aaron Spelling, 1981–9)

EastEnders (BBC One, 1985–)

E.T. (dir. Steven Speilberg, Amblin Entertainment, 1982)

Fame (dir. Alan Parker, Metro-Goldwyn-Mayer, 1980)

Fame (NBC, MGM Television,1982–3)

Family Guy (Fox/Channel 4/Sky1/BBC/ITV2, 1999–)

Friends (NBC, Bright/Kauffman/Crane Productions,1994–2004)

Fuller House (Netflix, Jeff Franklin Productions, 2016–)

Game of Thrones (HBO, 2011–)

Glasgow Belongs to Me (dir. Edward McConnell, British Transport Films, 1965)

Gogglebox (Channel 4, 2013–)

Grange Hill (BBC 1978–2008)

Grandstand (BBC,1958–2007)

Happy Valley (BBC One, 2014–)

Hill Street Blues (NBC, 1981–7)

I Love the 80s (BBC Two, 2001)

It Was Alright in the 1970s (Channel 4, 2014)

Ivor the Engine (BBC, 1975–7)

Jamie and the Magic Torch (ITV, John Hambley, 1976–9)

Jungle Run (CITV, 1999)

Katie Morag (CBeebies/CBBC, Move on Up, 2013–)

Knight Rider (NBC, Glen A. Larson, 1982–6)

Love Boat (ABC/BBC, Aaron Spelling, 1977–90)

The Man From U.N.C.L.E. (NBC, Arena Productions, 1964–8)

Mastermind (BBC One, 1972–1997; BBC Two, 2003–)

Midsomer Murders (ITV, 1997–)

Minipops (Channel 4, 1983)

Morecambe and Wise (BBC Two, 1968–71; BBC One, 1969–77; ITV, 1978–83)

Mr Benn (BBC, Zephyr Films, 1971–2005)

Multi-Coloured Swap Shop (BBC One, 1976–82)

Mysterious Cities of Gold (BBC, Studio Pierrot, 1982–3)

Nai Zindagi Naya Jeevan (BBC, 1968–82)

Nationwide (BBC One, 1969–83)

Parkinson (BBC One, 1971–2004; ITV, 2004–07)

Play for Today (BBC One, 1970–84)

Play for Today: Penda's Fen (dir. Alan Clarke, BBC One, 1974)

Play for Today: Dreams of Leaving (dir. David Hare, BBC One, 1980)

Pingu (SF DRS, 1986–2000; BBC Two 2003–06; Trickfilmstudio Otmar, original release 1986–2006)

Press Gang (ITV 1989–93)

Rainbow (ITV, Thames Television, 1994–7)

Six Wives of Henry VIII (BBC, 1970)

Stand by Me (dir. Rob Reiner, Columbia Pictures, 1986)

Stranger Things (Netflix, 21 Laps, 2016–)

Stupid (BBC, 2004–)

Sunday Night at the Palladium (ITV, 1955–)

SuperTed (S4C in Welsh, BBC One in English, RTE 2 in Irish, TF1 in French, Siriol
    Animation, 1983–6)

The A Team (NBC, Universal Television, 1983–7)

The Colony (dir. Phillip Donnellan, BBC, 1964)

The Enchanted Castle (BBC, 1979).

The Flumps (BBC One, 14 February–9 May 1977)

The Forsyth Saga (BBC Two, Donald Wilson, 7 January–1 July 1967)

The Gentle Touch (ITV, London Weekend Television, 1980–4)

The Goonies (dir. Richard Donner, Warner Bros, 1985)

The Great British Bake Off (BBC Two 2010–13; BBC One 2014–16)

The Money Programme (BBC Two, 1966–)

The Newcomers (BBC One, 1965–9)

The Scoop (YTV, 1996–9)

The Sooty Show (BBC/Thames 1955–75, 1976–92)

The Trap Door (ITV, Channel 4, Queensgate Productions, 1984)

The Wednesday Play (BBC One, 1964–70)

The Wind in the Willows (ITV, Cosgrove Hall, 1983–90)

The X-Files (Fox, Ten Thirteen Productions, 1993–2002; 2016–)

Thirtysomething (ABC, The Bedford Falls Company, 1987–91)

This Life (BBC Two, 1996–7)

This Week: Death on the Rock (Thames TV,1988)

Tonight (BBC, 1957–65)

Ulysses 31 (FR3, 1981–2)

Union World (Granada/Channel 4, 1985)

Upstairs, Downstairs (ITV, London Weekend Television, 1971–5)

Weekend World (London Weekend Television,1972–88)

Whicker's World (BBC/ITV, 1958–94)

Willo the Wisp (BBC One, 1981–2005)

Women – Which Way Now (BBC Two, 1975)

World in Action (Granada, 1963–98)

Worzel Gummidge (ITV, 1979–81; 1987–9)

INDEX

organizational memory 55–60
producers-turned-academics 45, 50, 51
'prosthetic memory' 117
public engagement projects 164, 170

queer theory 2n4, 3
Quinton-Tulloch, Jo 102n8

Rainbow 107
Reading, Anna 10
regenerative milieu 8, 68, 79, 89, 159,
    160–6
regenerative TV memory: *Dr Who and Me*
    exhibition 151–68
regional television 121. *See also* Northern
    Ireland; Scotland; Wales
remembering well 100
reminiscence sites 145–9
'remixology' 154
retro-memory 51
Rigney, Ann 89
Roberts, Justine 114
rogue archives 37, 149
Rollins, Peter C. 5, 9
Root, Jane 29
Rothberg, Michael xii, 38, 114–15
Ryder, Winona 135

Sandon, Emma 35, 58
Savile, Jimmy 42n9
Schoell-Glass, Charlotte 3
science fiction 135
Science Museum 91, 94, 99
Sconce, Jeff 102
(The) Scoop 55–6
Scotland 6, 7, 80–1, 84
Seaton, Joe 10, 33, 37–8
Seiter, Ellen 112n9, 128, 129
Sennett, Richard 47, 48
sexual harassment and violence xiii
sexual politics xiii, 49, 127, 143–5
Sharp, Elsa 52
Shooting Stars 148
Shubik, Irene 47
Silverstone, Roger 131
Singh, Anita 107
(The) Six Wives of Henry VIII 50
Smith, Janet 42n9
Smithson, Janet 114
social frameworks 7
socialist realist drama 19

social media 115, 123, 125
social memory 9–13, 20
Sony Technology Centre 69
(The) Sooty Show 107
Spacey, Kevin 42n9
spectrum scarcity 14
Spigel, Lynn xi–xii, 29, 36–7, 38, 39, 75,
    92
Stand By Me 135
Star Wars 118, 126
Steirer, Gregory 23–4
Stewart, Kathleen 136
Stranger Things 135
strategic forgetting 37, 101
Stupid 108
Sunday Night at the Palladium 57
superfans 156, 158
SuperTed 107
Sydney-Smith, Susan 12

Tankel, Jonathan David 158
Taylor, Charles 31n4, 75
television
    contemporary relevance ix
    materiality x, 58, 94–8, 103, 133, 136,
        146
television drama xiii
television exhibitions 91–4, 151
    Doctor Who and Me 152, 153, 155, 156,
        157, 158, 159, 161, 162–6, 168
television fans. *See* fan studies; fans
television genealogy x
television history 12, 15, 32–6, 42, 70
    official and unofficial histories 37–9
    popular memory and 36–7
    TV studies and 29–32
television memory xi, 8, 76, 170. *See also*
    memory studies
television studies 28, 29–32
    archives 39–41
Terwey, Michael 87, 94, 96, 97–8, 102, 104,
    133, 165
textural memories 84
Thirtysomething 137–8
This Life 138
This Week 55
Thomas, Matthew 148
Titley, Patrick 44, 48, 56
Tonight 54
transcultural consumption 89
transcultural memory 88